Angels Along the River

Retracing the Escape Route of Mary Draper Ingles

Foreword by James Alexander Thom

Author of *Follow the River*

By

E. M. LAHR

authorHOUSE®

AuthorHouse™
1663 Liberty Drive
Bloomington, IN 47403
www.authorhouse.com
Phone: 1-800-839-8640

First published by AuthorHouse 12/28/2011

ISBN: 978-1-4567-6415-9 (e)
ISBN: 978-1-4567-6416-6 (dj)
ISBN: 978-1-4567-6417-3 (sc)

Library of Congress Control Number: 2011908059

Printed in the United States of America

Cover design by Beth Arnold
Credit: © Thomas R. Fletcher
Location: Grandview, New River Gorge, West Virginia
Map created by John Lahr
Interior photos by Debbie Klene, Lisa Lahr, and Eleanor Lahr
Author photo by Mark Gines, Kirkwood Photo Lab

Dedicated

To all angels who wear everyday clothes,
especially those who are forced to pick the black crayon.

Author's Note

Before you read this book, you might find it helpful to read *Follow the River* by James Alexander Thom, *Trans-Allegheny Pioneers* by John P. Hale, or *Escape from Indian Captivity* as told by John Ingles Sr. Then it will be easier to understand my experiences and maybe my frame of mind. You could read them afterward, but do yourself a favor, go beg, borrow, or buy a copy and read one of them first. *Follow the River* is a fictionalized account of Mary and Will Ingles' experience. *Trans-Allegheny Pioneers*, a biographical history of several Virginia (which include West Virginia) families, is written by Mary and Will Ingles' great-grandson and includes their experience. *Escape from Indian Captivity* is Mary's story as recounted by her youngest son, John. *Follow the River* is still in print. *Trans-Allegheny Pioneers* and *Escape from Indian Captivity* are available at the Glencoe Museum, (540) 731-5031, and Radford Tourism Center, (540) 267-3153, in Radford, Virginia.

Throughout the book I use quotes from *Follow the River*, First Mass Market Edition: November 1983.

Foreword

More than two hundred and fifty years ago, as the starving, cold Mary Ingles slogged, scrambled, and crawled through briary thickets and over jagged boulders on her long trek home through the dire Appalachian wilderness, surely she implored her Lord to explain why she was being put through this ordeal. She had never earned such punishment. For what purpose was she being so tormented?

It's a question that sufferers do ask their deity, and so, when I wrote the novel *Follow the River* more than 25 years ago, I had her ask the question, more than once. Not presuming to know God's motives or intents, I didn't try to give her the answer. Perhaps eventually in her long life afterward, it was answered to her satisfaction, maybe not. Survivors who have sufficient faith tend to stop asking the desperate question after their deliverance from the desperation.

In the years since the novel was published, though, an answer to her plea has become apparent to me, the reteller of her story.

I began to receive letters from readers. A dozen at first, then scores of them, eventually hundreds. And at lectures and book signings, readers came up to me and told me face to face the same thing the letters told me.

That fervent message was:

"Mary Ingles' story inspired me more than anything else I ever read!"

Cancer patients and their families would tell me that they read and reread the novel to bolster their courage.

Men would tell me they had never realized how strong women are until they read of her toughness and durability.

Women would tell me that the story had cured them of all self-pity, and that they would never whine again.

One woman, obviously much battered by life, waited in a long line at a book-signing, and when she stood before me at last, she had no book for me to autograph. She just put forth her hand and took mine and said, "Thank you for saving my life." I asked her how I had done such a thing. She gestured toward her scarred and toothless face and said, "A while ago I decided I couldn't take any more, and I got ready to put myself out of my misery. But then someone told me to read *Follow the River*. I read it and told myself, 'If that little lady could get through that, I can sure get through this.' And I haven't considered suicide since."

That was the greatest reward I've ever had as a storyteller.

But, of course, I was only the storyteller. Mary Ingles and her achievement were the inspiration that changed that woman's life and made her decide she could go on. As a storyteller I was merely the instrument through which the brave song was played.

My motive for investing years in a book is simply the oldest urge in human communication. If a story moves me powerfully enough, I want to pass it on in hopes of sharing my awe with others. We all need inspiration; inspiration is contagious, and I'm privileged to be a carrier.

I can say with truthful humility that I was just simply lucky to run across that obscure old Mary Ingles survival tale while researching for another book. The sketchy account struck me as a story that shouldn't be forgotten, and I made a mental note to research it further when the work-in-progress was finished, and see if I could persuade my editor that it was worth the telling.

By good fortune, it happened that my editor had grown up in that part of Appalachia, and had long ago marveled at the Mary Ingles story when it was told in her family. Without that happenstance, I might never have gotten it written or published at all. One and a half million readers should be glad that editor, Nancy Coffey, had heard that story as a girl in the hills.

I said inspiration is contagious, and it affects us all in different ways. One of the most delightful and heartening manifestations of that inspiration came in the form of Eleanor Lahr, who read the novel several years after it was published. She was about 50 years old then, and was a smart, physically fit employee of the Indiana Department of Natural Resources, who lived in the next county east of the hill farm where I live. Eleanor got in touch and came out to tell me that the book had inspired her to try to reenact Mary Ingles' trek, the same route, in the same length of time, in the same season. I gathered from her character and the look of her that she probably could do it if anyone could, even though she was, she admitted, nearly twice the age Mary was when she did it. She laughed that she might fill the part of the old Dutch woman, and maybe someone closer to Mary's age would join her.

Eleanor's story, of her motivations and her need to make the trek, are in this book.

She found, as I had while researching the book years before, that the folks living along the route loved the story and were generous in helping along anyone who was trying to retell it by whatever means. A reenactment is a retelling by other means.

And she succeeded in walking the distance in exactly the time it had taken Mary.

The landscape was much different, of course. She had comforts and hospitalities that Mary didn't have. Newspapers and broadcasters caught on and publicized her progress. She maintained her humility and good humor. She got to be another carrier of the contagion of inspiration. Her life was changed by the journey, in ways she tells in these pages.

Eleanor and I have become like kinfolk, due to our respective ways of doing tribute to a magnificent, frightened, suffering little heroine of long ago.

As for Mary Ingles' anguished question, "Why me, O Lord?"

One evening in Virginia, at the exact place where she had finished her desperate journey and was rescued by men of the Harmon family, I sat in the home of Harmon descendant Jim Connell and talked with Jennifer Jeffries, a great-great-great-great-great granddaughter of Mary Ingles. Jennifer had just reenacted that final day, in a local pageant annually staged by Mr. Connell on anniversaries of her deliverance. My wife, a member of the Shawnee tribe that had abducted Mary so long before, sat nearby, making diplomacy with other Ingles descendants.

Jennifer Jeffries and I talked about what God might have had in mind when he put Mary through the ordeal.

We spoke about Eleanor Lahr. And I spoke about the woman who hadn't committed suicide. "Maybe that was God's plan for your ancestor," I said. "To have her inspire women, more than two centuries later, to keep on moving and to keep on living."

Jennifer was quiet for a moment. Then she nodded, her face aglow. "Yes. That must be what it was for."

James Alexander Thom

Disclaimer

Ask any lawyer or police officer. Memories are not dependable. Try as we might, we forget, misconstrue, and color events from our particular life's perspective. With the aid of photos, letters, newspaper articles, tapes, a trail journal, and many conversations with those who were present, this is as accurate as the author's fallible memory can make it. This book is not great writing, but it is her best. And no one else would write the story.

This book describes the author's experience and reflects her opinions relating to those experiences. Some identifying details of individuals mentioned in the book have been changed to protect their privacy.

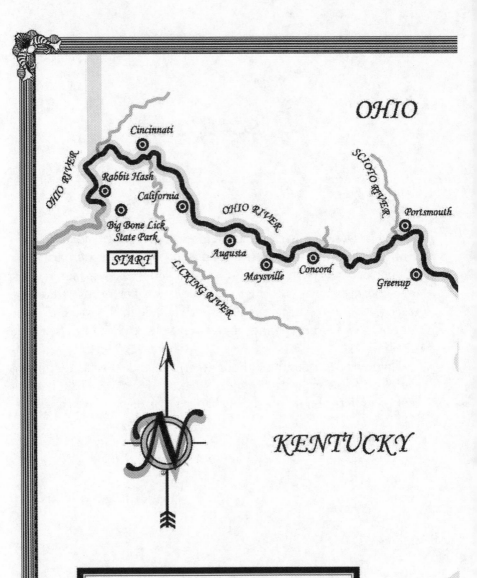

OHIO

Cincinnati

Rabbit Hash

California

OHIO RIVER

SCIOTO RIVER

Portsmouth

Big Bone Lick
State Park

START

Augusta

LICKING RIVER

Maysville

Concord

Greenup

N

KENTUCKY

Route of the 1987 retracing of
Mary Draper Ingles' escape.

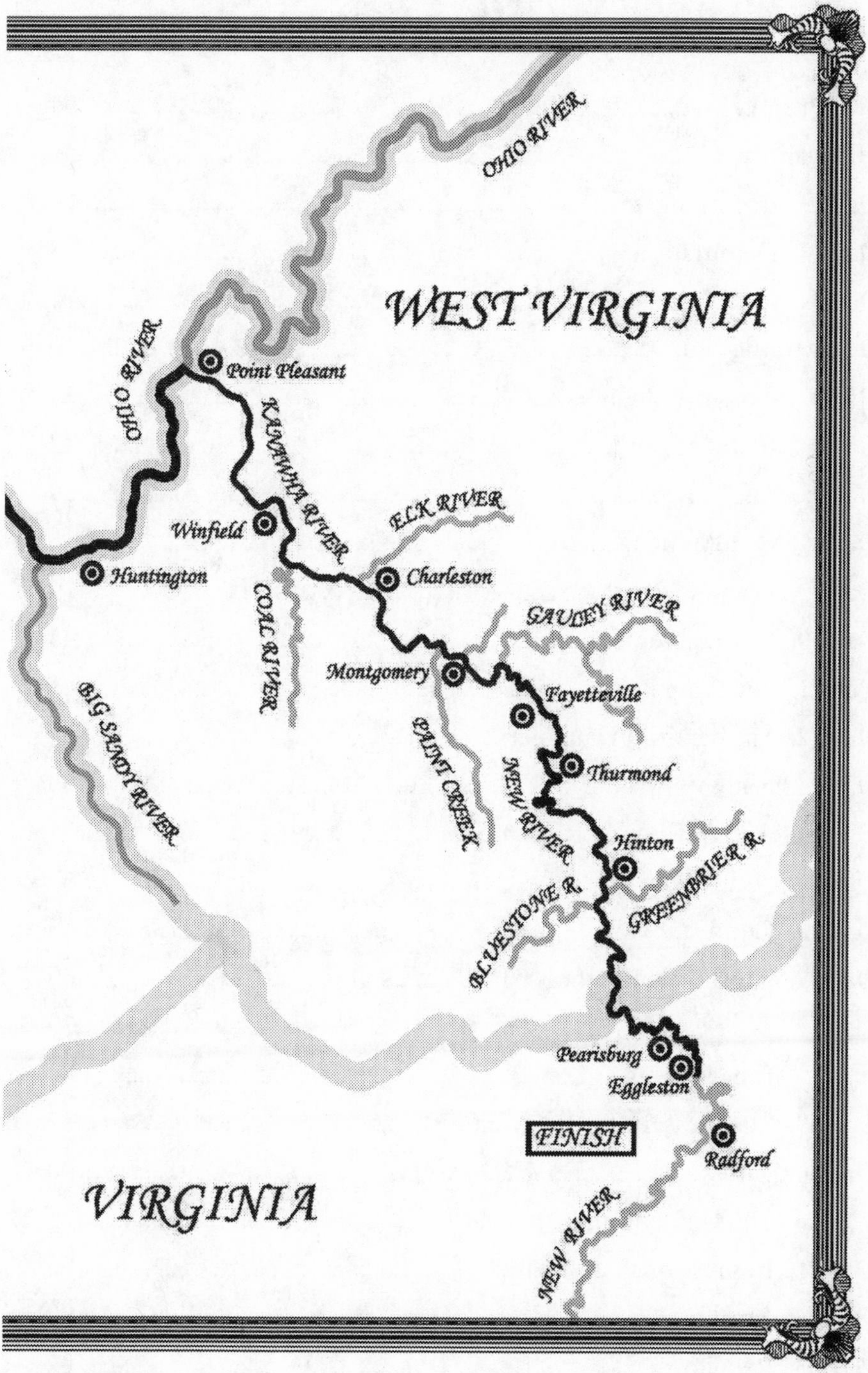

WEST VIRGINIA

OHIO RIVER

OHIO RIVER

Point Pleasant

KANAWHA RIVER

ELK RIVER

Winfield

Huntington

COAL RIVER

Charleston

GAULEY RIVER

BIG SANDY RIVER

Montgomery

PAINT CREEK

Fayetteville

NEW RIVER

Thurmond

Hinton

GREENBRIER R.

BLUESTONE R.

Pearisburg

Eggleston

FINISH

Radford

VIRGINIA

NEW RIVER

Contents

Wind blew in gusts, freezing my tears. Tent walls snapped. Pegs pulled loose. The tent came down. I crawled out from under it. Each fight with the cold and frustration slowed body movements. Anxiety and self-doubt mounted. Was some invisible hand trying to fling me off the mountain? Was some force saying I should not be there? I fought tears along with the wind and snow and tent. If it came down again, I'd just let it lie on top of me. A collapsed tent was more shelter than Mary had in 1755. On this night 232 years ago, necessity forced Mary Ingles to lie naked on the ground. I fought wind and cold by choice. So WHY was I crying?

The Dream

Everyone dreams. Some say babies dream before they are born. Some dreams we remember. Most we forget when morning sun opens our eyes. Think about your dreams. The ones you had as a child. A teenager. An adult. The ones that share your ride to work, spark up a dull job, ease you through the latest disappointment or just pop up out of nowhere. Think of the ones you replay year after year, night after night, where sleep imprints them on your soul. Did your dreams change over the years or stay the same? Did you ever share them with anyone? Did you make any of them come true?

From the time I was a small child, I dreamed of having an adventure. Any adventure. Being a good little girl, which meant being seen and not heard, I'd sit in the background and listen as my father and uncles planned deer and bear hunts in Canada and Montana. Sometimes they took their wives. Uncle Lee took his son and daughter. I waited for someone to take me. No one did. Well, that's not quite true.

When I was about ten, my father asked me to go squirrel hunting. Oh boy! My dad and I were going hunting! Excitement bubbled as I skipped proudly beside my father, the hunter. We left the house, walked past the barn and chicken coop, through the vegetable gardens and orchards, into a small deciduous forest behind our southwestern Michigan farm.

Hunkering down, we waited. Light played through leafy branches. Shadows danced. Birds twittered. Leaves rustled. There wasn't a sign of a squirrel. After what seemed too short a time, we gave up and walked back to the house. We wouldn't have squirrel for supper, but it didn't matter. I was riding cloud nine. I'd been hunting with my dad. We were a team.

As I burst through the door, Mom called out, "Get anything?" I opened my mouth to say, "No, but it was a great time." But, before words could form, behind me the sharp anger of a frustrated man unable to provide meat for his family cut the air and pierced my soul. "No. She wouldn't sit still! I'll never take her again!" And he didn't.

But the dreams didn't stop. Every book, magazine, and TV special about wilderness adventures had me glued to it. *The Boxcar Children. The Bobbsey Twins. Huckleberry Finn. The Adventures of Ra. Arizona Highways. Life. Look. Boys Life. National Geographic* specials. All were full of adventure seeds planted in a waiting brain. I'd dream for days afterward of jobs I could have done as part of the crew. I'd do anything. Cook, clean, swab decks, carry gear, be camp medic…if someone would just ask me.

With the naiveté of youth, I kept asking. There were always reasons why I didn't fit. I was too young, didn't have the skills, that piece of paper (a degree), or, worst of all, I was *a girl*. Then, with what seemed only the blink of an eye, I was the mother of four, helping them have bicycling, skiing and backpacking adventures to faraway places, and putting them through college. All at once I was 50 years old. Now the excuse for not taking me was that I was too old. What happened? What happened to me? What happened to my dream? Then I read a book.

For a year my daughter's best friend's mother kept saying, "Eleanor, there's a book you should read." Then she finally handed me *Follow the River,* by James Alexander Thom: the gripping story of the love, courage, strength and determination of an ordinary woman. Mary Draper Ingles, a mother, uneducated, and untrained (like me?), could not read or write, yet she did something no one else had ever done.

On July 30, 1755, a raiding party of Shawnee Indians kidnapped 23-year-old Mary and her two sons from their home in Virginia. Mary and an old Dutch woman escaped from Big Bone Lick, Kentucky, with only a hatchet and a blanket. They followed the Ohio, Kanawha, and

New Rivers from Big Bone Lick, Kentucky, to Adam Harmon's corn field near what is now Eggleston, Virginia, a distance of well over 500 miles.

Reading that book filled me with a burning desire to see the places where Mary walked, to experience her spirit, and capture some of her strength. All I had to do was find out who had retraced her route and talk to them. Then I could visit where Mary, with only the memory of a kind, loving husband to pull her through, had walked out of a Shawnee camp, trekked for 42½ days, detoured around tributaries, survived starvation, escaped from being eaten, and struggled up cliffs. My experience was that there aren't many men who care for their partner as much as Mary's husband cared for her. I wanted—no, needed—to be in the presence of such devotion.

People retrace adventurers, such as Columbus, Lewis and Clark and Sir Edmund Hillary, all the time. Surely someone had retraced Mary's escape. After all, it was over 232 years ago. I just had to find out who had done it. Unfortunately, there appeared to be no record of anyone even attempting to retrace her steps. Was it because it was too easy, that she was a woman, or just because no one ever had thought of it?

How difficult could it be? Just walk out of Big Bone Lick and follow the river.

The Plan

"Say, 'The plan is.'"

"It's not a plan."

"Just say, 'The plan is.'"

"But it's not a plan. It's only an idea."

"That's okay. Just say, 'The plan is...' and tell us what you plan to do."

"But it's only an *idea* of what someone *could* do. If I say it's a plan and never do it, I'll look silly."

"Eleanor. It doesn't make *any* difference if you *never* do it. *Just say*, 'The plan is...' and then tell us what you would do."

"The plan is..." With those words, wrung out of me by Wayne Sourbeer of WSWP-TV in March, 1987, an airy idea crystallized into a plan, and a plan was something possible.

Weeks earlier, when talking to James Alexander Thom, Wayne had learned of a woman who had an idea to attempt the first retracing of Mary's river route. With persuasive professionalism, Wayne called me and asked if I'd meet him at Big Bone Lick to "just talk." Earlier that morning, as part of his docudrama *Mary Ingles: Indian Captive* project, Wayne and his camera tech from Beckley, West Virginia, drove to Big Bone Lick State Park in Kentucky to film the site of Mary's escape. "Just talking into the tape recorder for a few minutes" turned into "just a little videotaping" and then "just a little hiking" in the sticky mud of Big Bone Lick Creek.

A bright sun warmed our backs as Wayne and I walked down the hill, to where a life-sized, cement mammoth reared its head and tusks to the sky (for just a little more videotaping.). It was easy to imagine a Shawnee salt-making camp with two white captives planning their escape. In fact, I could almost feel their spirits.

> *"Mary and the widow Stumf were put to work at dawn the first morning at the big bone lick and they worked until the sun set. They scooped out a shallow well at the place where the brine burbled vigorously out of the ground..." (FTR, p. 141) When gathering nuts, "They wandered out of the valley, onto the wooded slopes. Mary looked back from the brow of a hill and saw the Frenchmen and Indians loafing...To the west she caught a glimpse of shining water: the O-y-o. Her heartbeat sped up. It would be so simple to walk away..." (FTR, pp. 143, 144)*

In the middle of a place dripping with history and spirits, Wayne wanted my plan. With a deep breath I plunged in. "The plan is...for two ordinary women to just walk out of Big Bone Lick and retrace Mary's escape route. Following the Ohio, Kanawha, and New Rivers, they will walk from where she escaped along Big Bone Lick Creek to where she was rescued in Virginia. It would be women trying to reach back to touch Mary's experience."

Women, and maybe men, would attempt to draw close to this strong, courageous woman, while trying to find and prove themselves. The Walk will begin in the fall, the same time that Mary escaped. Camping out and living off the land (by stopping at gas stations and grocery stores for necessities), they will ask only for a place to pitch a tent and use of a restroom. If lucky, like Mary, they will finish in 42½ days.

To feel close to the 1755 experience, I'll carry a blanket and hatchet and keep track of days by tying knots in a yarn belt. Wearing a watch and personal grooming habits such as putting on makeup, shaving my legs, and curling my hair will be left behind. Baths may be rare. If we stink, too bad—gas station restrooms have sinks.

Finding a safe place to pitch a tent might be difficult. If we were lucky, people hearing about the retracing of history in their own back yards might offer us safe lodging. "No Trespassing" signs must be respected. Detouring around private property may be as much of a problem in 1987 as detouring around tributaries was in 1755. A few difficulties, but nothing daunting, that I could foresee.

So, thanks to Wayne Sourbeer, I left Big Bone Lick with a plan. However, like expectations and rivers, plans take abrupt, disappointing, and surprising turns.

My first idea was to invite a Draper/Ingles descendant to walk with me. Unfortunately, the only descendant I could find responded with a crisp, "None of us would think of doing a publicized hike. You are being exploited for advertising purposes." Devastated that I had offended the very family I was trying to honor, I gave up on the whole idea and wrote an apology to Jim Thom. After days of silent tears and self-recrimination, absolution came in another letter. Jim wrote: "You have done nothing out of place." So the plan changed.

It's a free country, I reminded myself. Anyone can go wherever they please, as long as they don't offend or interfere with someone else. I could just walk down the road and be close to places Mary passed. Instead of taking a member of Mary's family, I'd take a friend.

Easier said than done. Most friends and relatives smiled indulgently and brushed the concept off as another of Eleanor's nutty ideas. A few were encouraging. It sounded like fun, but they couldn't take the time away from work or family.

Maybe a national group. Because Mary is an excellent model of female strength and courage, I was sure the Girl Scouts would be interested either in having girls walk part of the way or in helping me find safe lodging. Not so. A friend who worked with the local Scouts checked with a regional office. "She can't do it without offending the Indians." Afraid of negative publicity, they refused all involvement.

There were those who didn't want to participate directly, but who found the project appealing and worked to find help. Such was the case of John Taylor, a firefighter colleague from West Virginia. He thought his athletic friend Susan Williams might be interested.

When Susan called, encouraged by her interest, I babbled on for half an hour trying to convince her to join me. When she said she couldn't walk but liked the idea and would try to find someone who could, I thought: Yeah, sure. Disappointment turned to confusion when she talked about a story appearing in the Sunday paper. Too late, I realized I had inadvertently given a newspaper interview. By giving Susan an interview I had reneged on my promise to Bloomington friend and reporter Larry Incollingo that he could have the first story *if* I ever went public. Like it or not, the plan was no longer my private little idea that I could back out of at any time. The Scripps Howard News Service picked up Susan's story, and the project took on a life of its own. Now, at the very least, I had to walk out of Big Bone Lick and make an attempt.

Soon letters, notes, and phone calls arrived from people interested in walking a few days, but none for all forty-three. Remembering all the people who had refused my desire to join a project, I hated turning them down. I wanted a single companion for the whole way, but no one appeared. In late August it shaped up as a solo effort. Then it dawned on me. By accepting all comers, I might make both their dreams and mine a reality.

If Brenda Hartman walked the first two days; Patti Dillard three days the next week; Phyllis Hyde a week or so in the middle; Rick Ransom a day near St. Albans, West Virginia; Susan Wood, Eleanor Henson, and Becky Straight a week beginning in Charleston; a volunteer from the Mary Ingles Trail Club through the New River Gorge; and Steve Trail from Hinton, West Virginia, to the Virginia state line, I'd have at least one person with me most of the way!

In addition, there was sag wagon support to check on me and give me a rest from carrying the pack. My daughters, Janette and Lisa, committed themselves to drive from Indiana to try to find me each weekend. Louise Kemp from Cincinnati and my cousin Kate Crossman from South Carolina would cover the first two weeks. John Taylor, from the first time I mentioned it, insisted it was possible to safely walk through "wild" West (by God) Virginia. He promised to coordinate the West Virginia volunteer fire service to move gear and help find safe lodging. Even my parents in Florida offered help.

Then there were those in Kentucky who wrote with food and lodging invitations: Pat Ackerson offered breakfast; Marsha and Gary Epplen and Bill and Ann Pladies offered campsites. I would not walk alone. Many hearts and eyes would be there for me. Different from the original idea, but definitely a plan. Until the last week in August.

John Taylor, who was coordinating the longest segment, unexpectedly needed heart bypass surgery. He couldn't help. My heart sank. Ever the friend, John said he'd ask Chip Stallard to take over for him. Since I was beginning my trek in less than four weeks, I had no alternative but to trust John's judgment and hope Chip bought into the project. Then, unexpected connections began clicking together. John Arrasmith, a Native American from Kentucky, heard of the Girls Scouts' refusal. He called and said, "When you leave, I'll be there for you."

The first week in September, Debbie Klene, a young mother from Indiana, was handed a newspaper clipping about the project by her mother-in-law. Soon Debbie called me, begging to walk the entire route. Although I agreed, I questioned her ability to get physically fit on such short notice. (I had been training for four months.) However, she was only 28, so I reasoned it would be much easier for her than for me at 51.

On Labor Day Sue Kennedy, Mary's great-great-great-great granddaughter, and her family were driving from Georgia to Cincinnati. On a whim Sue turned off the interstate to see Big Bone Lick and signed her name on the visitor log as a Draper/Ingles descendant. There she saw the WSWP-TV docudrama and learned of my plan. On September 5, she called me and offered help. (At least one member of Mary's family *was* interested in the effort to retrace her ancestor's escape.) Could she walk—even a short way? She'd like to, but there was a family get-together in Cincinnati at the end of the month. When was it? September 27. I caught my breath. The Walk would begin September 26. Sue would be there the first day.

Five days before leaving, I still had no lodging for if and when we reached Virginia. However, when my Radford University contact said that Mary was rescued near what is now Eggleston, Virginia, I decided, if that's where Mary stopped, that's where I'd stop. To end near the site of Adam Harmon's cornfield, where she was found, rather than going all the way to Blacksburg, Virginia, the site of Draper's Meadow or even further to Radford, Virginia, the site of Mary's home and Ingles Ferry, would save me several days of walking.

On September 23 I received a call from Mary Lewis Jeffries, another member of Mary and Will's family. She apologized for not answering my letter sent in August. Her husband died. But, in spite of her loss, if I made it all the way, she wanted me to sleep at Ingleside, the home that Mary's son John built on a hill above his mother's cabin! (Mary Lewis promised to have hot water for my feet.) Like Sue, Mary Lewis sounded enthusiastic, caring, generous, and gracious.

As the plan shook out on September 25, a young woman (Debbie), one of Mary's and Will's offspring (Sue), a Native American (John Arrasmith), and an old woman (me) would meet at Big Bone Lick. I would walk along the Ohio, Kanawha, and New Rivers. Occasionally, someone would transport gear or provide a safe campsite for me and any companions. If I made it to Mary and Will's farm, another descendant would welcome me. If the plan succeeded, I would visit Mary's grave and would know that I had reached back in history and made a dream come true.

It just might work.

My goal was to reach back in history to, somehow, touch an inspiring event. With a distance of 232 years, was there any possibility of feeling the smallest perception of the fear, anxiety, excitement, pain, longing, exhilaration, and accomplishment of an historic feat? In a few hours I would begin the search.

Recreating Mary's journey of capture and escape from the Shawnee was a physical and emotional impossibility. Forests had been cut, dams and power plants now clog rivers, and I did not have the emotional drive to walk 43 days in late fall, eating only bugs and berries, while sleeping on the ground without clothes, as she did. However, feeling some of what the escapees felt might be possible.

There could be similarities. Leave Big Bone Lick in the fall. Walk the same shorelines. Struggle up the same hills and valleys and tributaries. Carry a hatchet. Sleep in a blanket. Count days on a belt of knots. Watch the same sun set and moon rise. Maybe...maybe I could feel a small piece of Mary's experience, and with the similar experiences, a little of her courage might strengthen me. Lord knows I needed it.

Someone suggested I go in costume; an idea quickly squelched. I would make no pretense of being Mary. The old lady maybe. Definitely not Mary. The Walk was a retracing, not a recreation. However, in the spirit of a frontier woman, I packed no makeup, razor, curling iron, blow dryer, or clock, and wondered how the unadulterated Eleanor would be received.

Since childhood, I flinched at the sidelong glances people use when they think they are superior to the poor kid on the block. My clothes were hand-me-downs or handmade from feed sacks. And I never was sure, if there were more than one of each, which fork, knife, or spoon to use. Now I was saying, "Accept me as I am or go away." Would anyone even speak to me? In a few hours I'd find out.

Beginnings

Curled in a ball, I shivered as cold, damp air crept in among the blanket folds and down my neck. Each time I rose to consciousness, I thought how anxious Mary and Ghetel must have been in the sleepless hours before their escape. No more planning. No more training. This was the real thing.

I wouldn't need Janette's travel alarm to wake me—I slept hardly a wink. It was still pitch black when I decided I'd had enough tossing and turning. The light from a small Maglite eased that awkward dressing-while-sitting one does in a tent. I fumbled into jeans and T-shirt, then stumbled out and picked my way across frosty grass to the deserted shower house.

Ah-h-h. The caress of warm water flowing over a naked body. Only 42 days to go without another real shower or bath. It is amazing how special ordinary things become when you think they may be the last. Deliberately, I pulled on a yellow **GIRL SCOUTS DON'T LIVE BY COOKIES ALONE** T-shirt that was left over from my days as a Girl Scout leader. I liked the message and the Girl Scouts, even if the bigwigs had declined my request.

Trying to save my hiking boots (from what I haven't the foggiest idea), I put on an old pair of Aigners. Wet grass soon soaked through both shoes and socks. My feet were freezing. Idiot! Moisture is one of the prime causes of blisters. In over 400 training miles around my hometown of Bloomington, Indiana, I had never done anything like this. Now, on Day 1, before taking one step, I do something truly stupid. It was not a good beginning.

1

My two-daughter support crew, Janette and Lisa, struggled to start the Coleman stove while I shivered in the early morning chill. A rosy-pink sun began its climb in a clear blue sky. Good hiking weather. Bacon and eggs slid down easily and began warming my innards. But it took forever to heat water for coffee. While waiting, the girls covered Janette's homemade, cream-cheese, pecan coffeecake with candles. (Though not all 51.) Then, ever so softly, for it appeared we were the only campers awake on the hill, they sang "Happy Birthday, Mom."

Hands on the clock inched toward 7:00. I couldn't give the clock up yet because I had told several people I'd leave between 7:30 and 8:00. I had to be on time, and time was slipping away. The girls were tense. In an effort to reduce the strain, I walked to the edge of the hill. As I looked at the sun-drenched sky, my project became pitifully insignificant when compared with the wonder of a sunrise and the miracle of Mary's accomplishment.

Understanding the real risks of this trip, the night before, I had written a farewell letter to my children, attached a copy of the song "It's My Turn," and cried my tears. Now, on the brink of a final good-bye, I wanted desperately to be close to them. But it wasn't working. Son John was in Indianapolis and son Jerry in California. Janette and Lisa were physically near, but emotionally distant. Through shivers, sniffles, and strangled sobs, I whispered a gut-wrenching plea, "God...It's almost here...Please, help me...."

Debbie and I had planned to meet in the campground the previous night. However, arriving after dark, the girls and I couldn't find the campsite the park reserved for us. A quick search in the morning and still no Debbie. In three weeks of marathon telephone conversations, she sounded enthusiastic. However, she canceled every joint training hike we had planned. If Debbie was late, I would leave without her. This was one activity in which I refused to act as someone's mother. Come, follow the rules, take care of yourself, and keep up was all I asked. I wondered how many of the people I had talked to would actually show up.

Seven o'clock and still no boiling water. Park manager Bob Lindy expected me to be at the shelter at seven and leave between seven-thirty and eight. I was not where I had said I would be. As I paced around camp, my nervous tension was showing. Intuitive Lisa offered to stay and break camp. A last check for Mary's essentials: hatchet, blanket and belt, and mine: money, Mace, and MasterCard, then Janette drove me down to the shelter.

A small crowd greeted us. Randy and Linda Barlow, friends formerly from Bloomington, now lived a few miles from the park. Brenda Hartman, the teacher who would walk the first two days and who had arranged permission for us to camp outside the Loder House this night…if we make it that far. Marsha and Gary Epplen, who were providing tent space and supper on Day 2, came with smiles, enthusiasm, encouragement, and children in tow. A woman with bushy, jet-black hair who said she was a friend of Chip Stallard's pulled up in a white Corvette. A gal with short red hair and freckles smiled in the background. (Years later, I learned she was Patti Dillard, checking me out before joining us in Maysville.)

Just as I had hoped, Mary's family was there in the form of Sue Kennedy, her husband Christopher, and daughters Lynn and Anne, and also Sue's sister Patty Hons. Regina Villers, free-lance writer for the *Cincinnati Enquirer*, came with a photographer.

Others arrived whom I did not recognize. Each was important. I tried to remember everyone, but there were too many for my brain to take in. Names began to blur. A few names made it onto the yellow legal pad I carried in my backpack. It was amazing. Cold and shivering, total strangers had pulled themselves out of bed, early on a Saturday morning, just to see someone (me!) begin a walk.

John Arrasmith appeared, wearing authentic, Native American clothes he had made himself, in the style of those who lived in the eastern part of the country. His right eye and forehead were painted black, his left eye white, and he carried a rifle. He wore a blue shirt, brain-tanned buckskins with feathers, and braided decorations. Representing the natives who raided Drapers Meadow and kidnapped Mary, her sons Thomas and George, and her sister-in-law Bettie, he was also a symbol of those who had raised Thomas in such a good life that he was reluctant to return to his parents. To protect me from those who said that I couldn't do it without offending the Indians, this man with Native American blood in his veins said, "I'll be there for you." To keep that promise, he left his daughter's hospital bedside. Though a stranger, he felt like family.

With all the laughter and hugs, it looked as if a long awaited reunion was taking place, not a gathering of strangers. On this day, Mary's family and the Native Americans moved the pain of the past into the background. They met with goodwill and mutual admiration.

Warm feelings. Freezing air. Chattering teeth. Tingling toes. To thaw out and get acquainted, we took turns piling in and out of Randy and Linda's van. Seven-thirty and still no sign of Debbie. I would wait until 8:00 and no longer.

Concern for what lay ahead had me strung tight. I knew I could walk 20 to 30 miles for one day. But could I do it day in and day out? Could Debbie? (If she came.) I kept asking people to check on Debbie. Had she called? Had she checked in? If she backed out, the way she had on all other planned hikes, I might as well stop this dawdling and start.

In the middle of the hubbub, Sue called everyone to attention. Out of a paper bag she pulled a white sweatshirt with bright red lettering emblazoned across the front:

**THE LONG
WAY HOME
1755–1987**

and on the back:

**IN MEMORY
OF
MARY INGLES**

It captured the essence of the project, and I had another clothing layer. People seeing it would understand the reason for The Walk. With brimming eyes, I struggled for words of thanks; then the crowd broke out in a rousing, "Happy Birthday." Fifty-one is a *great* age.

Janette walked off for one last Debbie search. Silently I called for her, Come on, Debbie. Time is running out. At 8:00 I'm out of here with or without you.

Excitement mounted. Families and individuals were deciding who would walk the first steps, yards, or miles as part of the historic event. Sue Kennedy, her daughter Lynn, and sister Patty would walk Big Bone Lick Creek to the Ohio River. On the spur of the moment, Gary Epplen asked to walk. Why not? He was providing tent space tomorrow.

My watch showed 8:00. No Debbie. Disappointed, I turned to leave, just as Janette ran up, excited and breathless. "She's here! She'll be right down!" Tired of cooling my heels, I thought, She better hurry.

Janette explained that, arriving after dark, we had missed the WELCOME DEBBIE AND ELEANOR sign on a reserved campsite. Debbie had been where she was supposed to be, but had forgotten about the Indiana/Kentucky time difference. As Debbie sat on the "john," her mother-in-law ran in yelling, "Hurry up! She's leaving. NOW!"

Being late or waiting for someone (after I've made an effort to be on time) is a pet peeve of mine. It was after 8:00. I paced. I fretted. If she was coming, where was she? Janette insisted, "She's coming, Mom. She's coming."

After what seemed an eternity, a van drove up. A brief flurry of good-byes around the door. Then up walked a young woman in her late twenties. She wore blue jeans and sweatshirt, a small day-pack across her back, and a camera slung over one shoulder. A black, felt hat flopped over long, dark brown, wavy hair. She looked shy, scared, and sad. "Are you Debbie?" "Yes." "Let's do it." With that brief greeting, Debbie and I turned, stepped out of the parking lot, and headed toward Big Bone Lick Creek. An Indian, holding a rifle, stood off alone, watching.

Before reaching the trees, I noticed Debbie's reddened eyes and her efforts to hold back tears. Only then did I realize that, like Mary, this young mother walking out of Big Bone Lick had just turned her back on her young children.

Walking beside Debbie, I put my arm around her. The tremors I felt were not from the cold. Could she force herself to walk away? Softly, so no one else could hear, I asked, "Are you all right?" Through a sniffle came, "Yes. I'll be okay." "Are you sure?" A slight nod of her head. "Then let's go."

> "...*with an anguish that surely would kill her, she rose to her feet and stumbled, tearblinded, to the edge of the camp, her lungs quaking for release, her throat clamped to hold down the awful wail of despair that was trying to erupt....Oh dear God help me! Mary's heart felt the way her loins had felt when the baby was being born. But ten times worse...They were far into the woods before she could see or hear or feel anything, and what she became aware of first was the old woman's strong arm across her back helping her along...." (FTR, p. 156)*

Detours

"…when they were perhaps a fourth of the way back down the shore of the tributary, they were dismayed to find still another obstacle before them: a deep creek flowing across their path into the river. Mary sighed. They would have to make a detour from their detour. This was worse than ever she had expected." (FTR, p. 167)

Over and over on Day 1 as we hiked away from Big Bone Lick, we asked people, "How far is it to Rabbit Hash?" No one would admit they didn't know. Everyone tried to be helpful. However, we soon learned that "about five miles" was a guess. In a car, five miles is five minutes. Being off a mile or so is no problem. On foot, "about five miles" is an hour or two, depending on terrain, how tired you are, how many blisters you have, and how many people you have in tow.

One fellow suggested, "If you cut through the woods, you can save seven miles." *Save seven miles?* What happened to "about five miles"? We were on a treadmill running backwards! We collapsed beside the river in Rabbit Hash at 3:00. Three hours late. That evening I estimated that we had covered about 28 miles. A tough first day. The lesson I learned was to be skeptical and believe only a woman who had just clocked it by car or a grizzled, old farmer who'd lived there all his life.

On Day 2, determined to put the "about five miles" curse behind us, I carefully studied road and topographic maps. It looked like three miles of shoreline from Route 20 in Petersburg to the beginning of Route 8 (known locally as the Mary Ingles Highway), just north of I-275.

The Captain Moore House, shown on the 1883 map, still stood at the beginning of Route 8. Easy to reach by car and close to the river, it would be a convenient place to meet Janette and Lisa for lunch.

The first night out, thanks to Brenda's connections, the Loder House, a house-turned-restaurant, allowed us tent space in its yard beside the Ohio River. This morning, with stomachs full of its chef's steamy breakfast and anticipating a pleasant river walk, Debbie, Brenda, and I headed out from the nearby boat ramp. On the opposite bank, Indiana's blue-green hills, brown cornfields, and smoke-spouting power plant looked enticingly close. Upriver, a light fog blurred the outline of the I-275 bridge. Just beyond the bridge another power plant stood across the river from the Moore House. Three miles. An easy hour.

The Ohio River guided the other walkers and me for 19 days.
Like Mary Ingles, I carried a blanket and hatchet.

The firm riverbank was a treat, even if we were stepping over and around tires, plastic bottles, trees, and dead fish. Around the first riverbend, reality hit. Hard-packed, level sand gave way to slippery, slate-like rocks the size of tabletops. Stacked at steep angles, they threatened us with a twisted or broken ankle at every step. So we moved inland, only to fight dense undergrowth.

Narrow animal trails were a treat to follow though they inevitably petered out. At times they led to a tree canopy that retarded the growth of bushes and seedlings. A thin rabbit trail felt like a four-lane highway. More often, an animal trail led to a tangle of blow-down and trash that we'd stumble and scramble over or through. Then we'd stop short, captivated by masses of yellow flowers waving their petals atop six-foot-tall stems. A stranded, rundown houseboat made us edgy. Did it run out of gas, or had drug dealers parked it in this God-forsaken place?

Briars and tree limbs caught and tangled my blanket. Was the undergrowth this thick in 1755, or did the virgin forest provide Mary with a four-lane highway? Did she struggle over these rocks, or were they erosion-preventing measures put in after the dams? Was this day harder for us than it had been for Mary and Ghetel?

An hour passed. The bridge appeared no closer. We seemed to move in slow motion, like one of those nightmares where you are trying to hurry but it feels as though you are slogging through Elmer's Glue.

At noon, two and a half hours after leaving Petersburg, we walked under the I-275 bridge. Janette and Lisa would be worrying and waiting at the Moore House, but there was no way to communicate that we were okay. Although I anticipated a short walk to where they waited, we needed food and rest. So, while cars whizzed overhead and boats played on the river, like Huck Finn, Tom Sawyer, and Big Jim, three women laid back to rest on large rocks. According to the maps, we were over halfway there. One more hour. The worst was over. The power plant Janette and I had seen when we had scouted part of the Kentucky route loomed large and close. It was right across from the Moore House.

Cool morning air gave way to muggy afternoon heat. Sweat ran in rivulets. Wool from the blanket stuck to and scratched my sticky skin. Debbie lost the lens cap to her camera. To protect the camera, she stuffed it in her hat. But holding the camera in one hand and the walking stick in the other left her no way to hold on as she slipped, slid, and clambered over boulders. A loose rock, slick surface, or misstep, and we'd be dealing with a broken bone or someone in the river.

Suddenly, Brenda slipped, and with a cry fell flat on her back. Her arms and legs stuck straight up, waving and struggling like a giant, overturned insect. My heart stopped. Then she burst out laughing. We were fine. Our collective hearts rejoiced when a cultivated field appeared through the trees. The end was close! Near the field was a house. Not the Moore House, but we had broken through to civilization. It couldn't be far now. Then a man stepped out of the doorway, strode toward us, and erased all joy.

Large and muscular with a long, shaggy beard and unkempt hair, he wore faded and torn jeans and a frown. For uncomfortable seconds we eyed each other. Was I mistaken, or did he feel as threatened as we? Had we inadvertently stumbled into something...like a pot field? No other houses or even a road could be seen. He could rape, murder, and pillage and no one would know.

Quickly, I tried to explain about Mary Ingles' escape and our walk from Big Bone Lick to Virginia. My words sounded crazy...even to me. Debbie and Brenda chimed in as we tried desperately to make him understand we didn't care who or what he was. We just wanted to move across his field.

More than my explosion of words, Debbie's young, good looks and "what the hell" attitude seemed to be what calmed him. When he offered us a turtle (which we admired and politely declined) and warned that we probably couldn't get through the creek on the other side of the treeline that edged his field, I felt we would leave in one piece. As we walked away, I had no doubt that he watched our every move from inside the house.

Our steps grew lighter, because across the creek and around the bend we'd find my daughters, when we entered the trees. However, when we reached the stream that emptied into the Ohio, we discovered a manmade drainage ditch—too wide to jump and too deep to wade. The man who so frightened us was right. Another detour.

It wasn't fair. We were so close. I *knew* I had seen the power plant last summer. The girls were waiting on the other side. I was sure of it. Heat, tired muscles, and now another disappointment seemed to cause Debbie and Brenda to physically sag. Sounding more bright and positive than I felt, I called for a break. Sitting in the shade beside flowing water and our "friend's" field, we regrouped.

Neither Debbie nor Brenda complained, but rising temperatures and fatigue were taking a toll. I could feel their tension and wondered how much pushing they would take. However, when Debbie began cracking jokes, I knew things would be okay...at least for a while. And that little while would put us further upstream and closer to Janette and Lisa. But first this detour.

Following the dredged stream led us to another tributary coming in from the right that was also too deep to cross, which led to another and another. Struggling up and down several feeder streams, soon I wondered if we were going in the right direction. Was this the right one, or was it the other one? Frustration, pain, and the stress of trying to make correct decisions through a branching maze were certainly part of Mary's experience, and now ours. We were separated by 232 years, but just as close as this detour.

At every break in the trees, I'd look up, trying to see a smokestack. Beside it would be the river. Mary didn't have a smokestack landmark, but neither did she have a friggin' dredged canal and a river driven higher by dams!

Finally we broke into an area relatively free of trees. Though full of bushes taller than our heads, it felt like a clearing, because we suddenly had blue sky and clouds overhead. Enthusiasm at seeing the sun turned quickly to despair when Debbie and Brenda, then I, stumbled into a field of holes. It was like traversing a minefield. Before taking a step, we'd stab our walking sticks through long, uncut weeds. This technique prevented many a fall and made enough commotion to scare away sunning snakes. Inevitably, some holes were missed.

In a split second my right leg plunged with a thud into a knee-deep hole. Surprise and pain elicited an involuntary "OH!" I felt as if The Walk had just come to a halt in the middle of nowhere on Day 2. Sharp pain shot up my leg. Definitely an injury, but a carefully placed step took weight. As long as I could walk, my job was to get us safely back to civilization. Fortunately, uneven terrain disguises a limp.

Tired people make mistakes. I was tired and in pain. After struggling across that pock-marked field, I realized we were following the wrong tributary. Backtrack. Again. My companions handled another detour better than I. Without complaints or criticism they turned around, negotiated the potholes a second time, and turned up a different stream. I fought back tears.

To get in condition before leaving on this adventure, I had trained by walking over 400 miles without an injury. Debbie had trained by pulling on her new boots after Labor Day and walking around her kitchen. Brenda had expected a leisurely two-day hike along the Ohio. The physical and mental challenge we faced was more than any of us had expected. And there I was, the blind, dumb, and lame leader.

Road maps show roads. Topographic maps show elevation, some buildings, roads, and most streams. Maps do not show boulders, blow-down, scrub, or holes. Strangers may or may not be helpful. With all my resources I was as lost and frustrated as Mary would have been in 1755. Sometimes all you have is gut instinct. At my lowest, I glanced up. Peeking through a small break at the top of the canopy, I spied a tiny piece of smokestack. We were heading in the right direction!

Slipping and sliding, we groped along the side of a creek bank that grew to a steep hill. While Debbie and Brenda rested, I explored anything that looked like it might be the Moore House. On one side trip I discovered an old roadbed. Though they had a steep climb, Debbie and Brenda joined me. The road petered out, but we had crossed the last tributary and were back to the Ohio. We were not lost. Janette and Lisa would be waiting beside the river. Just a little further.

Any minute the white, two-storied Moore House would come into view. Any minute. Then another manmade tributary, too wide to jump, but shallow enough to wade, blocked our path. All it would take to reach the other side was one step in the water. Going around would mean another hour—if we were lucky.

To prevent blisters, my theory on feet was this: Keep 'em dry at all costs. During most of our breaks, I removed my shoes and socks and rubbed my feet with alcohol. On the other hand, Debbie was of the "I'm not taking one more step than is necessary" attitude. Without hesitation, she sloshed through the water, stood on the bank, and looked back at me.

One big step. Cold water poured over and down into one boot. Using the walking stick for balance, I swung the other foot up on dry land. With only one wet foot I was across. However, for a week afterward I would rue that decision.

Now we stood directly across from the power plant and there was *still* no sign of the Moore House. Back down river, the bridge loomed close. We had struggled so hard to come so short a distance. Calling another break, I deliberately spread the blanket. If anything happened to us, one of the boaters running up and down the river might remember three women sitting on a red blanket.

Moving on, we enjoyed walking under a canopy clear of undergrowth and over what appeared to be four-wheel-drive trails. How did they get there? Where did they lead? Like the game trails, these tracks all dwindled into nothing. The only sure guide was the river. No matter how tired or emotionally drained, I felt secure with the river in sight. We were not lost. We would make it.

We all saw a dilapidated two-story house perched up on the hill. It had what appeared to be a wall behind it. Debbie and Brenda opted to rest by the river while I explored. Like tattered wallpaper, the house's floors and walls hung at weird angles. At one time it had been a lovely, gracious home with children running and laughing and flowers in the yard. It was the pride of its owners, who probably thought it would last forever, but it didn't. A hundred years from now, someone may stand outside my house and think the same thing, and they'll be right.

It occurred to me that I should hike up to look at the wall on the other side of the house, but I was tired. More exploring meant tackling another tangle of brush. Besides, Debbie and Brenda found another "four-lane highway" and called me down. Sooner or later we *had* to break through. It would be later.

After another hour of hard walking, I saw sunlight stream through the trees. While Debbie and Brenda took another break, I checked it out. As if trying to regain strength, I walked in slow, deliberate steps. During Day 1, I had worried about my companions. During Day 2, the emotional strain of uncertainty, leg pain, and the responsibility for the others wore me down, until I broke through the trees and all stress disappeared.

A field! A large soybean field! No buildings, but a farm that size requires equipment, and equipment requires a road. Suddenly we all had energy. Like Dorothy and her friends hurrying toward Oz, we each picked a row and moved quickly toward the top of the hill. Brenda saw a car off to our right. Although our legs were only walking, in our heads we were running.

A level path! A smiling Lisa was walking toward us! And a distraught Janette minding the car. *Everything* was all right. We had made it! We would make it through the weekend! Amid hugs and laughter, Lisa lifted the blanket off my shoulders and onto hers. Strain and pain melted away.

We learned that Janette and Lisa had been under the bridge before we arrived for lunch and that the "wall" behind the tattered house was the side of the road that the girls were driving up and down, looking for us. Once they even glimpsed a flash of red between the trees in front of the power plant. (My blanket?) So near and yet so far.

As we struggle through life's detours and disappointments, how many times are we so near and yet so far?

Sag Wagons

"Mary estimated that they were covering twice as much distance each day as they had before acquiring the wonderful animal, partly because the horse could carry them both across creek mouths and shallow rivers they would have been afraid to wade on foot." (FTR, p. 191)

When I rode the Hilly Hundred bicycle tour in 1983, a sag wagon followed behind the group to check on bicyclists' progress and offer first aid, a spare tire, or a lift if someone became too tired to finish. I didn't need sag support; however, it was reassuring to know it was there, if necessary, to pick up my broken bike and/or body.

So, when I began thinking about The Walk, an important element was to have sag support to check on my status, carry my 40-pound backpack, and drop it off wherever I happened to be at day's end. When the Kentucky State Police recommended that I have a support vehicle and suggested ways to protect myself against the most feared predator— the human male, I realized the potential for danger was real. I wanted an adventure, but I wasn't stupid. Sag support seemed the best chance for me to return in one piece.

The police were pleased that I was using a walking stick and would hang a hatchet from my belt. I would appear strong and able to defend myself. They advised posting an identifying sign on the sag vehicle. So Janette and Lisa taped **"RETRACING MARY INGLES' WALK"** signs to the side windows of the car.

14

My daughters agreed to sag on weekends. No light commitment. The one-way drive from Bloomington to Big Bone Lick was three hours, seven to Charleston, West Virginia, and twelve to Radford, Virginia. The girls were both working, and Lisa was also taking graduate classes. With their pledges that someone would come and look for my bloody body at least once a week, I had begun serious planning.

Kentucky Governor Collins' office wrote and said that the State Police would drive by each day to check on me. Kate Crossman, my cousin from South Carolina, would drive her van up to sag for one week; which meant that if safe lodging wasn't available, we could sleep in the van. (Better safe, dry, and cramped than cold, wet, and vulnerable.) When Louise Kemp's daughter read a newspaper article about the walk, she declared, "Mother, Mary didn't carry a backpack. Eleanor shouldn't either." So a 69-year-old woman from Cincinnati decided to sag five days for a woman she had never met.

With Janette and Lisa on weekends, Louise the first week and Kate the second, that meant someone would be looking out for me each day for the first two weeks. By then I would know what gear worked and what didn't, how many miles a day I could walk, and how realistic it was for an ordinary woman to, as Mary did, walk from Kentucky to Virginia in 43 days.

John Taylor thought that because I was a volunteer firefighter, the West Virginia volunteer fire service would help. If he was right, I'd have a virtual cast of angels watching out for me clear through West Virginia. Virginia was not a concern because, if all went well, we could easily cover the distance from the state line to Eggleston in two or three days.

Early Sunday evening, September 27, my daughters completed their first weekend as their mom's sag wagon staff and dropped our backpacks beside the Licking River. After warm hugs, and a lump in my throat, I waved good-bye and wondered if I'd see them again. Then Debbie and I pitched our tents on the lawn of Marsha and Gary Epplen's home, near where it is believed that Mary and Ghetel had crossed the Licking River. In addition to providing tent space, the Epplens also cooked up a lip-smacking spaghetti supper.

I telephoned Louise to tell her where we were and that we'd be ready for a 7:30 a.m. pickup. Although I wanted to leave the clock (that silent controller of our lives) behind, all the help we were receiving demanded a schedule. Perhaps later, like Mary and Ghetel, we could rise and go to bed with the sun.

Monday morning, a half hour early, a tan Honda hatchback pulled up. Out hopped perky Louise Kemp. She wore bobby socks, tennis shoes, a skirt that stopped at her knees, and a smile that stretched across her face. She had the infectious, happy spirit and sense of humor I longed for. Louise may have had a wrinkle and a gray hair or two, but she was 69 going on 21. Without hesitating, she pitched in to help fold our dew-drenched tents and appeared totally unconcerned that they might dirty her vehicle.

Thankfully, the Epplen work and school schedules pressed us to leave. There was no time for long farewells, which I found harder to negotiate than asking for help. In addition to Gary walking the first day and Marsha feeding us, they had made us part of their family, and even found a lens cap to replace the one Debbie had lost the day before. "Thank you" was not enough. Would leaving ever get easier?

When Louise asked where we were starting, without hesitation, I said, "Raven's Hill Orchards," where we had quit the day before. Debbie immediately began a good-natured, but serious, objection. "These feet do *not* go backwards." Backtracking appeared more than she could emotionally, and perhaps physically, handle.

I was torn. I *knew* I could walk it. The dilemma was whether to park Debbie and do the segment alone or begin here at the Licking River. Would not walking every step of the route cheat me and the intent of the project? After much mental argument I decided that Mary did not walk *every step* from Big Bone Lick to Adam Harmon's. She had a horse for four or five days. The few miles between Raven's Hill and the Licking River could easily have been covered by a horse in one day. The car was our horse. It was okay to start at the mouth of the river and walk over the bridge. With my companion visibly relieved, I decided I could live with the rationalization. But it highlighted a worrisome element—that Debbie needed to walk slowly at first to "break in" her feet.

I did not question Debbie about the state of her feet or how she cared for them. The fact that she kept up was all that concerned me. If she did not like the pace or conditions, the decision to leave was hers. However, it was obvious that if her feet did not begin improving, she would never make it a week, let alone 43 days. In spite of her problems, we slowly moved upriver past signs and through towns.

Route 8 runs near the Ohio River in northern Kentucky. We read all the historical markers along the way—ones that people in cars pass without thinking. A bronze plaque brought us up short.

MARY INGLES
Said to have been the first white
woman in Kentucky. Captured by
Indians in Virginia, July 1755, and
taken to Ohio. Later she escaped
a salt-making party at Big Bone
Lick and made her way across
the Kentucky wilderness back
to Virginia.

We were making The Walk for the same reason that sign stood there—to help people remember the accomplishment and love of an ordinary woman.

At noon, Louise joined us for lunch. Scouting out a shaded, grassy area, she parked the car at a wide place, where there was room to spread out our bodies, gear, and food. She thoughtfully brought and shared water, cheese, crackers, sandwiches, bananas and oranges. A grand supplement to the water and gorp Debbie and I carried. She also had her friend Marilyn Hooper in tow. Before eating I took off my shoes and socks, the hiker's effort to dry feet and help heal blisters. Debbie kept hers on.

As we discussed what time Louise should pick us up if we did not make it to California (a small Kentucky town), Marilyn asked about our schedule. Tuesday Augusta and Wednesday Maysville. Where did we plan to stay? Tent beside the road. "Well, I know someone in Augusta, and there is a women's crisis center in Maysville. I bet they'd let you stay. I'll call." Amazing. Out of the blue, without my asking, this stranger came along to arrange safe lodging. Mary may have had spiritual angels help her find food and shelter, but our angels were flesh and blood. This particular angel was a striking blond, wearing a pink sweatsuit.

With Louise's nutritious food and Marilyn's good news, I was charged for the afternoon. On the other hand, Debbie slowly eased into her stride. Gingerly, limping a little, she eventually began a steady pace, but considerably slower than in the morning. How much longer could she walk on what must be expanding blisters?

About a half mile down the road, passing a gas station and glancing at the newspaper dispenser, we were shocked to see *our* photos with the headline "**MARY INGLES' LONG WALK FROM CAPTIVITY RETRACED**" clear across the front page! A couple of customers recognized us and enthusiastically began videotaping as though we were celebrities. A store clerk let us use a restroom. (A privilege not always accorded strangers.) And afterward, Debbie kept up with me—at least for a while.

As the afternoon wore on, Debbie lagged. I'd slow down and "reel her in." But soon she'd be far behind, and as the distance between us grew, Debbie became more and more quiet. Ann Pladies, driving home from work, saw her evening guests beside the road and stopped to introduce herself. Ann's encouragement was another temporary rejuvenation to Debbie, as was the offer from a couple in an old blue-and-white car.

Bill and Pauline Kelsch wanted us to stay at their Augusta home the next night. "We're right on the river...where Mary walked!" But Marilyn Hooper already had that night lined up. When I refused the offer, their joy at meeting us and making the invitation changed to such visible disappointment that I asked, "How about the next night?" I had not planned any rest and relaxation days, but a day of R & R in Augusta might calm Debbie's feet enough for healing to begin. Looks can be deceiving, but with the state of their old car and tattered blue jeans, this couple did not appear as polished as Marilyn and Ann; however, their sincerity was apparent.

Debbie seemed to require periodic adrenaline charges of encouragement just to finish the day. I wanted a companion, but not to the point of crippling her. It was late in the afternoon, and we were still four miles from California when Louise drove up and stopped. I could make the distance in about an hour and wanted to go on. Debbie made a beeline for the car. Realizing I could not get another step out of her, reluctantly I consented to "ride the horse."

Frustration and anger at myself for once more giving in tightened my stomach. I could rationalize using the sag wagon this day and the day before, but I would not let my goal of walking the whole way go down the tubes by starting the habit of riding the last few miles each day. Debbie was making a Herculean effort to walk 20 miles on severely blistered feet, and she deserved a lift. However, for me the car rides had to stop. As far as I was concerned, the horse was dead.

Louise downshifted her car up the steep, narrow drive to Ann and Bill's mountain home above the river, and then negotiated tight switchbacks up to the meadow. This sprightly, senior imp forever crushed my stereotypical image of the older woman.

The campsite, a flat clearing in the mountain forest, offered a fire ring, picnic table, and hammock. But best of all, after we unloaded Louise's car, made pickup arrangements for the next day, and waved good-bye, we were *alone*. Alone to set up tents, rest our feet, and enjoy the peace and quiet. No reporters or well-meaning, but prying, eyes.

Ann came by to invite us down to their 100-year-old log cabin for a delicious supper of red beans and rice. We became acquainted with our hosts and related our day's experiences. Of particular note were incidents when people who stopped to talk or walk with us were narrowly missed by speeding cars. A sudden tragedy might be closer than we realized.

When Ann offered the use of her bathtub, I jumped at it. (Only 40 days to go without bathing!) While I prepared to scrub and soak, Debbie called home. It was obvious that the person on the other end of the phone was applying pressure for her to stop this foolishness. Turning her back on us, Debbie talked quietly. After hanging up, she never complained or explained. I ached for her. After baths, we thanked our hosts and headed back to our camp. Debbie seemed enveloped in a cloud of gloom.

Against a dark dome, twinkling stars were our only lights as we gingerly felt for each stone step up to our home-away-from-home. Leaves rustled in a warm, gentle breeze as we climbed into our individual tents. We were not nestled side-by-side as Mary and Ghetel were, but we were alone in the night. Basking in the glow of hospitality, new friends, and people looking out for us, all was right in my world.

> *"...the evening was mild, so they did not have to huddle together for warmth. Each rolled up in her own blanket...and lay in her private hopes and fears in the creaking, hushing, owl-hooting darkness above the murmuring river...." (FTR, p. 163)*

Endurance

"...they put weight on their feet, groaning with the returning pain and then getting used to it, and started to move on." (FTR, p. 263)

It never ceases to amaze me what humans are willing to suffer. Equally surprising is human reaction to the difficulties of others. Take Debbie Klene.

A 28-year-old mother of two, Debbie had learned about my plan to retrace Mary Ingles' escape when her mother-in-law handed her a newspaper clipping three weeks before I was to start. A few days later, she telephoned me and begged to join The Walk.

Although I doubted someone could get in shape in so short a time, Debbie was much younger than I, and I assumed that she was working on her own crash-course training program.

What I did not know was that Debbie's husband was less than enthusiastic about his wife taking off for 43 days. His words to her were, "You can go if you make 43 days' worth of food before you go." Now, that was not 43 meals, but 43 days' worth of food. Consequently, instead of preparing for The Walk by going out and working the kinks out of her new equipment, Debbie put on her boots and clomped around the kitchen preparing freezer meals for her husband and two children.

Now if my husband had said that, I *think* I would have given him money and said, "Go to McDonald's." Not Debbie. She cooked and baked and packaged while her boots remained new, unscuffed, and stiff.

On Day 1 Debbie was quiet. She brought up the rear but never complained. Day 2, she started well, but began dreaming up every opportunity possible to stop walking, from taking photos of dead snakes to relieving herself in a cornfield. It was frequently necessary to slow my pace to let her catch up. In camp the second evening she admitted to having blisters. There were no complaints, but Debbie and moleskin were becoming tight friends. On Day 3 Debbie stopped several times to add moleskin and adjust her socks. She dropped farther and farther behind, but still no whining.

All this time I did not look at Debbie's feet or make suggestions. I took care of my blisters; she took care of hers. Debbie was a big girl, and one decision I was firm about was that I would not "mother" anyone. In this project, it was all I could do to take care of myself. I would not be responsible for others. Help and advice would be given if asked for. Debbie asked for none.

The morning of Day 4, my blisters had healed to an occasional twinge. Debbie was another story. After walking less than five miles, she limped badly. I was not sure how much longer she could withstand the pain of putting one foot in front of the other. Then, just as I reached *my* limit of watching her agony, in the middle of nowhere, a little Shop Kwik grocery appeared just ahead of us. Debbie immediately sank onto the gas pump's cement sign support to check her feet. This time I took a look...and my stomach turned.

"Rucking" socks produce enough heat to make blisters on even toughened feet. Debbie's soft skin must have started bubbling the first day. She had put moleskin on top of moleskin, on top of blisters too numerous to count. Moleskin adhesive, which stuck to and pulled at broken, tender skin, complicated the problem. Her feet and toes were a mass of raw, oozing, bloody blisters. For all I knew, gangrene might have set in. That she could stand up, let alone walk, was a feat in itself. It was time for me to get involved.

I dug out my first aid kit and handed her the scissors, with instructions to cut away the moleskin and her own torn flesh. Next I handed her Neosporin to spread on all raw areas before wrapping her toes and feet in lambswool. (Was it just an accident that last summer my neighbor happened to praise the blister-healing virtues of Dr. Scholl's lambswool, a product I'd never heard of, and that this out-of-the-way store had a single, dusty package hanging on a peg?) Finally, I gave Debbie a pair of my "blister buster" socks (a double layer system that wicks away moisture while the two layers of cloth slip on themselves rather than on skin).

As Debbie pulled on socks and boots, more smile than agony now shone on the face of this young mother. Standing up, slinging the day-pack on her back, and leaning heavily on her walking stick, she gingerly eased into a limping gait. With a broad smile she sang out, "Just give me a little time 'n' I'll make it…. Feet shouldn't have labor pains!"

Gossip and Gifts

"...they would take the bread that was offered to them, (and) eat it while nodding in appreciation...." (FTR, p. 4)

A raised eyebrow. An exchange of looks. One sentence of gossip. After a night in Gertrude Schweier's rooming house, the sunny R & R day which was designed to rest Debbie's battered feet began to hang tarnished and heavy. Wandering past shuttered, pre-Civil War houses diverted us but did not dissolve our doubts. It was gossip. Ignoring it didn't shake the worry. Should we pass up this offer of food and lodging? What was more risky: camping beside the road or accepting the invitation of strangers? Perhaps it would reduce the tension if we checked out the house of the couple who had stopped us beside the road two days before and had issued the invitation. It didn't.

The old, two-story, brick house with a front lawn kissed by the river was obviously historic. But it didn't have the cheery clutter of Gertie's rooming house. Bill and Pauline's house was dark. It seemed to be in the middle of a minimally funded restoration. The master of the house, wearing a day-old beard and torn overalls, had sleepy eyes and a somewhat seedy appearance. He invited us in. His wife wasn't home. Something felt amiss. Using the need to wash clothes as an excuse to leave, we headed up the street to find a Laundromat and consider our options.

Reacting to a nagging gut feeling, we decided to tell Bill and Pauline that we'd eat in a restaurant and set up our tents in their backyard. That way, we would accept their hospitality while still protecting ourselves.

23

No sooner did we come up with this brilliant compromise than a cheerful Pauline walked into the Laundromat with a list of places for us to visit: the Civil War cemetery, Rosemary Clooney's house, and the film site for *Huckleberry Finn* topped the list. She even offered to show us where Confederate soldiers were buried. (The Civil War was fought this far north?) Pauline bubbled with enthusiasm and sincerity. Did she notice our reticence?

Certainly Pauline's house was not in the style of Gertie's, but her excitement at finding and maybe hosting pseudo-famous guests stifled my carefully rationalized refusal. The most I could get out was that we hadn't decided what we would do. Debbie threw me an "I can't believe you said that!" glance, then stared at the floor. Too bad we couldn't wash away the dirty dilemma as easily as we did body odor from our clothes.

An hour later Pauline found us, above the town, exploring a mountainside cemetery and offered a ride. Before I could decline, Debbie snapped up the invitation so she could rest her feet. So we piled into Pauline's rusted and rattling '69 Oldsmobile.

As I held onto the door to keep it from flying open and watched pavement rush under my feet through the hole in the floorboard, the doubt-clouds darkened. However, in spite of my continuing concerns, Pauline was so pleasant and kind that I heard myself say that we'd eat with them, but would sleep in our tents. Debbie glowered.

In late afternoon we returned to Gertie's to pick up our gear. A local lawyer had paid for our one night at her rooming house, and neither of us could afford another. It was accept Pauline's offer or sleep beside the road. Debbie dawdled. She admired a wall of commemorative dishes, looked at photo albums, admired Gertie's designation as a Kentucky Colonel, and copied her recipes. Debbie didn't want to leave. Neither did I. But we had to move on. Slinging on my backpack, I headed up Riverside Drive by myself.

A strong wind pushed me up the street. Perhaps the impending storm was the reason for our increased anxiety. Looking back down the street, Debbie was nowhere in sight, but I did see dark clouds boiling above the river. In the morning we'd be piling muddy tents into Louise's car.

Arriving back at the two-story, white shuttered, old-brick house, my pack and I were invited in by an excited Pauline. "No thanks," I insisted, "we'll camp outside." She was incredulous. "But it's about to storm! Your tents will be a mess in the morning."

"We'll sleep on the porch. All we need is the use of your bathroom." I couldn't tell if Pauline was disappointed or she thought I was nuts.

While I walked back to help Debbie, gusting wind whipped my clothes. The temperature had dropped precipitously. Rain was imminent. It would be miserable outside. But we didn't know these people...and there was that feeling. Cold and wet was surely better than being inside at night and carrying out critters in your clothes in the morning. And what if "they" were right, that she had put her husband in jail?

With backpacks propped reassuringly on the porch, Debbie and I walked inside, met the children, and were ushered over threadbare rugs and past sparse furniture into an old-fashioned eat-in kitchen oozing good smells. Pauline bustled around, loading the table down with roast beef, mashed potatoes, string beans...and only two place settings. "Please sit down."

Bill and Pauline leaned against the kitchen cabinets as three big-eyed children shuffled their feet and watched. Debbie and I took chairs across the table from each other and pleaded with our hosts. "Please join us."

"Oh no, we've already eaten."

Catching my breath, I looked into the children's eyes. Suddenly I was six years old. Back in another kitchen where I was standing and watching visitors eat as my mother said, "Oh, we've already eaten"...only we hadn't. I remembered my words to my children when there was only $5.00 to buy a week's groceries for a family of six. "I've already eaten."

Not 30 minutes before I had not wanted to step into this home. Now guilt almost closed my throat. Pauline had worked so hard, and I felt so ashamed. What had this family given up so that Debbie and I could eat this feast? How could I ever repay them?

I began looking around the kitchen. An old icebox that Bill had refinished was just like my grandmother's. Pauline had made the kitchen curtains, as I had made curtains for my home. Bill was a railroadman. He offered to call and warn the railroad that we might be on the tracks, even though he had been laid off for months. Months? I'd experienced a husband out of work for months, with children to feed and clothe, and money scarce.

The pain of my prejudging, misjudging, snobby attitude was acute. To please these kind people, I swallowed past the lump in my throat and ate until I thought I'd burst.

Just when I felt I could not be more shamed, Pauline brought out gifts. Gifts? Two pewter mugs. "So you will remember Augusta." Debbie and I exchanged glances. Out of their struggles, this family gave two strangers everything they had. Remember Augusta? I would always remember the strength and enthusiasm of a woman and her family who worked against difficulties, many of which were beyond their control. Never have I been more contrite.

With all reservations gone, Debbie and I happily played Trivial Pursuit with the children. Then we accepted Bill's offer to brave the pouring rain and see a restored house, where slaves were hidden during the Civil War. As we stooped in a cramped, pitch-black underground railroad tunnel under the kitchen, I suddenly had a tiny appreciation of how desperate slaves must have felt. I also realized that the people of Augusta had a long tradition of taking in strangers.

When, once again, Pauline asked if we would like to sleep inside, without hesitation, Debbie and I pulled in our packs. We climbed stairs that Bill and Pauline were refinishing by scraping off layers of old paint with broken glass. As I laid my blanket on the twin bed and wrapped it around me, rough wool caressed my skin. Rain beat on the window. Warm and dry, I almost burst from gratitude and humble-come-tumbles.

Rich or Poor

"Mary felt the child stiffening his back against her in terror as the warrior stood by the horse. She stroked the little boy's hair and spoke to the Indian." (FTR, p. 35)

An early morning fog rose up from the river, spilled onto Route 8, and immediately swallowed Debbie and me as we walked away from Augusta's warm hospitality. The icy 34-degree temperature raised giant goose bumps on my bare legs. The R & R day had helped Debbie's feet to the point that she was able to keep up with a brisk pace designed to warm us from the inside out.

As if to take our minds off the frosty air, conversation also moved along rapidly. We marveled at how close we had come to giving in to fear and missing the generosity of a family willing to trust and share their home with strangers. Every day challenged our personal assumptions, impressions, and judgments. Carefully built protective walls tumbled down, as strangers opened their hearts and homes to us. What before had been easy to judge now became difficult. What was rich? Who was poor?

The road pulled a little way from the river as it moved out of Augusta, and we traveled past isolated farmland. Short, neat hay rows and weathered, red tobacco barns were the only civilization between the road and the tree-lined river. Then our paved path wove through a tunnel of abandoned farmlands overgrown with scrub trees, bushes, and a tangle of undergrowth. Buildings were few and far between. There seemed to be no cars on the road. And with the isolation rose a growing uneasiness. For reassurance I felt for the Mace in my pocket and hatchet hanging on my belt.

Ahead, on our left between the road and the river, stood a rundown, one-story, peeling, white house—it was the only building in sight. Glassless windows gaped as black rectangular holes. Roof shingles waved. A broken door stood ajar. The overgrown yard probably hadn't seen a lawnmower in months, maybe years.

Expanding on our philosophy about family struggles and courage, Debbie and I conjectured about the rundown farm and house, and wondered what had happened. Where did the family go? Did the father lose his job? How were they making ends meet? Would the children finish school? Debbie had had several conversations with teenagers who felt certain that dropping out of high school to get a job was the thing to do. I suppose, if I'm honest, I even felt a little superior at my "objective" assessment that anyone who really wanted to could work and get an education and make it. And that the so-called poor, leeching off welfare, are probably the lazy, no-good, dregs of society.

As these holier-than-thou thoughts and words flowed forth, we drew even with the house. Then, without warning, a small boy, maybe four years old, stepped into the doorway, stood still, and stared at us. A child? Someone *lived* in that hovel? How could they? It was uninhabitable. There were no windows. No source of heat. Winter was coming on. It was literally freezing out. That wretched dwelling was someone's home?

Before Debbie or I could say a word or even react to the boy, a young woman appeared, framed in the doorway. Tall and thin, wearing a shapeless, worn dress, she stood beside her son. And with the pride and bearing of a princess, she gently reached down, lovingly pulled him to her side, and ruffled his hair.

It could have been Mary and Jesus in Nazareth, or Mary and Tommy before the massacre. Any mother. Anywhere. Yes, they were poor. But also strong, courageous, and full of love and pride. I wanted a photo. But pointing a camera would have been intrusive, even patronizing. In the presence of such courage, one should show respect. So, as if passing royalty, Debbie and I nodded, acknowledging our mutual presence, walked past the house, and with a whoosh, let out the breaths we'd been holding in.

The Mayor

"The way was easier here in the valley of the O-y-o River...through the rich bottomlands, through soft-floored forests and sunny canebrakes along the base of the bluffs." (FTR, p. 75)

In the second-floor bedroom of the old-moneyed house, our safe haven for the night, Debbie paced back and forth and hissed words that dripped anger and sarcasm. "Don't put your shoes on the front hall rug!" She pleaded, "Can't we go to the women's shelter? Do we *have* to stay here?" Almost bodily I pushed my increasingly agitated companion toward the door.

My immediate problems were to calm Debbie, who was more comfortable with Kmart plastic than the crystal and silver surrounding us, and to reassure Maysville Mayor Harriet Cartmell, who was justifiably nervous with two scruffy-looking strangers under her elegant roof.

We were in her home by default. Marilyn Hooper had recommended the Maysville Crisis Center as a place of safe lodging, but the publicity surrounding The Walk made the staff nervous. Someone in their office contacted the mayor, who, in a weak moment, agreed to put up two strange women. Our meeting, minutes before, was inauspicious.

The 200-year-old Cartmell home sat near downtown Maysville. A large American flag fluttered above our heads as we stood on the porch, before a heavy, wooden door. A tentative knock. The door opened and framed a woman, casually dressed in slacks and sweater. Because of the political climate of the area, that I am Caucasian and that, until this day, we had only been helped by Caucasians, I was surprised that the mayor

29

was of another race. Well, as it turned out, the gracious, smiling lady ushering us inside was the housekeeper, pre-warned by her employer of our arrival.

Wilma led us into a large foyer of brocade, walnut, and crystal. This was more than a home, it was a mansion filled with generations of family antiques. My only association with houses like this was on museum tours. Our backpacks, walking sticks, hats, Debbie's Diet Coke and presents, etc., filled the window seat and spilled over a good portion of the foyer. We had created a junk pile in Buckingham Palace.

Trying to keep my dirt and sweat away from all the valuables, I sat on a rug just inside the front door. If I couldn't make a good first impression, at least I didn't want to make a bad one. Just then the door opened. Mayor Cartmell, took one, shocked look at the hot, smelly, ragged women in her home and, before I could say more than "hello," she curtly instructed me to remove my shoes from the rug. It was an antique oriental. So much for a good, first impression.

Harriet Cartmell, a 64-year-old, quintessential southern lady, who just happened to be mayor, wore a perfectly coifed, blond pageboy, elegant clothes, and gold jewelry that definitely was not costume. Her southern accent softened, but did not hide, her doubts about allowing two grubby strangers into her house. She immediately and firmly set rules that announced who was in charge. In spite of obvious doubts, she directed Wilma to put us in an upstairs bedroom.

Up a curved staircase, Wilma led us into a room with a four-poster bed, fireplace, seven chairs, a desk, two end tables, two chests, and a coat rack...all expensive looking antiques. It wasn't Tara, but we were definitely in the South. I was in awe. Debbie wanted out. "Don't put your feet on the rug!" She repeated.

I too felt the sting, but understood both Debbie's and the Mayor's positions. It was like being between two bandy roosters. However, I felt that if Mayor Cartmell saw that I was honest and sincere she would relax. It would be a long, miserable time unless we gained her trust. What I said and did when I descended the stairs would be crucial. In the meantime, I had to keep Debbie and the mayor separated. "Debbie, go outside and smoke a cigarette! I'll handle the mayor."

During my shower (only 36 days to go without a bath!) and while pulling on clean clothes, I developed a strategy. The mayor must feel that I appreciated her and her home, and that I was interested in her town. It was also vital that Wilma like us. There was not a doubt in my mind that the mayor would discuss us with the trusted employee who looked after her home.

When the clean me descended the stairs, the game plan was simple: Explain about Mary's escape. Ask lots of questions. Keep the mayor talking about herself. Be sincere and honest. Don't touch anything. Keep off the oriental rugs.

And it worked! Icy hostility and defensiveness melted, the tightness around the mayor's eyes and mouth relaxed, and her voice softened. Though the mayor was obviously a smart, tough, no-nonsense woman, we were now on a first-name basis. Harriet made dinner reservations and invited her friend Anne to join us. She brushed off my protests that Debbie and I had only hiking clothes, nothing appropriate for a nice restaurant. "You're just fine."

While I was inside getting to know the hostess, Debbie was outside making friends with Erica, a little girl from down the street, who just happened to be a good friend of the mayor. I saw no frowns from Wilma, and Sheba, the family dog, wiggled and sniffed happily. The housekeeper, dog, and neighbor children liked us. Things were looking up.

Caparonies, several notches above McDonald's, sat close to the river. Boats floated up and down the water highway, and trains switching tracks or clickety-clacking past provided moving entertainment. Across the table Harriet and Anne bantered over who would pay for tickets to concerts and football games. In diametrically opposed positions, these strong-willed women stated their opinions firmly and stood their ground, yet came away friends...an interchange I usually associate with men. Women *could* disagree without being bitchy, petty, whining, and catty. Amazing.

Debbie's tension eased in direct proportion to the amount of alcohol our hostesses consumed. After two glasses of wine, conversation relaxed. Laughter was easy and frequent. Where hours before we didn't know these women existed, now we were comfortable and laughing like friends. It would be okay.

Phone calls always came before bedtime. I checked in with the amateur radio operators who were helping to report our locations, gave Lisa detailed directions so she could find us Saturday morning, and asked Glenda Morrison (a friend who worked for Bloomington's mayor) what was the proper etiquette for a mayor's house guest. Newspapers wanted to be called, and lodging arrangements were made for the days ahead. Eight calling card charges. The mounting phone bill was an unexpected expense. That all happened yesterday.

By the time I came downstairs Friday morning, Harriet had left for meetings in Lexington. We wouldn't see her until evening. However, Thursday she had recommended historic places in Maysville for us to visit and, just in case we needed help, she called friends to introduce us.

Eating a breakfast of the local specialty, transparent pie (kind of a pecan pie without pecans), Debbie and I plotted the day. We'd wash clothes (Harriet insisted we use her washer and dryer rather than the Laundromat), take Carol Stivers up on her offer to drive us around nearby Washington, Kentucky (another long distance call), then take a walking tour of Maysville.

For me the car was a twentieth-century intrusion. Debbie, on the other hand, appeared relieved, enjoying the advantage it gave of going further, seeing more, and being off her feet. Washington was within walking distance, but Debbie's feet needed rest.

Referred to in Maysville as "Up the Hill," Washington seemed to be revitalizing by rebuilding its history. We stood on the Buffalo Trace that ran between the Ohio and Licking Rivers. (Four days before we had slept beside the Licking.) We saw houses built from flatboats that were floated down the river (30 years after Mary's escape). We wandered through Simon Kenton's store and in the log post office we learned we were standing on the site of the original canebrake lands (the ones shown on my 1784 map...the ones Mary walked through or around). We had indeed reached back to touch another time.

Back in Maysville for lunch. Wilma offered us refrigerator privileges (We were accepted!), then took us next door to tour the three-story home of a neighbor, if possible more beautiful than Harriet's. As we left, Viola Parker called from across the street and invited us in. What friendly folk.

Warm and homey, I doubt Viola ever met a stranger. Widowed twice, she appeared undecided if moving to her husband's home or selling the family's 200 acres was the thing to do. I felt a sinking feeling when she said she had already sold the family property. I hoped it was right...for it was done.

Personally, I feel cheated that all the land my great-grandmother worked so hard to pay for after she immigrated from Russia was sold out of the family. If asked, I usually caution people against selling the home place, but Viola didn't ask. Only time and point-of-view would determine if the decision was "right." Viola's situation touched me as I realized a part of me, through Viola, Wilma, and Harriet would remain in Maysville, just as a part of them would forever be with me. Perhaps that connectedness is a form of immortality.

In addition to beautiful homes and people, Maysville has a three-storied, white-shuttered jail. Daniel Boone had run a store in town, before he left for Point Pleasant. (Our destination in 12 days, if we were lucky.) Slowly walking the streets, I felt a spiritual tie to the men and women who settled this area. For Mary had walked through the forests and canebrakes long before Daniel Boone and others cut them down to build a town called Maysville. A day of rest, friendly people, and history rejuvenated us, body and soul.

As usual, the evening meant phone calls and planning. I checked in with Patti Dillard, who was scheduled to join us the next day. Even though I asked only for a place to set up a tent and the use of a toilet, it would be more difficult to find a place for three than for two. Louise found us lodging for Saturday with the retired mayor of Concord. Harriet suggested the Catholic church's home for transient poor for Sunday. (The lady I spoke to did not sound thrilled, but she agreed to let us come, I believe largely due to Harriet's recommendation.) Then I called my cousin Kate in South Carolina (our sag support for week two) to tell her where she might find us. Calling Bloomington, I learned that the *Louisville Courier-Journal* had carried an Associated Press story about us. We were getting famous.

Debbie, who had had the bed the previous night, was asleep on the floor as I sat propped up on pillows and sighed a deep sigh of satisfaction. We made it through Week 1 in one piece, Debbie's feet were on the mend, strangers were unbelievably kind, and safe lodging was falling into place. We just might make it to West Virginia.

At about 11:00 o'clock, I heard the front door creak open as Harriet walked into the house. In case I missed her in the morning, I wanted to be sure to thank her for her hospitality and friendship, so I threw aside the covers and headed downstairs.

In my navy-blue, polypropylene long johns, without inhibition or embarrassment, I sat on the curved stairway and chatted comfortably with the mayor. Wearing a red-and-white suit, red feathered hat perched jauntily on perfectly arranged hair, Harriet laughed and described her day at the statehouse. (She was arguing for the legalization of marijuana.) What a sight. Complete opposites were talking, laughing, and enjoying each other, because 48 hours before they each gave a stranger a chance.

Abruptly, Harriet blurted out in a stage whisper, "I've got to go pee-pee!" She dashed around the corner to the bathroom and from there continued the conversation, the way one does with someone they feel particularly comfortable with. It was difficult to submerge a smile when Harriet, still talking, emerged from the bathroom, skirt hiked up to her waist, tugging at her nylons. Men show their acceptance and equality by standing and talking in front of a urinal. Women do it with pantyhose.

Day 8
Saturday, October 3, 1987
Maysville to Concord, Kentucky

Old Women

"—there was something formidable and even noble about her. She was standing there apparently unbeaten by the ordeals she must have survived, grinning happily...." (FTR, p. 87)

Preparations for leaving Maysville were fraught with emotion. Harriet, Wilma, Debbie, and I had overcome grave reservations to become a "family" for two days. Now, in all probability, we would never see Harriet and her friends again. The sadness of good-byes did not become easier with repetition. If anything, it grew more difficult.

Waiting for Lisa, who was driving in alone to provide weekend sag support, and for Patti Dillard, who was to be a new walker, fueled my anxiety. I glanced repeatedly at my watch. At 7:15 Patti drove in, with her carrot-red hair, open arms, and warm laughter. She would be fun. A little pressure off, but still no daughter.

I knew my gut-tightening pacing and fretting were making the others nervous. But my "baby" might be lost, or could not find us, or maybe she had an accident and was in a hospital, or worse, she might be dead in a ditch! And it would all have been my fault! Fifteen minutes later, Lisa, her smile and my red Olds Firenza arrived, all in one piece, right on time for our scheduled 7:30 departure. Guilt and worry climbed back into their boxes.

Time to load up and leave. Though I would never be able to repay Harriet, I would forever carry her as a role model of the older woman as a polished and accomplished leader. As we walked out the door, I fought back tears.

E. M. Lahr

Prior to 1987, I had thought of old women as cranky and grouchy, wrinkled and ugly, complaining and bitchy, and dumb and dull. Of course, that was before I met Harriet Cartmell, Louise Kemp and the other older women along the river. Harriet, the refined but tough lady, and Louise, a lively imp, were as different as night and day. It came as a surprise to find that I admired and even wanted to emulate these women who were in their 60s, 70s, and 80s.

This night I had planned to sleep in a field. However, Louise talked her 85-year-old friend and former mayor of Concord, Kentucky, Daisy Sprigg, into letting us bunk with her in her home near the river. Another mayor. This rubbing of elbows with the rich and famous was fun. But before we could be society dames, we had to walk about 20 miles.

The biggest accomplishment of the day was coaxing Patti over a railroad trestle. Only after she inched safely across what to me was a low bridge did Patti reveal her terror of heights, as she exclaimed, "Now I can drive across the big bridge into Cincinnati!" We were breaking down all kinds of barriers.

Lisa and Louise's Cincinnati friends, Fran and Regina, joined Debbie, Patti, and me for the last few miles into Concord. As we approached Daisy's one-story house, it was obvious that this would not be the "old money" lodging of Maysville. With a picket fence and front porch, the little white house with green shutters resembled a 1930s Sears mail-order house. The society dames were put in their place. We didn't need fancy. We needed safe. And Daisy was stepping up to the plate.

In response to my knock, Louise opened the front door. We stepped directly into a small living-dining room area, the kind that is separated by a wide archway and leads straight through to the kitchen. To the left of the living room was a bedroom, and to the right of the dining room was a bathroom. One glance took it all in.

As the six of us crowded through the front door, we saw an orange, stuffed recliner against the far wall. In it sat a gray-haired, petite, toothpick-thin woman who couldn't have weighed more than 90 pounds. Wearing a loose-fitting pink dress, she was so short her feet didn't touch the floor. Without a word, she hooched herself off the recliner, rose, walked toward us, and stopped under the archway. After the pregnant pause was not filled with the "hello" that I expected, I started to fill it with my own greeting and appreciation to the woman I assumed was Daisy Sprigg.

Without a word of acknowledgement, she bent over, reached down between her legs and up under her dress. Then, with a sudden motion like throwing a baseball, she spit out, "If you gotta take a dump just catch it in your hand and throw it out the window...'cause my toilet's broke!"

We stood stunned into shocked silence, until Louise started to laugh. When all of us nervously joined in the laughter, Daisy's eyes twinkled in delight. She obviously loved to shock and be the center of attention. With my female band of walkers as a live audience, Daisy was in her element.

Louise made introductions. Then she, Regina, and Fran loaded the kitchen table with food they had brought. Sitting scrunched around the table in Daisy's tiny kitchen, where Styrofoam plates and paper cups replaced the china and crystal of the day before, we laughed and laughed and laughed! Women could be funny. They could be old and funny. They could be old and intelligent and funny. They could be old and intelligent and funny and sexy. They could be wonderful! And they didn't need lots of money to do it.

Daisy Sprigg held court before her admirers. Pictured left to right: Daisy Sprigg, Louise Kemp, Fran Wirthlen, and Lisa Lahr.

Looking around the modest home, I noticed a hutch and curio cabinet stuffed with old china, crystal, and family heirlooms. Daisy obviously appreciated the pretty and fine things in life. Like Gertrude Schweier and Harriet Cartmell, Daisy was a Kentucky Colonel, the highest honor bestowed by the state. After a supper befitting the highly honored, Daisy sat on her recliner like a queen on a too-large throne and held court.

Daisy entertained us with stories of her life as midwife (22 years), police judge (24 years), and mayor (25 years). Looking around, I saw eight women whose ages ranged from 22 to 85 enjoying themselves and each other. Faces glowed as we laughed and hugged our aching stomachs. It was women at their best. And I wished, oh how I wished, that Janette were there. But at least my daughter Lisa would see what women could really be.

Daisy had been married four times and was looking for number five. "What happened to your husbands?" we asked. "They all died except my first. He fathered a child by another woman." (Moans of sympathy.) "Oh that's all right. I wasn't puttin' out for him!" (Howls of laughter.)

A wealth of history flowed with Daisy's conversation. I wondered if her family appreciated her for the treasure she was. Would they sit down to listen and record her stories before memories and soul evaporated in the wind? Do any of us appreciate our family before it is too late? So often it is only after a stroke or heart attack or death that someone says, "I wish we had asked about why and how Grandma emigrated. What was Grandpa's life like before electricity? Why did Mother quit school? What was it like to give birth at home?" History, both past and present, is important.

A born leader, Daisy had been a police judge until she refused to accept the job one more time. Though fiercely independent, she was on the lookout for another husband. "But not any ol' guy with baggy pants. I want one with a tight tush!"

And I want a brain and attitude like Daisy Sprigg's!

Fear and Trust

"...she and the old woman suddenly froze." (FTR, p. 180)

One of the reasons I wanted an adventure was that I was tired of being told, by word or inference: People have become dishonest and cruel. It's dangerous. Particularly for a woman. Don't go out alone. You can't trust "those" people.

Because I carried the sting of many painful rejections, acceptance was important to me. I was determined to welcome whoever wanted to participate, as long as they were no threat to me or the group. Most who walked with me appeared to join without preconceived judgments. I never knew, nor did I care, if someone were Gentile or Jew, Protestant or Catholic, Buddhist or atheist, gay or straight, rich or poor, or what their racial background was. If they wanted to walk, contributed to the sense of group cohesion, and obeyed my simple rules of "ask only for a place to go to the bathroom or pitch a tent, and honor 'No Trespassing' signs," I welcomed them. If they made us laugh, so much the better.

That is not to say that differing and strongly held beliefs, such as religion, were never discussed. However, there were no put-downs. Just interested questions. There was respect for the speaker's position. I learned not to fear expressing my ideas. These new friends respected me, even if our beliefs differed. Amazing.

And amazing was the word for the human generosity we encountered. Of course, the first thing I noticed was the way strangers came along each and every day to offer food, lodging, and sag support. I never dreamed there would be gifts, such as pins, books, T-shirts, caps, jackets, keys to the city, and proclamations. Each weekend I would send my collection back to Indiana. Not that I did not appreciate the offerings, but they added weight to my backpack.

One thing I carried every step of the way was fear. Sometimes it stayed tucked away, deep under laughter and accomplishments. But it never entirely disappeared. I remembered the warnings of the Kentucky State Police and the women's shelter: Look strong. Most killers look like the guy next door. If need be, the walking stick can be a weapon.

Fear raised its red-hot anxiety most often when we walked along a road. I felt more vulnerable out in the open than I did deep in the woods. When a car slowed down, the same car passed us several times, or a car stopped ahead of us blocking our way, Debbie and I would instinctively tense and tighten our grip on our walking sticks. I would reach for the Mace hidden in my pocket, my finger on the release button. Then, with our "don't mess with us" attitudes and stern faces, we kept a firm, straight-head pace. Such was the case as we walked on an isolated road on the way to Vanceburg.

Early that morning, Daisy, wrapped up tight in her blue chenille robe, had waved good-bye from her front porch. Her last gift was to personally call and second Harriet's recommendation to Sister Connell, a nun who supervised the Christian Community Center in Vanceburg, assuring her that it was safe to take us in for this night. After one last look at Daisy's spunky smile, Debbie, Patti, and I stepped into the murk of a heavy fog that hung over the river and spilled onto nearby fields and roads.

The only indication we had of a mountain was our steady uphill climb. Except for the chirps of awakening birds, the road was quiet. No cars. It was an idyllic walk. The frosty air necessitated gloves, and the blanket was a warm weight around my shoulders. Our breath hit the air in puffs of white mist until the sun slowly pulled the fog up and away. Orange and yellow trees dotted distant mountainsides, foretelling the approach of even colder weather. As we crested the long grade, the two-lane road grew flat. Fields of grain ran ahead, merging into the mountains. Few houses and almost no traffic made us feel as though we were among the last (or first) people on earth.

Late in the morning, a big, light blue Mercury, with three people inside, seemed to appear from nowhere and pulled to an abrupt stop several yards in front of us. I tensed and gripped the Mace canister. There were three of us, too, but we were miles from help. The driver's side door opened and out stepped a balding man with something in his hand. Out of the passenger side emerged a woman who also carried something. They both walked toward us while the third person climbed from the backseat. As the distance between us closed, my hand holding the Mace slowly eased from my pocket and hid behind the fold of my blanket. I was tense as violin string. Then my brain clicked, and I realized who I was seeing. It was Tom and Beverly Arnold, my neighbors from Indiana...and Lisa was with them! Fear scuttled away.

Tom and Bev had traveled to Cincinnati for their son's wedding shower and then decided to try to find us on their way back home. They had serendipitously spotted Lisa in a Vanceburg phone booth. And here they were bringing us coffee and doughnuts and even a Diet Coke for Debbie, who was a walking Diet Coke advertisement during our entire journey. As if mirroring our spirits, the sun suddenly came out in full force. The gloves came off as we sprawled beside what appeared to be an abandoned farmhouse to eat a special-delivery breakfast from drive-by angels. Fear was gone, for the time being.

Another day, about an hour after lunch, found Debbie and me looking for a pit stop, as usual. There wasn't a tree, bush, barn, or cornfield in sight. Then as we walked along the road a weather-beaten, whitewashed block building, which appeared to be a tavern, came into view. Pick-up trucks and old cars were parked in the weedy, pot-holed parking lot. Normally I wouldn't set foot in such a place, but nature was calling with increasingly strong "gotta go!" urgings. The Willow Inn appeared to be a major port in a storm.

It took a while for our eyes to adjust to the tavern's dimly lit interior. Several men sat nursing drinks at the bar and small, assorted tables. They eyed us up and down as we entered. However, with walking sticks in our hands and a hatchet at my belt, Debbie and I were anything but typical looking pick-ups. We stood at the bar as Debbie bought us each a soft drink. Then we sank into chairs in a far corner to rest our weary bones. Curiosity got the best of a couple fellows, who asked us the "Where are you going? What for?" kinds of questions, but generally we were ignored.

I was surprised to see so many people in an isolated bar on a Sunday afternoon. But it wasn't up to me to figure out or criticize whatever was going on. We had bought a drink for the privilege of using the facilities. So, after taking turns in the restroom, we finished our drinks and walked out, relieved physically and emotionally. The uneasiness I felt about the men in the tavern evaporated when we emerged from the dimness into the sunshine.

We had walked about a quarter of a mile down the lonely road when a car pulled up and stopped right beside us. The driver appeared to be one of the scruffy-looking guys from the bar. Anxiety, apprehension, and fear erased all afternoon fatigue as adrenaline-charged energy filled my every muscle. Were we about to be attacked? No one would know. There wasn't a car or house to be seen.

As we assessed our fight-or-flight options, the man leaned toward us and reached out his arm. Instinctively we drew back. His fist opened and on his palm was a small change purse, "Is this yours?" Before I could say "no," a visibly shaken Debbie reached out for it. It contained *all* her money. When Debbie had paid for our drinks, she laid her purse on the bar and walked off. All we could do was offer profuse thanks and hope this stranger understood our appreciation.

Once again, fear was spanked back into its dark hole, and we learned that angels sometimes appear as "those" people.

Grandparents

"Elenor Draper loved to take her grandsons berry picking in the summer, and herb gathering and mushroom and wild-grape hunting in their season, mostly because little Thomas had such an inquisitive mind and imagination." (FTR, p. 11)

We had a place to stay this night thanks to my cousin Kate, who drove her blue-and-silver conversion van up from South Carolina the day before. Late in the afternoon she found us and our backpacks sprawled beside a stream in front of the Vanceburg Christian Community Center. A gregarious person, Kate would drive ahead of us and stop at stores to talk to people about The Walk. You could call her our unofficial advance person.

It was late morning when Kate parked her van beside the Garrison, Kentucky, IGA parking lot. She pulled out red-and-white-striped folding chairs to set up a mini-camp and waited for Debbie, Patti, and me to arrive. There was understandable tension when John and Sherman, the big, burly, bearded storeowners, approached to question our interloping intent. After a brief explanation, they were soon posing for pictures, allowing us bathroom privileges, and offering camp space for the night. The idea of setting up tents beside the Conestoga wagon in their front yard was tempting, but to keep on schedule we had to move on upriver.

About 3:00 in the afternoon we walked into Quincy. The town consisted of a grocery store, a post office, a yard sale, and not much

43

more. Patti sank down on the step in front of Davis' Grocery Store. Her aching legs were calling for a break.

Earlier in the day, Kate had stopped at the store and engaged its owner, Zoni, in a long conversation. So when we arrived, Kate knew Zoni, and Zoni knew about us. With Patti needing rest just as we reached Zoni's store, Kate hot-footed it inside to announce our arrival. The door swung sharply open, and a gray-haired woman wearing dark sunglasses stepped onto the porch. We heard, "I want to see these CRAZY women!" Zoni may have been interested in us, but it was obvious she thought walking from Kentucky to Virginia was not the activity of a sane person.

While the yard sale next door drew Debbie like a magnet, Patti didn't move from her seat. Kate urged me to check out the store. Small, dark, and dusty, it was a hodgepodge of shelving, cases, canned goods, and books. Shelves and boxes brimmed over with second-hand, paperback, romance novels—probably someone's getaway from reality.

As our eyes adjusted to the darkness, we wandered to the back and found the meat case. Kate took one look at the fat and meat buildup on the meat slicer and instantly opted to avoid purchasing any dead animal products. I decided frozen, wrapped, ice cream bars were safe. And although the store was not one I would normally stop at if driving through the area, once inside, it felt like a fascinating step back in time.

Zoni, a chain-smoking, 60-year-old, sported short-cropped, straight, once-blonde hair that now hung mostly gray and thinning, parted at the side, long bangs brushed across her high forehead. Her polyester outfit of aqua-colored slacks and yellow-black-and-red-patterned jacket could have come from the yard sale outside. Aged beyond her years, Zoni shied from the camera. Was it because she appeared to have no teeth? Perhaps. On the other hand, maybe she remembered when she was young and pretty, without wrinkles and worries, and dreamed dreams. Now it seemed that all Zoni had was struggles. Kate and I pieced together part of her story.

Zoni's husband had died three years before. For reasons she did not explain, fifteen months before our arrival, Zoni's son and daughter-in-law brought their four children to her and left. The pain and frustration in Zoni's voice as she described trying to care for four active elementary-age children by herself, and her efforts to avoid governmental assistance, broke my heart. One of her grandchildren needed medical care. Zoni wanted a little help with *one* medical problem. However, according to her, "the system" insisted that she sign up for total assistance or nothing. And Zoni appeared equally determined to care for her grandchildren without the stigma of welfare. I wanted to scream at the bureaucrats: "Help her! For God's sake, help her! Can't you see how hard she is trying?" It seemed to me that this grandmother had the same stubborn determination that kept Mary and Ghetel going when they faced extraordinary hardships. There *must* be a way to help people without taking away their dignity. Suddenly, making some—*any*—purchase before we walked out took on a new importance.

While we were in the store, Patti had climbed into the van to elevate her feet. Her aching legs would not let her hike any more on this day. I knew Patti was hurting badly because in the morning she had been eagerly talking of walking well beyond Quincy. I could have walked another hour or two. However, the week before I had slowed up for Debbie, so as long as we were pretty much on schedule, there was no reason not to stop early for Patti. Like Debbie, Patti was a good sport, and I wanted to keep her with us.

So I approached Zoni for permission to park the van and set up tents between her store and her house next door. At first reluctant, she relented when I assured her we only needed parking space for the van, a small area for three tents and access to a toilet.

Zoni said all she had was an outhouse. Not a problem. Then, just as I thought everything was set, she hesitated. "Well, I guess I could give you a key for the night." "A key? For what?" "The outhouse *has* to be kept locked!"

Now a lock *inside* an outhouse is common. But I had never heard of a *padlock* on the *outside*. I must have looked confused, for Zoni then explained, "My grandson fell in one time. So I have to keep it locked…. He's a little slow."

I thought someone falling through a toilet seat into the crud below was just the stuff of poor jokes. Here was a real-life incident. As I assured Zoni that I would keep the outhouse door locked, I stifled mental images and laughter at the thought of the ruckus that must have happened when her grandson fell in. Then I walked out and gave my companions the news that someone who had so little, gave us a gift of great value…a safe place to spend the night. And the key to the outhouse.

In turn, we became Quincy's entertainment. Children gathered around to stare as we set up chairs, table, and Coleman stove and ate supper. They were probably familiar with the boxed Chef Boy-R-Dee spaghetti and homemade chocolate chip cookies like the ones Janette had sent along with Lisa on the weekend. But the smoked salmon that my Dad had caught in Alaska and had given me just before I left was a rare treat for all. When the local "puzzle man" came by with more puzzles in his mind and pockets than we could imagine, it was hard to say who was entertaining whom. And, although I did not experience it, Debbie insisted that the outhouse walls had half-inch wide cracks and that the children peeked and giggled whenever she used the facilities.

We amused ourselves by admiring three sweaters that Debbie bought at the yard sale, and "chewed over" the social problems of poverty, sex discrimination, and men. After eating, to avoid the chilling air, we climbed inside the van and were greeted by hundreds of swarming flies. Fortunately, Davis' Grocery carried bug spray. We were slowly learning that solving one problem frequently put us face-to-face with another. And, another day without a bath. Could I go the remaining 33 days without one? Well, there was always the river.

As night began to fall, the thought of setting up tents among the flies and beside an outhouse became less and less appealing. So, when Kate suggested that we all sleep in the van, we jumped at the chance. Debbie curled up on the driver's seat. To prop her leg, Patti lay sideways between the front and back seats. Kate and I, the shorties of the group at barely five feet, folded down the back seat and slept spoon-fashion on the small bed that ran the width of the van. We either had a great deal of patience, a supreme sense of humor, were gluttons for punishment, felt terribly desperate, or all of the above. We knew we would not sleep well, but we were together and safe. As we talked and laughed and held our aching sides, we were able to look past our personal struggles to find humor, and I wished that everyone could experience such a slumber party.

The next morning as I handed the key back to Zoni and said, "Good-bye," she cocked her head to one side and, through a toothless grin, firmly announced, "My grandson is slow, but *you're* crazy!" We didn't win them all.

Touching Back

"This village in which they were now sojourning was called Lower Shawnee Town, and the river on whose bank it stood was called Scioto-Crepe, the Scioto River." (FTR, p. 107)

Raindrops pinging on the van roof woke us at daylight. We had thought sleep would be hard coming, but we not only slept, we slept soundly. For when we looked out the window to see how much it had rained, we saw a huge semi parked right beside us in a tight space between the van and Zoni's house. None of us had heard a thing. It had been a smart decision to sleep in the van. There were no wet, muddy tents to pack up.

Patti wrapped her legs, from ankles to knees, in Ace bandages. The previous day she had blamed her leg pain on shin splints. This morning she blamed her Achilles tendon. All that leg wrap gave her an awkward gait that would, almost certainly, cause stress and discomfort in other body parts. She decided to walk for only an hour or so. If her legs hurt "really bad," she'd climb into the van with Kate. However, each time Kate drove back to check, Patti said she could walk a little farther.

Using any excuse to rest, each day we'd stop to read all roadside historic plaques. Not far out of Quincy I read, "First village in Kentucky built by Shawnee Indians and French traders. Was visited January 1751..." 1751? The village was probably active when the Shawnee brought Mary through in 1755. They may have stopped near this spot. During their escape, Mary and Ghetel would have had to make a wide detour to avoid detection. Again, a little piece of history made us feel as though we really were touching Mary and Ghetel's experience. Suddenly, I swallowed hard to fight back unexplained tears.

In the afternoon, Kate came by to say that the women at a little store up the road wanted us to stop to see them. Stifling my "we have to stay on schedule" thoughts, I reluctantly agreed. Between customers, the clerk peppered us with questions. I tried to ease us out and down the road. However, before I reached the door, a female customer, in faded jeans and long-sleeved shirt, maneuvered close to me and quietly asked, "Would you like to see the everlasting spring?" The everlasting spring? The one the pioneers and Indians used? The one that Mary may have drunk from? Suddenly we had all kinds of time.

Another serendipitous meeting. This time because Nina Duncan stopped at the store, overheard our conversation, and was willing to share her life with strangers. As a result, we visited a stream that, according to local history, is never muddy and never runs dry. I drank cool, clear water from a source that existed as long as people could remember. It quenched my thirst as it had for countless others before me, and I felt as if we really were reaching back in time. And this spot felt, for lack of a better word, sacred. Since leaving Big Bone Lick, we had made daily connections to people past and present.

Patti toughed out the rain and the pain through lunch. Then she decided she would continue to walk, but only in half-hour segments. By mid-afternoon the rain had stopped, the sun came out, and Patti was still picking 'em up and putting 'em down. We packed away our raincoats, and my Mickey Mouse T-shirt and walking shorts became the perfect, free-and-easy hiking outfit.

We entered the community of South Shores on Route 23, which runs beside the river and widens into four lanes. Broad, hard-packed shoulders made for easy walking. We could relax and not fear that at any moment we'd be hit by a speeding car or truck. The downside was that we could not find a campsite, so Kate drove ahead to search out a spot.

Kate's van was barely out of sight when a car driven by a large man pulled up and stopped beside us. No smiling eyes twinkled behind his glasses. It was evident that this was no friendly, "Are you Eleanor and Debbie?" inquiry. A starched shirt with matching tie and jacket gave him an official look. His bearing was stern and threatening. A deep voice sharply asked, "Where are you going?" In an attempt to melt his hostility, with my sweetest apple pie voice I replied, "To Virginia." The look he shot me could have iced the water in my jug. Without a word his face said, "Yeah. Sure."

We trekked where the road, the railroad, and the river
offered hard-packed shoulders and easy walking.

Mentally, I reviewed our day's activities. What had we done that was so wrong? We hadn't broken anything and, as far as I knew, we had not trespassed. Did this area have a law against walking beside the road and river? It was obvious that this man was grim and more than a little skeptical.

I hurriedly tried to explain about Mary Ingles and that we were retracing her escape route, how we began at Big Bone Lick in September and hoped to finish in Eggleston, Virginia, in November. As I gushed on, the tension eased. When I stopped for breath, a smile broke across the man's broad face. "I'm Chester Bruce. The truant officer. I thought you were running away from school." Fifty-one years old and I'm picked up by a truant officer! We laughed and thanked him for the ego boost. As Chester drove off, Patti announced, "No matter how much I complain, make sure I walk tomorrow. I wouldn't have missed this for anything!" Mickey Mouse turns everyone into a kid.

Soon Kate returned with an update. The bad news was that there was no campsite or motel on our side of the river for miles. However, the good news was that she had found a motel across the river in Friendship, Ohio, and a bridge was nearby. A motel was an unforeseen expense, but

E. M. Lahr

with all of us sharing a room, the cost would be reasonable. Besides, we were feeling and smelling ripe from three bathless days.

To reach Reiser's Country Inn, we had to cross two rivers: the Ohio and the Scioto. The motel sat between Shawnee State Park and Raven-Rock (the lookout rock, shaped like a raven, that the Shawnee used as they watched for invasive flatboats). As I surveyed the rivers and the lay of the land, I realized that serendipity was once again at work. We would be sleeping at or near the site of the village where the Shawnee had taken Mary and her sons as they traveled to Big Bone Lick. In my mind's eye, I could almost see domed, bark-covered huts beside the mouth of the Scioto and natives carrying birch-bark canoes over their heads, and I could smell their wood-burning fires.

The owner of the motel, well versed in local history, urged us to visit Raven-Rock. However, it was on private land, and we couldn't make the necessary connections. We settled for a visit to nearby Shawnee State Park, where huge paintings portrayed the people and life Mary would likely have experienced when she and her sons were here. We gazed up at Shawnee lookouts high above the river and studied paintings of a family sitting in front of a round-topped hut, women at work, and portraits of Blackfish, the Prophet, and Tecumseh.

Debbie snapped pictures. Kate and Patti explored. I wandered alone and wondered at circumstances that put us in this place. Since 1755, this land had experienced an unimaginable amount of life changes. Not all bad. Not all good.

Debbie, Kate, Patti, and I had had a rewarding day and an enjoyable evening as free spirits. However, Mary and Ghetel did not have a good time on this land near the mouth of the Scioto. For it was here that Ghetel ran the gauntlet, and Tommy and Georgie were ripped from Mary's arms.

Georgie, two years old at the time, probably died shortly thereafter. It would be 13 years before Mary's arms again reached out for her son Thomas. By then he would resemble a 17-year-old Shawnee, and would have all but forgotten his parents and the way of life he was born into.

When we leave home, even for short periods, change is inevitable. After 43 days of new experiences with new people, the changes in me would be more difficult to discern than they were in Thomas. However, in a few years, the seed of self-confidence that took root in 1987 would blossom into a happy woman making many of her dreams come true.

Mothers and Daughters

"They had been gone two weeks from the salt camp when, toward evening Mary glanced over the O-y-o and saw a canoe moving northward across it. The canoe was at this distance a mere sliver of sunlit gray on the green water. Mary stopped and the old woman almost stumbled over her. Mary pointed at the faraway moving shape. They watched it head straight for the northern shore and then it disappeared.

She recognized the spot then. It was the mouth of the Scioto....

'Ghetel! That means...we've come along a hundred and fifty miles!'" (FTR, p. 179)

No doubt Mary would have recognized the mouth of the Scioto. However, more than rejoicing at her mileage marker, I believe it broke her heart when she realized that her sons were within sight and she couldn't reach them. Perhaps Mary stood and strained to catch a glimpse of Georgie and Tommy running around the huts or playing at the water's edge, just across the river.

A mother's love is not erased by time and space. It spins an invisible web and builds a place for both mother and child. Love creates boxes and strings. It can be as painful for those building the boxes as it is for those struggling to break free. It seems that we continue to spin the string while simultaneously struggling to hack it away. It is as if those we love the most are the ones who must leave.

Those who care desperately seem destined to do the very thing that will push the object of that affection away. Daughters, who unconsciously use their mothers as role models, refuse to acknowledge the legacy they simultaneously hold onto and toss away. Good parents understand that the child must leave the box and break the string. However, as in childbirth, it is almost never without pain.

My mother and I never had what you would call a bad relationship. It's just that she never seemed to understand my dreams and desires. We were always on different wavelengths. I wanted a life different from hers, and that appeared to cause a constant, negative tension. Now it appeared that no matter how hard I tried, I was doing the same thing to my children. I wanted our relationships to be better, I but didn't know how to make it happen. Patti taught me lessons in communication that I hoped to try on my own offspring.

A divorced, single parent, Patti had written to me in the summer and asked to walk with me for a weekend. After I talked to her on the phone and listened to her wit and upbeat attitude, I cajoled until she rearranged work and vacation so she could walk for five days. This day we would say good-bye.

Patti's vibrant Kentucky accent colored her personal anecdotes. It seemed that no matter how difficult the problem, without criticizing or blaming, she found humor. If life knocked her down, she would pop back with an in-your-face, "That was *not* nice of you. Let's think about this and try again." By not fitting my stereotype of a divorced mother as irresponsible, careless, and selfish, she exactly fit my concept of a 1987 woman of strength and courage.

Kristina Lee Dillard, as Patti referred to her seven-year-old daughter, was the apple of her eye. At times Patti referred to Kristina as an equal, and I envied them that relationship. At other times Patti was the in-charge parent—the only status I seemed to have with my children.

As Patti prepared for The Walk, she was not concerned about who would care for Kristina while she was away. Kristina had a regular sitter, and if she were unavailable, there was Patti's mother, who routinely helped out. One of them, she assumed, would take over. When the regular sitter refused to take Kristina, because she disapproved of Patti walking around Kentucky with a stranger, Patti turned to her mother. Rejection from a sitter whom she had counted on disappointed her, but the sharp criticism her mother dished out delivered a painful, unexpected blow.

In one testy exchange Patti's mother (referring to me) snapped, "You don't even know that woman! She might be a lesbian and have AIDS!" To which Patti replied, "Mother, I want to *walk* with her, not *sleep* with her!" This criticism was particularly distressing because in any other circumstance, such as job, illness, or "regular" vacation, both Patti's mother and sitter would have gladly helped.

Likewise, Kate found that her mother-in-law was critical when Kate announced that she would help me. And her mother-in-law had known me since childhood! It appeared that because Kate and Patti had stepped out of their expected roles, they were punished. In the end, Patti found a different sitter, and Kate followed her instinct to help. As a result, I was blessed with invaluable assistance, encouragement and inspiration.

If the experiences of my companions were typical, it appeared that parent-child struggles were the norm. Normal doesn't mean fun. For me it seemed that the harder I tried, out of love and concern, the further my daughters and I grew apart. If I talked to them, I was preaching, and they pushed away. If I kept my mouth shut, I was negligent and blamed for not warning them. The ol' "damned if you do and damned if you don't" dilemma was always at work. Most frustrating was—at least it seemed to me—that my children did not confront their father with the same ferocity. What was I doing that was so awful? Maybe nothing. For after walking with Patti, and sharing our mother-and-daughter struggles, this single parent, 10 years my junior, parented me and left a legacy for her own daughter.

At day's end, after walking 17 miles in rain, sleet, and snow, Debbie, Kate, Patti, and I sat in a booth at the Super Quick store near Greenup and reviewed the day. Judy—another contact of Kate's—was so enthusiastic about our little project that she had arranged for us to have complimentary drinks and, most important, to sleep on the floor of her church the next night. We had made amazing progress and friends. Debbie and I begged Patti to stay. But she had to return to work and was thinking of reunions; "When I get home, I think I'll tell my mother, 'You know, Mom, I tried that lifestyle...and I think I like it!'"

Just before Patti walked away to climb into her boyfriend Jim's car, she stood in front of me at arm's length. A Daniel Boone-style coon-skin cap perched jauntily on her tousled, short-cropped, red hair. The cold rain and snow of the day's walk had brightened her freckles. Eyes that usually twinkled were uncustomarily serious as she seemed to look deep into my soul. "You did this *all by yourself!* Whatever you want to do after this, you *can* do." And, with a hug, she was gone.

Patti showed me that it is possible to love and help without turning the string into binder twine. You can also leave without breaking the box.

Naughty 'n' Nice

"And she remembered him kissing her in the mornings and rolling onto her for what he called "a bit o' brawdry" before the children awoke.... I wonder how many a woman spends the time I do athinkin' on her husband...." (FTR, p. 143)

Walking along a road puts you up close and personal with life's used, abused, intimate, and abandoned: bottles, cans, clothes, toys, paper, and dead animals. All dirty and used. Usually broken. Stepped over, or beside, or on. After walking for two weeks, we found life's trash had become unimportant and uninteresting. Then two incidents forever changed my outlook.

The first occurred the day before Patti left us. My companions' spirits and bodies were sagging. Patti raised pain with each step, while Debbie complained of a stomachache. They lagged behind. Hoping to speed them up, I hiked on and caught up with Kate's van about a quarter mile ahead. Looking back, instead of seeing Debbie and Patti trying to catch up, we saw two red-faced women beside the road, holding their sides and laughing hysterically.

Patti squatted over something while Debbie snapped rapid-fire photos. Not wanting to miss out on the joke, Kate and I retraced my steps. I looked uncomprehendingly at discarded plastic toys: a small sunflower, a ribbed baby bottle, and a long narrow tube with a tongue. To my blank, ignorant stare Debbie exclaimed, "Condoms!" Condoms? Not in my world. I had married into a minister's family. Debbie knowingly and irreverently quipped, "I think I'll box them up, send them to Carl (her husband) and say, 'Having fun. Wish you were here.'" Unlike me, Debbie, Patti, and Kate were honest and open with their sexuality, even laughing and having fun with it. Although married and the mother of four, by comparison, I was inhibited and uneducated.

Gone were the lagging steps. Our bodies, minds, and spirits suddenly revived with our laughter. Miles zipped by unnoticed as we made up stories of how that trash happened to be beside the road.

The second incident happened six days later, after Patti was gone. Downtown Ironton, Ohio, had prepared another opportunity for me to loosen up. It was the end of the day. Kate was driving us around, looking for a place to eat supper. Debbie spotted a store with a "Naughty 'n' Nice" sign. She lit up like a Christmas tree, "Let's stop!" Kate zipped into a parking space.

"It's open!"

"Let's go in!"

"If you think I'm going to get caught going in Naughty 'n' Nice, you're nuts!" I protested.

"Nobody's going to see us."

"I have no intention of going in there." But I did.

In my "good and proper" upbringing and marriage, "nice" girls and women didn't think about such things, much less *go into* "adult" stores. It was acceptable for men to enjoy X-rated movies, but women were not supposed to…or at least not admit it. However, here were two women I liked and admired who thought it was a lark to see what was inside Sandy's Midnight Delight with its naughty and nice merchandise. While I was racked by guilt and concerned about what someone would say if Mary Ingles' name were linked to women checking out the steamy side of life, Kate said, "El, you're taking this walk too serious." But…we were spending the night in a church! I had to keep reminding myself that God was the one who invented sex.

It lowered my embarrassment and anxiety level to discover the manager was not some dirty old man but a pretty, young girl—a gentle, kind person. Why would she choose such a business? The answer was easy. She couldn't find any other job. It was a way to support herself.

"What does your mother think?"

"Not much."

I admired this young woman's courage.

"Look! Look! Take my picture!" Kate and Debbie were having uproarious fun perusing inflatable dolls, nude playing cards, sexy lingerie, creams and lotions, and *huge* dildos. Discomfort held me in its grasp. Was I naive or dumb, or was it religious guilt? Kate and Debbie were planning what to buy and send to their husbands. Since I had not shared my marriage bed for years, I had no one to buy for. Even when I was sexually active, I had never felt comfortable speaking of my desires with my husband. My companion's attitudes seemed honest and healthy. I envied them their freedom and feelings. It must be an exceptional experience to share such intimacy and humor with someone you love, who loves you back and respects you in that love. Perhaps that's another reason *Follow the River* so captured my soul. Jim Thom had made Mary a sexual being who remembered and longed for her husband's physical affection.

It seemed that Kate and Debbie had many a willing and happy memory as they laughingly paid for presents to take home, and dreamed of skin-on-skin sharing. I walked out empty-handed, but with a smiling heart and a new awareness of what could be.

An Unremarkable Day

"And the smell of the hickory smoke here under the salt kettles: It made her remember the little log smokehouse, where Will would hang up the salt beef with ropes to cold-smoke for three or four days. Oh, all the happy autumn hours and days they had spent, after the harvests, working like one, putting food and firewood by for the winters!" (FTR, p. 142)

Rough, male conversation rumbled just beyond the blanket of sleep. Gently, Judy Justice's soft voice tried to shush it. At 5:30 a.m. the New Life Fellowship church had an apple butter-making project at hand, and there would be no tip-toeing around three women sleeping on the floor. Debbie, Kate, and I tried to ignore the voices and return to the Land of Nod. No luck. So we roused ourselves and ambled outside into a pitch-black morning to join the work party.

As part of Greenup, Kentucky's "Old Fashioned Days," the women and men of the church had worked for days harvesting and cooking apples and running them through colanders to make gallons and gallons of applesauce. This day they were busily engaged in the final step of cooking away the liquid to make apple butter, a cooking-down process similar to the salt-making operation at Big Bone Lick in 1755.

Like witches at a cauldron, two dark forms stood beside a copper kettle, three feet in diameter, suspended above a small wood fire. One man tended the fire while the other stirred the contents of the kettle. The flame had to be hot enough to evaporate the liquid but not so hot that the applesauce would scorch and ruin the entire batch. The fire-tender shone a flashlight on the simmering liquid, while the stirrer slowly moved a long-handled, wooden paddle back and forth. Taking a turn at the stirring paddle, I soon learned that it was more difficult than it appeared. As the sauce cooked, it thickened, and this increased the resistance and the possibility of scorching. The stirrer had to keep the paddle constantly moving. While the men were cooking down the sauce, the women were scalding glass jars to hold the thick apple butter that would spice up many a winter breakfast biscuit.

As I watched the women working, Judy talked of her hopes for an adventure. A dreamy look came over her face when she spoke of a trip that could take her *one hundred miles* from home. We invited Judy to join us, but she was quick with reasons why that would be impossible. By providing us with food, shelter, and assistance, she had become a part of The Walk. And that appeared to be all the adventure Judy could handle.

Just as we started to drive away from the church and head for breakfast, a reporter drove up alongside. Paul Long had hunted for us without success the previous day and came within seconds of missing us again. He wanted to walk. But with river access blocked by business and industry, it promised to be an uninteresting day of hard road walking. I doubted that anything we would do on this day would be newsworthy or memorable, but he insisted on joining us. But first things first—breakfast. People at the church had recommended the YMCA.

YMCAs of my experience did not serve meals. However, this one served food in a room the size of a gymnasium where men sat on benches beside long tables. The smells of biscuits, gravy, bacon, cooked apples, and coffee wafted through the air and started our stomachs growling. After eating, I noticed a pay phone and decided to make one last try to contact Phyllis Hyde, a teacher from Michigan.

Back in the summer, when I had talked to Phyllis, it sounded as though she strongly desired to join me in West Virginia. Before I left, the plan was for her to call Janette or Lisa if she could make it. Neither had heard a word. The coin dropped. The phone rang and rang; then, as I was about to hang up, she answered. In response to my greeting came the excited and relieved voice of someone who might have "space cadet" leanings, explain that she had lost the phone numbers and just happened to be in the house when I called. Phyllis planned to meet us Sunday afternoon. I gave her the name, address, and phone number of the couple who had offered us tent space for Sunday, wished her luck, and dropped the receiver in the cradle.

The day's nature interest was Paul rescuing a black-and-white kitten from busy Route 23. The day's human interest was my first experience in a unisex bathroom outfitted with urinals and a condom dispenser. And conversation again centered on the problems of education, illiteracy, and pollution. So much for adventure.

By early afternoon, Paul left to file his story: *"Sometimes, hard gravel crunched beneath their feet, at other times their hiking boots trod upon soft, dew-covered grass. But no matter the surface, Eleanor Lahr and Debbie Klene trekked forward..."* (*Kentucky Post,* October 12, 1987). Debbie and I walked on into Catlettsburg.

The attendant of a gas station located between the river and the road agreed to make space in the parking lot for Kate's van. The location would be easy for Janette and Lisa to find at their scheduled midnight arrival.

Rather than explore the area, Debbie shopped. When she found and shipped presents to her children, she glowed. However, her phone calls home continued to cast a dark cloud. Josh had vomited. Her mother-in-law had broken her hip. In spite of this news, Debbie appeared less depressed than she had after previous phone calls. However, for the first time she spoke of leaving The Walk before the end, maybe in a week.

Though stung by the real possibility of continuing alone, I did not encourage Debbie one way or another. I was afraid to. The decision had to be hers. I did wonder if Debbie's nervous stomach and badly chewed fingernails were indications of enormous emotional pressure. And, while I sympathized, I carried my own tensions.

This was our last, full day in Kentucky. While making logistical phone calls, I strained to hear over the motor and gear shifting sounds of the busy gas station. The next morning we would cross the mouth of the Big Sandy. Would people in West Virginia be as kind, and would we be as lucky as we had been in Kentucky?

Back in August, my firefighting friend John Taylor had planned to coordinate West Virginia sag support. Unfortunately, his heart attack put him on the sidelines. John then tapped his friend and colleague Chip Stallard to take over. As a result, I spent a lot of phone time with, and depended greatly on, someone with whom I had only once shaken hands at the Fire Department Instructor's Conference in Memphis.

Chip had good news. To keep us off a narrow, treacherous bridge and avoid a long detour to enter West Virginia, a state legislator had rented a boat to carry us over the Big Sandy and had organized an "official welcome." (Whatever that was.) Chip also sounded confident that someone from the Emergency Medical Service (EMS) would transport gear for us on Monday.

Adding to the good news, Sharon Ferguson, a descendant of Mary and Will, had made arrangements for us to have a room at the Radisson. And George and Joandel Jackson, in whose yard we planned to pitch our tents on Sunday, invited us to go to church…even though the only thing we had to wear was a pair of unsoiled jeans and a T-shirt. Fourteen days ago I would never have considered wearing jeans to worship. (My priorities were certainly changing.) Where earlier I thought nothing could beat Kentucky hospitality, now it seemed that West Virginia goodwill would be just as warm. However, amid all the reassurance and gratitude, sadness and tensions churned.

In 12 hours Kate would leave. On this day we had proven the legitimacy of our project by completing The Walk through Kentucky. From a 43-day trek, only 29 days remained. Only two states to go. There should have been a celebration. However, instead of a party, after a "spit bath" in the gas station restroom, we curled up in the van and tried to sleep. Like a street person, I was learning to manage.

The darkness of night deepened a growing apprehension. With each car that pulled in for gas, I'd rise up and peek out. When it was not the red Firenza with Mary Ingles signs on the side windows and my daughters inside, my uneasiness heightened. Thank goodness Kate was there for Debbie to talk to, because I was miserable company.

While I drifted off to sleep, sounds from truck motors and people drowned the sound of the Big Sandy lapping at its bank. But like Mary, I knew it was one of the last, large river mouths to be crossed before we saw the Kanawha River (Mary called it the New River) flow into the Ohio.

It was an unremarkable day. The kind I would later play over and over in my mind, because of one seemingly insignificant phone call.

Politics and Parties

"...they came to a sandy-bottomed tributary that Mary distinctly remembered from the trip down in the captivity of Captain Wildcat. The Indians had crossed it in a canoe..." (FTR, p. 192)

In the morning, I rose up and looked out the van window to discover the happy sight of my red Firenza parked next to us. Janette and Lisa had had no trouble driving in from Bloomington. (I was slowly and happily realizing my daughters were capable young women.) Their safe arrival took the edge off my swirling emotions. I hugged the girls hello, bade farewell to Kate, and prepared for an early morning boat ride that would lead me away from Kentucky and into West Virginia.

West Virginia State Representative Walter "Lefty" Rollins had planned for us to cross the Big Sandy by boat, and to be met with an official welcome. This would keep us off the Big Sandy bridge. Designed for motorized traffic, with no shoulder or sidewalk, this narrow bridge forced anyone crossing by foot to take her life in her hands. I was grateful for Mr. Rollins' offer of a boat ride, even if it was (as it seemed to me) an obvious ploy for his political publicity.

Mr. and Mrs. Rollins greeted us on the Kentucky bank. Their plan was for Mrs. Rollins to accompany Debbie and me on the little blue-and-white houseboat, while Mr. Rollins drove over and waited on the West Virginia side to head the welcome party and to direct reporters. The slow and easy ride on the deck of a little houseboat that sunny day relaxed both my mind and body. Cares and tensions floated away on sun-sprinkled ripples. Debbie and I, temporarily isolated from the hubbub, leaned on the rail and watched the Ohio River flow from the northeast and then make a sharp turn northwest. We floated across the large, dusky-green mouth of the Big Sandy as it flowed into the south side of the Ohio.

Mrs. Rollins, Debbie, and I watched seven pairs of dark mallard ducks play around the boat and follow the lead of a much larger white duck. The largest duck would gather the smaller mallards together, quack instructions, and then lead them in a miniature flotilla. When the line inevitably disintegrated, the big duck would quack-quack again. The flotilla would regroup, and then he'd guide them off in a new direction. I enjoyed watching the follow-the-leader display, until the wife of our benefactor quipped, "Just like people. The white one leads the dark ones."

An icy chill ran through me. This was a different world, where the attitude of white supremacy was alive and well. Maybe the warnings about "*Deliverance* Country" were justified. Fear kept me from protesting the racist comment. Like many good people who fail to speak up, I implied consent with my silence.

At the official welcome, West Virginia presented me with a citation from the House of Delegates, a proclamation by Treasurer of the State A. J. Manchin, and a letter of congratulations and Godspeed from Governor Arch A. Moore Jr. It appeared that my worries about West Virginia were groundless. The state was a friendly place. So, through a day brimming with generosity, reporters, interviews and welcomes, I carefully kept to myself my belief that women and people of color can be equal to—and even superior to—white, Protestant males. The official welcome was nice, but the best part was the pride shining in my daughters' faces.

Then Debbie and I headed out for Huntington. We stopped in front of a statue about 10 feet tall and took pictures. The engraving read, "St. Christopher. Patron of Tourists. Pray for us." We didn't know it then, but in 72 hours, we would desperately need all the help this saint could muster. But, for the time being, help was coming from Mary's descendants. Sharon arranged for a room for us in the Radisson Hotel. (Another bath!) Al Castonali invited us to a fancy "reverse raffle" at Robby's restaurant, to raise money for a Catholic school. (Free food!) The raffle gathering looked like the cream of Huntington society, and there I was wearing blue jeans and a gray Patagonia pullover, trying to be appreciative and sociable, even though dead tired. I stayed what I thought was long enough to be polite, then headed to bed.

Stomach cramps, diarrhea, and a splitting headache, I guess brought on by nervous tension, ruined my sleep on a real mattress. This day's big accomplishment, of making it through one state and beginning another, was overshadowed by an off-hand remark…and my guilt at not making an appropriate reply.

In our days along the river, a housekeeper, a fireman, and a store owner, all of whose skin color was darker than mine, would come to our aid. Each time, they were helpful and generous, reaffirming my belief that we can be kind and gracious to those who appear different, if we just greet each other with honor and respect. And each kindness drove deeper the knife of guilt.

Connections

"She tried to smile away her anxiety." (FTR, p. 2)

A headache and knot in my stomach took the edge off the enjoyment of a night in a bed and an early morning shower. Downing two of Janette's aspirins and laughing with Lisa in the bathroom eased the discomfort of an unexplained sense of impending doom. We were preparing to meet our benefactress and her daughters. Maybe that was it.

Sharon Ferguson had learned of our need for safe lodging from a newspaper article. Through her former husband, she arranged for a double room at the Radisson. She had intended to walk with us the previous day, but we missed meeting her at the Route 60 bridge. Concerns that Sharon might be upset were quickly put to rest as we ate breakfast with her and her teenage daughters, Martha and Courtney.

Joandel Jackson, who was providing safe lodging for this evening, joined us. Beaming broadly, she handed me the Sunday paper. Again we made the front page. Joandel was as nice in person as she had sounded on the phone. I picked up the breakfast tab; it was the least I could do.

As I checked out, Debbie huddled over the telephone in another long call. From the look on her face, I doubted she would be joining Joandel and me at the Beverly Hills Methodist Church. Whatever was going on back home was not my problem, but I ached for my steadfast companion.

Because Joandel and her husband George sang in the church choir, I sat with their son Scott and his daughters Julia and Jennifer. (Joandel assured me that my "Sunday best" blue jeans, turtleneck and Patagonia fleece jacket were acceptable.) The service was a musical fiesta with a children's chancel and bell choirs, and a male soloist and oboist. My spirit swelled with gratitude that I was fortunate enough to be in this place of beauty.

At her home beside the river, my plan to attend the Ohio River Odyssey flew out the window, as Joandel whipped up a Sunday feast of baked chicken, carrot casserole, fresh green beans, potatoes, and Chocolate Delight for dessert. (We certainly were not starving as Mary and Ghetel had.) Joandel understood that Janette and Lisa needed to head back to Indiana by 2:00, so everything was ready. Then, as if she had not done enough, Joandel handed the girls grilled cheese "care packages" for the road. As phone calls and visitors began arriving, I settled beside the fireplace.

John Taylor called to welcome me to his home state. In the spring he had dismissed my concerns about making it safely through "wild," wonderful West Virginia and promised to coordinate safe lodging through his volunteer fire department connections, if I made it that far. Sidelined by quadruple heart bypass surgery, he had passed the job on to Chip Stallard. John's call showed that his finger was still in the pie. Who would have thought that meeting the casual acquaintance of a Delaware friend at a fire conference in Memphis over five years before would have turned out to be so important in my life?

A young family who had heard Debbie and I would be at the Jacksons' came to meet us. It turned out to be Rick Ransom's family, who planned to walk if/when we reached the St. Albans area. Rick asked about our West Virginia lodging. When I told him the only safe place arranged, after we left the Jacksons', was a place on the Cole River, he offered to see what he could do. He only planned to walk one day, but I was looking forward to it.

As the fire began to die, I stared into the flames and wondered what would happen next. It seemed that we were bombarded with striking happenings, with each day a unique jewel on a long necklace.

At 6:00 in the cozy family room, Debbie and I added some of Joandel's recipes to our collection, and thought about supper. The phone rang. The teacher from Michigan needed directions. I'd given them to her previously, but she seemed confused. My young daughters had followed my directions and found the Jacksons' home without a problem. But, to reduce the chance of error, this time I asked Joandel to explain them to her.

It's an easy 10-to-15-minute drive from Huntington to the Jackson home between the railroad and the river. So as Joandel began supper preparations, the new walker was included in the headcount. When the food was ready, about a half hour or so later, and she had not arrived, I told Joandel to go ahead and serve. Goodness only knew what had happened. With directions and a phone number, she should either find us or call.

We finished eating and still no teacher. Debbie decided to go outside to smoke a cigarette. (Her vow to quit was not working.) After helping with the initial pick-up of dishes, I watched Joandel and George continue their happy team effort at "readying up" the kitchen.

Sitting at the kitchen table and hearing footsteps, I looked toward the hallway. There, framed in the doorway was a strange woman, with Debbie standing directly behind her. (Debbie later told me, "I didn't want to miss your reaction.") The woman appeared taller and older than me. A stretchy headband held shoulder-length, graying-blond hair away from a face with a firm square jaw. Phyllis Hyde had arrived.

More than an expression, her face was a force. Here was not the bubbly Louise, professional Harriet, risqué Daisy, or lively Patti anxious to participate and join the team. As Phyllis looked at me, I felt an icy defiance and anger. And I had no idea why. No open-armed, welcoming hug would be accepted or offered. Forcing a smile over my reservations, I said, "Hello. You made it!"

A torrent of woes tumbled out. Phyllis described how she drove up and down the road trying to find the house. If Debbie had not gone out to the road for a smoke she'd still be driving around! Apparently Debbie saw the car going back and forth, stopped her and discovered the long-lost Phyllis. Instead of greeting Debbie with words of gratitude and appreciation, Phyllis snapped, "Why weren't you out here an hour ago?" Whew....

Although Joandel had just cleared the kitchen, the ever-gracious hostess offered Phyllis food and coffee. They were brusquely refused. Phyllis had food outside in her car and the Jacksons' brand of coffee creamer was not acceptable. She would use her own.

Although I didn't say anything, this brash social behavior made me bristle. Phyllis was a stranger, a newcomer to an existing program. And within the first few minutes she was rude to those who had bent over backwards for us. What was the matter? What was I missing?

Debbie and I had made it through 16 difficult days, largely due to the extraordinary generosity of strangers. If a member of the group went around offending people, the whole atmosphere of trust, helping and education I had worked so hard to build would be ruined. Not to mention the dishonor it would give the Draper/Ingles family. Maybe Phyllis was just upset from the long trip and her trouble trying to find the house. (But we all have difficult times.) Phyllis wanted to sleep outside, so I walked outside and offered to help with her gear.

Strewn under the tree beside her car was an array of camping items, including a huge cardboard box of food and miscellany. As Phyllis fussed around trying to find her cook stove and food, I stood and watched. My hands in my pockets, my mouth shut.

Jim Thom had referred me to Phyllis as one who had experience along the New River. In phone calls and letters last summer, Phyllis repeatedly talked of her experience as a camper and backpacker. I stared in disbelief. How was she planning to carry the cardboard box? With my little Olds Firenza as weekend sag support, a third backpack was all we could handle. We did not have room for boxes of groceries. And what about when there was no sag support? Would Phyllis carry the box in her arms? This person who could not follow well-defined directions to locate a big house along the river was the survival expert?

It would be an interesting three weeks.

Day 17
Monday, October 12, 1987
Huntington to Crown City, West Virginia

Sunshine and Storm Clouds

"Mary was anxious to get back down the east bank of this river and rejoin the O-y-o. She was worried about being out of sight of it." (FTR, p. 166)

As I stood looking out the upstairs bedroom window, a thick layer of clouds covered the sky. Reflected on the river, it gave the Ohio the look of dull mercury. Except for green hills on the horizon, water and sky blended together into an indistinguishable gray. What would we experience today as we followed the mercurial guide?

After 24 hours of R & R, I was anxious to leave. However, there were the inevitable last-minute arrangements. Joandel, providing the day's sag wagon support, would drop us at the Radisson, then pick us up wherever we happened to be at day's end. We'd have safe lodging, because when Joandel heard we planned to camp in a field beside the road, she insisted we stay with her another night.

A troublesome development was Phyllis' car. It wasn't running properly. She decided to take it to a garage, rather than walk with us. In addition, Phyllis privately kept asking me where she could park the car while she walked. Good gracious, I didn't know! It was *her* car. If she brought it, she should take care of it. I suggested Phyllis check with some parking lots or the police department, but frankly I refused to worry about *her* vehicle. It was all I could do to deal with moving us down the road safely, the unexpected media interest, and finding safe lodging, property access, sag wagons and, in many cases, food. "If you bring it, you tote it" was my principle. Whether Phyllis walked or drove was up to her. Just don't cause me any problems.

Just as Debbie's children, Gary's feet, and Patti's mother were personal difficulties for them to work out, Phyllis' car and backpack were her responsibility. However, I was adamant that people associated with this walk not impose on strangers who were already extending hospitality way beyond what one would expect. I could not believe Phyllis had come all the way from Michigan with no arrangements for her vehicle. She appeared as unorganized in person as she had sounded on the telephone, when I first talked to her last August. Well, there was no need for me to be upset. All groups seem to have one character who adds interest. When we arrived at the Radisson, I tried to stuff Phyllis and her problems deep in my subconscious.

Although several people we met over the weekend said they would like to walk today, no one showed up. We had too far to go to wait around for the well- intentioned. Promptly at 8:00, Debbie and I walked away from the hotel.

Though the day was gray and cloudy enough to rain, I decided to chance it and carry my blanket. Latecomers who wanted to walk might recognize us. Because of heavy development along the river, locals recommended a city route noted for its history and architecture.

As we walked through a neat, tree-lined, residential area, a car pull up, and a man call out, "Are you Eleanor and Debbie? Can we walk with you?" The middle-aged twosome was Muriel Stuart from Huntington and her brother, Clayton Varney, from Florida. They were total strangers, but conversation was easy and relaxed. Though the pace slowed considerably, I was honored by their obvious pleasure to be part of our little adventure. We'd walked to the corner when Clayton turned to Muriel and said, "I'll move the car ahead." Remembering how Carol Stivers drove up and walked into Maysville with us, I assumed they'd walk at least a mile, even though Muriel was wearing only light moccasins.

As Clayton was about to walk back to the car, I sat on the ground adding their names to my yellow legal pad, when another car pulled to a stop. Out stepped a petite woman, about my age, dressed in blue-jean skirt, turtleneck, and oversized hand-knit sweater. Her short-cropped, brunette hair, flecked with gray, framed a face of sharp, finely chiseled features and one of the most open, accepting smiles I had ever seen.

When she came around the car, her one word was both a question and exclamation. "Eleanor?! I'm Susan!"

Susan? Susan? Of course! The bronze sculptor! One of my West Virginia walkers! Instantly, as if we were long-lost college roommates, we were joyously hugging and laughing. What was she doing on *that* street, on *that* corner, just as Debbie and I arrived? Susan explained that after visiting her daughter in Huntington, she was making a mad dash to a 10:00 a.m. meeting in Charleston and just "happened" to see us.

Like proud parents watching babbling children, Clayton and Muriel smiled in the background while Susan and I hurriedly exchanged information. Words tumbled out and on top of each other. Yes, she still planned to join us after her exhibition in Charleston. Did we have a place to stay in the Point Pleasant area? No, not yet. If we needed help when we arrived, just call. And she was gone.

What a dynamo. Susan's enthusiasm, presence, and way with words were stimulating. Patti and Kate were gone, but if we were lucky, in a week we would have Susan. She would be great fun.

Before an anxious Clayton moved the car, Debbie took pictures as Muriel posed with my red blanket draped around her shoulders. But he moved it only to the end of the next block. As Debbie, Muriel and I approached the corner, Clayton opened the car door and called to his sister, "I think you better get in now." No doubt confusion washed across my face as I thought, Muriel only walked a block. How dare he boss her around? However, Muriel smiled pleasantly, said "Good-bye," and walked away. Then, as if reading the questions in my eyes, she turned and said, "I just had a heart catheterization. I just wanted to be part of this."

It is impossible to tell by looking what problems people are struggling with. An attractive blonde, dressed in black slacks, white blouse, and turquoise jacket, Muriel appeared the picture of health. Empathy flooded from me to this lady. Heart trouble makes one reassess priorities, and in the midst of her difficulties, Muriel desired to be part of my little project. I was overwhelmed. How do you thank someone for such an honor? The only thing I could do was remember another woman of courage and grace.

An overwhelming sense of humility swept through me. For various reasons, we all needed each other that morning. On a nondescript street corner, something put the idea of an Indiana woman in the right place to encourage a West Virginia heart patient. And that delay would obtain us needed assistance days later. It makes one wonder about invisible forces.

When we were alone, Debbie put my thoughts into words when she said she was glad Phyllis wasn't around and worried that if Susan had met her, Susan might have had second thoughts. Debbie nailed the problem. Phyllis was a different kind of personality than anything we had experienced. I couldn't put my finger on it. She was just...Phyllis.

Gawking at beautiful old homes, the likes of which we'd never own, we zigzagged along quiet streets and past an occasional store until we reached Route 2. Probably a former game or Indian trail, it would eventually follow the river all the way to Point Pleasant. At times like this, I truly felt we were walking in Mary and Ghetel's footsteps.

Enthusiastic people stopping us to talk, always encouraged Debbie and me. So, in spite of the delay, we were soon back on the riverbank looking down for the river to show us the way. In what was becoming an almost daily occurrence, at a wide spot in the road two local TV reporters caught up with us. If the interview were on the news that night, maybe we could see ourselves. Imagine, Debbie and me on the evening news! It must be a slow news day.

Then the sun began to peek from behind the clouds, and the Ohio stretched out as a silver ribbon between lush, green banks. Between us and the river, the railroad, with its white, rocky bed appeared as neat landscaping. Approaching the Jacksons' house, with the luxury of toilet privileges, this was a "do not pass" pit stop.

As we trekked across the lawn, Joandel walked out of the house carrying three large apples. She must have been looking and planning for us. While our original plan was to make quick use of the clean bathroom and be off, it didn't take much of Joandel's twinkling eyes and mischievous smile to tempt us to dawdle.

After pigging out on chocolate dream dessert, we took pictures of Joandel, and she walked around the backyard explaining how her and George's parents acquired and developed land that very likely Mary had walked across.

When Debbie made another trip inside, Joandel approached me with obvious unease at broaching a difficult subject. "Eleanor, Phyllis wants us to keep her car. I'm really reluctant to take responsibility for it." My heart sank and went out to Joandel while my blood pressure shot up with frustration at Phyllis.

Both George and Joandel had opened not only their home, but their hearts, to total strangers. When all I asked for was a place to put up a tent and the use of a bathroom, they gave us inside beds, bathroom privileges, family meals, and caring support. Now, within hours of arriving, a newcomer insulted Joandel's food, was making an intrusive request, and, worst of all, made Joandel uncomfortable. What could I say that would give Joandel the support she needed without sounding overly critical of Phyllis?

Standing in the garden, surrounded by flowers and sunshine, I looked into Joandel's eyes. "You have *no* obligation to keep her car. She was told not to make *any* requests other than a bathroom and tent space. If you *want* to keep the car, fine."

"I don't. We've had minor vandalism here, and I would worry."

"Do what you feel is best and *don't* feel guilty. You've done more than enough."

Though I didn't say anything to Debbie, I knew I *had* to have another talk with Phyllis. However, with Phyllis off with her car, that had to wait. So, after once again using the friendly facilities, Debbie and I chugged on down the road. Unfortunately, for me, the sun and flowers did not seem as bright, and my shoulders sagged as I felt the additional weight of a growing doubt.

We were barely out of sight of the Jackson house when the Ceems-Cabel Emergency Service vehicle stopped beside us. Gordon, a clean-cut, handsome, young man, was driving and would transport our gear through Cabel County. John and Chip's fire service network had snapped into service.

"Do you have a place to stay the night?"

"Yes."

"Tomorrow?"

"A field beside the road."

Big frown. "Would you like to stay in the home of a former Confederate general? It's right on the river."

"Sure! All we need is a place to pitch our tents and a toilet." Gordon left, saying he'd see what he could do.

Route 2, the Ohio, and railroad tracks follow each other as if they were in a choreographed dance. Sometimes the river is within spitting distance; at other times the road moves away. Then, the river is evident by a treeline weaving far off to our left. As long as the silver ribbon or the treeline was in sight, I felt comfortable; away from it, anxiety set in. The road, the railroad, and the river. Now we joined in the dance.

Without a doubt, Mary would have taken the Indian and game trail shortcuts between the river's serpentine curves. To stay on the riverbank would add useless miles. Mary would not have done it, and neither would I. But walking beside a busy two-lane road is dangerous. We were constantly on guard for traffic from both directions. However, ever-changing scenery relieved the strain.

Old barns nestled against hillsides. Purple asters grew in a profusion that suggested spring rather than fall. Nature is incredibly wasteful. All that loveliness, and the chances were no one would see, let alone appreciate it. Beauty sat silently by the roadside. Yet few, if any, looked her way. At least not in 1987, when most people flew by in cars. I wondered how many flowers and people go through their entire lives with no one appreciating them.

Without warning, we looked up and saw Phyllis walking toward us. A little way ahead she had parked beside the road and walked back. Wearing a trench coat and army-type hiking boots and swinging a small paper bag in one hand, she looked anything but the experienced hiker she claimed to be. I thought she planned to tell us about the car and would leave to put on her hiking clothes. Not quite.

There were no serious mechanical problems. Phyllis would just walk a little in the afternoon. Though a fresh walker, she brought up the rear and talked only when spoken to. Meanwhile, Debbie, finally walking without obvious pain, kept up and was in bubbling spirits. A striking contrast in personalities.

I couldn't figure out Phyllis. Hers was not the cheery, outgoing, friendly disposition of Debbie, Brenda, Patti or Susan. Phyllis seemed sad or sullen. Perhaps it was just the difficulty of meeting new people and concerns about her vehicle. Whatever the reason, she was not a happy camper.

When we reached her car, Phyllis announced she did not like the road and wanted to walk closer to the river. She climbed in and drove away. The rest of the afternoon, off to our left, we would occasionally see a lone, trench-coated figure with paper lunch bag dangling from a hand, walking down the middle of the railroad tracks.

River and hills pulled away from the road. The property between was private land, which, even without "No Trespassing" signs, I respected. The space between us and the river made for flat land, broad shoulders, and easy walking. There was plenty of room beside the road when a white Corvette came toward us and slid to a stop.

JoAnn Oakes (left) shared her maps, books, newspaper clippings, and bubbling excitement with me.

Out popped an excited imp, with bushy, jet-black hair and a smile that filled her face. Coordinated in black and white, she wore skin-tight jeans and looked like she just stepped out of *Vogue*. Rapid-fire speech, with a thick southern drawl, pulled o's, r's, and e's into expressions of wonder, apology, humor, and self-deprecation. JoAnn Oakes had landed. As I introduced Debbie, JoAnn began excitedly handing me books and papers.

A fistful of newspaper articles (about The Walk), a letter from Eleanor Henson (who wanted to have a cookout when we arrived near Charleston), a copy of *Trans-Allegheny Pioneers* (while exclaiming, "*This is the book! It has the true story*"), a booklet on the Battle of Point Pleasant and, last but not least, a message of welcome from the Point Pleasant mayor. JoAnn seemed to know everyone personally. Obviously excited by history, she was trying to educate us. And though I wouldn't hurt JoAnn's feelings by refusing her generosity, looking at the pile of gifts, all I could think of was that I'd have to carry all this stuff!

Debbie joined in the discussion and seemed as captivated by our new friend as I. Then, in a conspiratorial tone, JoAnn whispered that she hoped to walk with us in the New River area. But she didn't want anyone to know, just in case it didn't work out. Another enthusiastic walker? *Yes!*

As cars whizzed past, I spread road and topographic maps on the ground and tried to give JoAnn an idea of where we might be in the days ahead. I had the feeling she was having as much trouble comprehending my information as I was hers.

In the midst of JoAnn's enthusiasm, Phyllis drove by, parked her car ahead, and again walked back to us. She stood apart and silently looked down on JoAnn and me with cold, brooding eyes. I felt the same knot-in-my-stomach anxiety I had as a child or at home when my parents, husband, or children were disappointed in me. It seemed I had displeased Phyllis. However, I didn't have the foggiest idea of what I had done or why she was unhappy. Since Phyllis was a teacher, I assumed she would be interested in the history JoAnn was sharing. I tried drawing Phyllis into the conversation and camaraderie. Unfortunately, Phyllis' silent, rigid stance indicated she wanted none of it.

JoAnn bubbled on, seemingly oblivious to Phyllis' attitude. When she mentioned being at Big Bone Lick, it dawned on me that JoAnn was not a new person. She had been with us at the start. Another name and phone number were added to the yellow legal pad. As JoAnn zoomed away, I felt I had been hit by a friendly tornado.

In spite of Phyllis' disapproval, in that brief roadside encounter, a complete stranger swept away the doubts and fears gnawing at me. There is nothing like the "high" of being in the presence of someone who thinks you are significant. JoAnn left me feeling that we really could make Charleston. No matter what happened after that...if we made Charleston, The Walk would be credible.

Phyllis may have been distant and hostile; however, the Lesage grocery store was friendly. It let strangers use the restroom! Then, as we left the store, someone from the house across the road hailed us.

Roy and Maxine enthusiastically offered refreshments, which Debbie and I accepted. However, Phyllis refused, said the road was too noisy, turned, and walked away. So she missed Roy's root beer toast to our success and his recommendation for the next possible friendly restroom. A brief encounter. But, like sunshine peeking from behind a cloud or stopping to smell a flower, it brightened the long trek.

This day, hiking felt good. It was one of the first days Debbie was not dragging in the afternoon. Crown City or Gallipolis Ferry was our goal. However, the frequent stops slowed our progress. Though not a serious concern, it nagged at me.

Along with the delays, I worried about Phyllis. We had not seen her for some time. She gave no indication of what direction she was going or what she was doing. I tried reminding myself that she was a big girl and I wasn't her mother. I didn't have time or energy to go hunting for her. But what if she were hurt? I prayed she was safe.

With the publicity we were receiving, an injury or problem with someone associated with The Walk would negatively affect or end the project and, worse still, could offend or anger the Draper/Ingles family. I desperately wanted Mary's family to be proud of this attempt to honor their ancestor.

After leaving Lesage, rocky hills dressed in vibrant fall colors moved close to the road as railroad and river ran along side by side. Then, at a particularly large road cut with a marshy area between the railroad and the river, another car pulled in front of us and stopped. A delicately built, well-groomed woman approached. Wearing a feminine red-and-white blouse and navy skirt, she looked like a patriotic poster. Her first questions were cautious and guarded. But, after a few minutes, her attitude warmed and she became enthusiastic, even began talking about herself. It was then that I realized this was the person Gordon had mentioned: Clara, owner of Confederate General Jenkins' house.

Apparently checking us out, she must have liked what she saw, because she invited us not only to set up our tents in her yard the next night, but to join her for supper! Since Phyllis wasn't around, I explained there were really three walkers. Clara said that was no problem. Like the Kelsches in Kentucky, she came out of nowhere with help, just when it was needed.

Once more, when we were alone, Debbie said she thought it was a good thing Phyllis wasn't around, or the invitation might not have been made, and we'd be sleeping in a field. I hated to admit I agreed with her. But Phyllis wasn't with us. And we had a safe place to stay for one more night. Immediately after Clara left, Joandel arrived and the day's walk was over.

As Debbie and I climbed in the car, Joandel asked, "Where's Phyllis?" We shrugged our shoulders. Then, on the drive back to the Jacksons', we saw Phyllis trudging down the road toward her car. We three shook our heads. Nothing about Phyllis made sense.

Back at the house, I learned that Joandel decided not to store Phyllis' car. Phyllis was back in my lap, for she came to me with, "Eleanor, *we* have to get our heads together about this." My unhelpful reply was, "I don't know of anyplace." My goodness, Phyllis was a grown woman. *Her* car was *not my* responsibility!

Though bewildered by Phyllis' attitude, I was also sensitive to her feelings. It seemed The Walk was not exactly what she had expected. (In fact, it wasn't what *I* expected.) In a private chat with her, I tried to explain that while I was uncomfortable when she went off alone, she was free do what she wanted. However, I would not send search parties out after people who did not stay with us. It was her responsibility to keep us in sight. I repeated the rules: We do not trespass or make requests of people who, out of the goodness and generosity of their hearts, were donating lodging or transportation. The *only* things we ask for are a bathroom and a safe place to set up our tents. She was welcome to stay or leave, if the trip was not what she expected. Phyllis nodded agreement. I was not convinced she understood.

And apparently Gordon didn't understand Clara. For that evening he called to say he had talked with Clara, but it didn't sound like she would allow us to stay on her property. Imagine his surprise when I told him we had met her and had an invitation not only to pitch our tents but to join her and her husband for supper! With the sound of relief in his voice, he said that in the morning he would take our gear to General Jenkins' house and us to our starting point.

About 10:00, Phyllis retired to her car. Though exhausted, Debbie and I accepted Joandel's offer of using her laundry room to reduce the amount of sweat and dirt we carried. As we waited on the washer and dryer, we worked to keep each other awake.

Debbie asked, "Have you noticed Phyllis stops talking whenever you walk up?" How could I *not* notice? We decided that before leaving in the morning I should again talk to Phyllis, but with Debbie present. And the conversation would be taped. I had a strong feeling that I needed to make Phyllis understand the purpose and guidelines of The Walk and I had a gut-level urgency to document what was said.

Sleep finally closed a day filled with colorful people, extraordinary circumstances, and 18 additional miles. However, an uneasy feeling that Phyllis could be troublesome clouded the night.

Love

"...that great, dear, strong, hairy man whom she loved 'til her heart ached with the sweetness of loving..." (FTR, p. 3)

George and Joandel Jackson had come into my life a few weeks earlier, just after Joandel saw a newspaper article describing my proposed retracing of Mary Ingles' escape route. She courageously wrote to invite me—a stranger—to camp at her riverside home. Like many people who live beside the Ohio, she and her husband were convinced that Mary had walked right through their property (maybe even slept there), and they wanted me to do the same.

Upon meeting Joandel, the first thing one notices is her warm smile. It spreads a glowing warmth, like the rising sun, until it infuses not only her face, but her whole being. A fifth-grade teacher, she stands about five feet, three inches and has blonde hair that curls softly around her face.

A recently retired garage door installer, George helped around the house and kitchen as he supported and encouraged his wife. Like teenagers, they teased and played jokes on each other without a hint of meanness. Honest respect and love flowed out of them and enveloped all who were lucky enough to be nearby. I was fascinated.

Debbie and I were supposed to camp in their river-bordered back yard for one night. However, after we arrived, Joandel offered us the guest room. And when she learned we had no safe lodging for the following night, and that we planned to sleep beside the river, Joandel insisted on driving us back to their house after our day's walk. As a result, for two days, we became a family.

In that time, I listened as this couple blended their voices in the church choir and felt the intense pride as they presented a handsome son and two golden-headed granddaughters. I laughed until my stomach ached at their description of how a simple backyard pool project grew into an indoor pool and greenhouse addition to the house. All because Joandel kept saying, "Couldn't we just...." Yet their life was not without pain. From time to time, without apology or self-pity, I learned of George's business problems, their son's rocky marriage, and worries over their aging parents.

**Joandel Jackson took time from her busy schedule
to make serapes for Debbie and me.**

Although Joandel had a family, papers to grade, and lessons plans to make, she fed us sumptuous meals that included homemade bread. In addition, late at night and early in the morning the sewing machine hummed as she us made serapes. (She thought we did not have enough to keep us warm and dry.) All the while, Joandel made it seem, if not easy, at least a pleasure. I never felt I was a burden.

Perhaps it was the pain of my own tortured marriage that created the desperate need to be near and absorb the love I felt in this household. It was as if I were a spirit who was given the special privilege of watching an extraordinary event. So this is what love was supposed to be.

Watching and listening, I kept waiting for the cruel silences, belittling comments, and demeaning jokes. Although I looked closely, there was never a hint of meanness between them. I admired the way George spoke to and about his wife; with respect...even with pride. They had disagreements, but they were with respect, not one-upmanship. Watching them was 48 hours of wonder. The time to say good-bye came too soon.

When I wandered into the kitchen that morning, I was disappointed to learn George was already up and gone. Debbie and Phyllis were not yet stirring. So, sharing the early morning quiet, I sat at the kitchen table as Joandel worked at the sink. With clumsy words I tried to describe what it meant for me to be with her family. In particular, I wanted her to know that her relationship with George was especially meaningful and beautiful to watch.

As I babbled on, Joandel stopped her work, leaned on the sink and silently listened. Then, looking down at her hands, there was a pause and a deep breath. With a voice so soft the words would not leave the room, she said, "Less than a year ago I almost left him." I looked at her in stunned disbelief. No! Not *this* couple. They were my role models. They had the secret. They were the perfect example of happily ever after. They gave me hope. It couldn't be!

Looking at my stricken face, Joandel continued, "George has a drinking problem. It got to be more than I could handle. Before Christmas I told him, It's it or me...and he chose *me!*" With love-brimmed eyes and radiant smile she added, "Now, it's the way it was in the beginning!"

Inner Voices

"She shivered, despite the heat of the hearth, and glanced again toward the sunny rectangle of the cabin door. No one was there, not a shadow. But she felt that same uneasiness that had returned to her several times...." (FTR, p. 1)

As a "child of the Depression," I learned well the early lessons that were drummed into my brain. "Be seen and not heard." "Don't talk with your mouth full." "Keep your elbows off the table." "Don't speak unless spoken to." "Father, teacher, minister, policeman, husband, any authority figure (particularly male) knows best." Therefore, when Gordon Merry drove us to the day's starting point, and mentioned, not once, but several times, the dangers of Route 2, I listened.

Along this stretch, the road, railroad, and river lay beside each other like black, silver, and blue ribbons on the mottled back of Mother Earth. It was easy to remember that game trails had become Indian trails; had become wagon trails; then macadam blacktop, and in some places today, a four-lane highway or part of an interstate.

In this area, Route 2 was a narrow two-lane. To the left of the road's small shoulder, a steep embankment ran down to railroad tracks, and left of the tracks, another embankment led to the broad, ever-flowing Ohio. Road, railroad, and river bend back and forth like a giant, curved staircase.

An inner need made me keep the river in view. I was uneasy whenever I was not absolutely sure where it was. There was no need to clamber over its bank every step of the way. Choosing the road, a good path rather than struggling on the river bank, seemed like a decision Mary would have made. Whenever possible, I believed she would have taken the easiest, shortest route. More often than not, that would have been walking a game or Indian trail rather than stumbling through thick brush and rocks at the river's edge. Mary was no dummy, and neither was I. This day we would walk the shoulder of the road which, I had no doubt, had been a game or Indian trail in 1755—perhaps even one Mary and Ghetel had walked.

There were other parallels to 1755. While Mary labored to elude Indians, bears, and mountain lions, we struggled to avoid being mashed by speeding cars, semis, and dump trucks. On this day, not only was the road narrow, visibility diminished to almost zero. A thick layer of fog overlaid the river. Like shaving cream, it oozed into every nook and cranny of the valley. Visibility was close to the white-out of a blizzard.

As Gordon's truck pulled to a stop at an isolated intersection, Debbie, Phyllis, and I climbed out. Again, Gordon reminded us of the dangers from vehicles and described the mangled bodies he'd picked up along this stretch of road. Casually, and softly sarcastic, he mentioned that he'd really rather not be called out to scrape *us* off the pavement. While waving good-bye, his last words were: "I really think you'd be better off down on the railroad tracks. There are trains, but I'd feel better if you were not on this road." There was not a doubt in *my* mind that walking the railroad tracks was the thing to do. However, Debbie frowned.

She was unhappy. You don't spend two-and-a-half weeks, 24 hours a day, in someone's company without becoming aware of their moods. I tried reasoning. "We've come through pretty well listening to local experts. He's the local EMS director. He knows this area. He knows what's best. If we wait until the fog clears, it might be noon. We have to cover twenty miles today. We *can't* wait." Debbie fell in behind Phyllis and me as we walked down the middle of the railroad tracks, but her dejected countenance and silence left no doubt that she was not convinced.

An eight-foot embankment and a "keep-the-riffraff-out" fence separated the railroad from the road. We knew the road was only a few yards above us, by the sounds of speeding cars and roaring trucks that floated down. But a solid, engulfing, gray wall was all we saw.

After walking only a few yards, Debbie began acting totally out of character. Like a spoiled two-year old, she hung back, dragged her feet, kicked at stones, and pouted. "I don't like these railroad tracks. I don't want to walk on these railroad tracks." Again I tried reasoning. "Gordon is the local expert. He said it is best. It's only until the fog lifts." It didn't work. She became sullen, and silent, and dropped further behind.

We'd walked maybe a block when, at a break in the fence, Debbie suddenly charged past me. Through the fence and up the embankment she flung angry words at me, "I don't like these railroad tracks! I don't want to walk on these railroad tracks! I'm taking *my* chances with the cars!"

My stomach sank. This person I'd grown to love as a companion, buddy, and dear friend was putting herself in grave danger. Pleadingly, I called after her, "Gordon is the local expert. He said the tracks are safer. We should listen to him." Her back disappeared into the fog.

Now the dilemma was on my back. Debbie and I had spent 18 days as hiking companions. Healing broken blisters and strained muscles, sharing laughter and food, and searching for safe routes. We were never separated. My first inclination was to go after her and leave Phyllis to walk the tracks by herself, for it was obvious that Phyllis was as determined to not walk on the road as Debbie was to not walk on the tracks.

Phyllis was strong willed, but not a strong hiker. The day before she'd walked only a short way and she made it clear that her preference was to walk the railroad alone, rather than join Debbie and me on the "path."

Whether Phyllis was frustrated, disappointed, unhappy with me or The Walk, or something else, I couldn't tell. But as leader, I felt it was my job to help her feel comfortable and part of the experience, and also to have fun the way Brenda and Patti had.

Conversation with me seemed difficult for Phyllis. I wondered if it was because Debbie and I were so close, that Phyllis somehow felt left out. (Brenda and Patti hadn't had a problem with me, but this was a different individual.) Perhaps if I stayed on the tracks and it was just the two of us, Phyllis would relax. If we got to know each other, perhaps the invisible strain would melt away. So, feeling as though something were being torn out of my gut, I stayed with Phyllis and watched Debbie walk away. Then I set to work to engage Phyllis in conversation. I asked about her job as a grade-school teacher (she was having personality problems with her principal) and her training for this hike (a weekly Jazzercise class.)

Meanwhile up on the road, Debbie intended to hike speedily ahead to the first road/railroad crossing. She planned to sit down, have a cigarette, and wait for us. (Because railroad ties have such awkward spacing, railroad walking tends to be slow and laborious. You can always walk faster on the road.) However, every time Debbie glanced back, there we were, faint figures walking just below her. She was frustrated and could not understand why she could not outwalk us.

After a few minutes, Debbie again looked back. This time she saw Phyllis and me walking, side by side, down the center of the tracks, talking amiably, the way people do when they don't have a care in the world, while silently bearing down on us, came the single headlight of an oncoming train. Debbie screamed at the top of her voice, "*Train! Train! Train!*"

Down on the tracks, I heard one faint word drifting through the fog, "*t r a i n.*" Looking up, I saw Debbie's wild face mouthing words and jabbing her walking stick in the air. I looked ahead. Nothing. Looking behind, a huge, silent beast with a glowing white eye was almost on top of us.

I shouted one word at Phyllis, "*TRAIN!*" Then, with every ounce of strength in my body, I made one giant leap, hit the near vertical embankment, and the train thundered past. I clutched at tiny blades of grass in a desperate attempt to hold myself close to the vibrating ground and away from the roaring, pulling force. My only thoughts were, "Hang on. Hold tight. And, grass, please, *please* don't break."

Huge wheels clanked and bumped on metal tracks inches from my body. Clutching and crawling, while fearing each movement might be the one to topple me back onto the tracks, I scrambled up the embankment and over the fence as the last car clamored by.

Phyllis had also jumped and escaped without a scratch. Up beside the road, Debbie was collapsed in a quivering, almost hysterical heap, panting over and over, "You don't know…you don't know…you just don't know how close! You should have seen the engineer's face!" (Imagine him peacefully driving his train through isolated country when from out in front of his train jump two women. One in a trench coat, carrying a paper bag, the other clutching a four-foot walking stick with a red blanket billowing out from her shoulders like Superman's cape!)

Incredibly, I had no sense of fear. There was no time to be afraid; only time to react. What I felt afterward was exhilaration and peace. For beside a fog-shrouded river I received the most precious of presents: a new life.

After catching her breath, all Debbie wanted was to relax with a cigarette and a Diet Coke. I wanted an uneventful walk beside Route 2. Phyllis wanted to climb down and continue walking on the railroad tracks.

The Pleasant Point

"...they continued northward along the winter-gray O-y-o and came at last to the place where the mountain river came down and empties into it. Mary recognized it at once, despite the change the season had wrought. There was that wide river mouth coming down through the narrow but lush bottomland, between those steep and dark-flanked mountains. There on the opposite side of the mouth was that spacious grove where they had camped..." (FTR, p. 209)

Like Mary and Ghetel, Debbie and I watched the Ohio stretch out in front of us. But in 1987, houses dotted the riverbank and bottomland. Barges pushed up and down the wide stream. Two-lane Route 2 ran close to the river. When the road widened to four lanes, we knew something important was ahead. Around a long turn, we saw a bridge rise high above us and over the wide mouth of another river. Debbie and I ran to the middle of the bridge, looked upriver, held each other tightly, and laughed and laughed to keep tears from falling. (Phyllis did not join our little celebration.) We made it! We made it to the Kanawha! (In 1755, people considered this the mouth of the New River.) We made it halfway!

After gathering ourselves together, we crossed to the point of land where Mary, Thomas, and Georgie had camped on their forced journey to Kentucky. Known then as Tu-Endie-Wei (mingling of the waters), it is still a quiet, pleasant point of land where one can rest and contemplate, and watch two rivers converge into one mighty flow.

   Our euphoric plans to pitch tents and sleep at the same place where Mary had camped were dashed by Fred Taylor from the Sheriff's office and Alice Sauer at the Point Pleasant Park Mansion House. Both felt it was not safe for us to be there alone, overnight. As a result, I struggled to find a campsite and deal with other logistical matters while Debbie took Fred up on his offer of an historical tour and Phyllis went shopping. Fred had given me the name of someone who he thought would provide us with tent space. However, the hesitant tone of the person on the other end of the telephone line was such that I did not even ask. With no other option, I called Susan, the woman who had happened upon us beside the street in Huntington and had said, "If you need something, call."

   Not only was Susan kind and gracious, she sounded as though she actually wanted us. She lived a few miles away and agreed to pick us up on her way back from her store, Mountain Trading in Charleston. When I explained there was now a third walker, she graciously included Phyllis in the invitation. That resolved, I just wanted time alone to think and enjoy the peaceful park. Fat chance.

   Alice Sauer had generously allowed me free use of the Mansion House office. When I finished with phone calls, I had planned to relax or catch up with Debbie and learn about the area's history. It wouldn't happen. Alice asked, "Would you sit on the grounds and be available to talk to visitors?" Of course. It was payback time.

   After spreading my blanket on the lawn, I sat with my hatchet and walking stick while the warm sun and cool breeze caressed my skin. No visitors at the moment. Maybe I'd get lucky. I watched the two rivers intermingle at the edge of the lawn as they had for thousands of years. Unseen spirits seemed to be everywhere. In 1755, Mary and her sons had camped overnight on this point of land. (They might have sat on this very spot.) In 1774, Mary's son Thomas fought in the Battle of Point Pleasant, a battle some call the first battle of the American Revolution. And, it was here that the great Chief Cornstalk was murdered. I felt insignificant. This was really touching back to another time.

   Reverie ended when a busload of tourists arrived and I became the show-and-tell oddity. They appeared to be a senior citizens group from Pennsylvania. They hadn't heard about Mary, so they asked the usual questions, such as, "Where are you going and why?" What most struck me was their genuine appreciation, not only of Mary, but of my effort. A couple of them even understood that financing such a project in 1987 was an issue.

After they left, I had a little time alone, and I tried to figure out the schoolteacher from Michigan. She did not act like any of the others who had joined us. This was her second full day with us, and she seldom hiked with Debbie and me. She would drive away. Sometimes she'd park her vehicle, walk back to us and walk up to her car, and then climb in and drive off again, not be seen for an hour or more. Because of comments by people along the road, such as, "Oh we've already talked to the one ahead," it appeared that Phyllis would drive ahead, park, walk a little, meet people preparing for us, eat their food, then go off before Debbie and I reached them. Why did she drive all the way from Michigan, if she was just going to walk short pieces? If she didn't like me, or couldn't keep up with the pace, why pretend she was the out-front walker, when she was *driving* most of the way? It seemed that the only thing Phyllis liked about the activity was the free food and lodging that I arranged. Nothing made sense. As I watched thousands of gallons of muddy water flow past and lap at the bank, it made me philosophical and relaxed. Phyllis might be unorthodox but, at the moment, she wasn't causing me or The Walk any problem. I did not need to understand her. We live in a free country. The road is open to cars and walkers alike. We could all use the space…as long as we followed the rules.

Fathers

"Will Ingles looked happy and proud enough to burst." (FTR, p. 395)

Debbie and I made good progress down Route 35. Phyllis joined us shortly before noon, after driving to Winfield and asking Chip Stallard to bring her back. (I rankled at her imposing upon the hospitable folks she met, but saw no way to prevent it without making a scene.) Phyllis could not keep up with our pace, but since I'd slowed for Debbie, I did the same for her. Dropping down to two or three miles an hour felt like crawling. The day's goal was Pliney. So what if we were an hour or two or three late, as long as we finished before dark. There is nothing "wrong" with walking a slower pace. And while it surprised me that the person who claimed to have wilderness training experience was not in better shape, it was her social skills that truly confounded.

Earlier in the morning, Susan had spread out an assortment of bread, cold-cuts, and fruit for us to make a lunch. Debbie and I each made a sandwich and took a piece of fruit. Phyllis gathered up and took everything that was left. I was dumbfounded.

When we stopped for lunch under a tree in an isolated area, Phyllis did not sit with us. Rather, she sat apart and spoke to me only when I asked her a direct question. I thought I might be imagining things until Debbie asked, "Have you noticed she doesn't talk to you?" Notice? I'd have had to be extremely dense not to notice. Three days ago I had asked Phyllis to be honest and let me know what was going on. Instead of

90

getting better, she seemed more distant and withdrawn…at least where I was concerned.

At 4:30 in the afternoon, Debbie and I walked up to the truck stop in Pliney. Leaning wearily against the outside brick wall, we slid down and sat spraddle-legged on the sidewalk. Phyllis went inside. After an estimated 20-mile day, Debbie and I took a welcomed and deserved rest in the warm sun.

While I worked on cool-down stretches, Debbie drank her usual Diet Coke. Customers, mostly men, looked at us quizzically as they passed by when going in and out of the restaurant. We'd just smile and say, "Hello."

An old, rusted car pulled up and parked in front of us. The driver, a large man with grizzled beard and two arm canes, pulled himself out with enormous effort and slowly shuffled past. Looking his way, we smiled and nodded and hoped that we appeared to be the friendly and not staring type. He nodded in acknowledgement and moved inside. His effort, every minute of every day, dwarfed and put into perspective our 20 miles of easy walking. Though scruffy looking, he might well have been someone's beloved father.

Families come in many shapes and colors. Patti had told us that her father had been a hobo. So for her, the day we walked along the railroad was a day of remembering and touching back and appreciating. Debbie's grandparents and husband's parents were her family, close behind Carla and Josh.

Debbie and I ambled inside to join Phyllis and wait for the sag wagon. Shortly afterward, an official-looking Putnam County four-wheel-drive pulled up. I walked out to see if it was our pick-up. A tall, handsome, young man with dark hair and moustache walked toward me. Chip Stallard. The firefighter I had met briefly last spring in Memphis, and who was now organizer of all my West Virginia support. A cool, professional, handshake greeting? Not a chance. I wrapped him in a warm, "Boy, am I glad you are in my life!" bear hug.

After touching briefly on our progress and needs, I moved toward the restaurant to get Debbie and Phyllis. Chip stopped me with the soft voice of a man in love. "First I want you to meet someone special." Expecting to be introduced to a new wife or fiancée, I followed him to the passenger door of the truck. Opening it, he lovingly and formally introduced me, "Eleanor, I would like you to meet Lori Ann." At first I did not see anyone. Then I spotted the object of his affection, asleep in an infant seat…a beautiful, dark-haired, 10-month-old baby girl.

I had never seen a father so proud of a daughter. The men in my life reserved this type of open pride for their sons. Yet here was a macho firefighter so proud of his daughter that he took her everywhere. Even on fire and EMS runs. "Isn't it a problem at the scene?" I asked. "Naw," he replied. "There's always somebody to watch her for me."

And later in his office, I realized what a truly modern man he was. Chip was so sure of himself that his office was decorated with baby powder and jars of baby food. I watched in silent amazement as Chip became the in-charge administrator, answered questions from his staff, and made arrangements to walk with us for a day or two, all the while clipping an infant seat to the side of his desk and spooning baby food into Lori Ann. "I could leave her with a sitter, but we don't get to spend much time together."

What a lucky little girl. Her daddy not only loves her, he is proud of her.

The Unmentionable

"Ghetel got up and stepped a few feet away, squatted with the hem of her skirt drawn up around her waist and discharged her bowels into the leaves...A few minutes later Mary felt the call and went away to do the same." (FTR, pp. 164-165)

Everyone does it. Everyone. Several times a day. Yet the topic is avoided like the plague. And that's usually okay. We all manage by quietly excusing ourselves, disappearing for a few minutes, then dropping back into the conversation as if nothing happened.

For Mary and Ghetel traversing the wilderness it was equally a nonissue. They just stepped off the trail, lifted their skirts, squatted, and grunted. For us, walking through developed communities, attending to the necessity of body elimination became an unforeseen problem.

Most of the time, we didn't have the luxury of cover when we "had to go." Therefore, we soon learned to "go" at every opportunity that appeared, whether or not we had the urge. Surprisingly, many stores had "Employees Only" signs on their restrooms. Even without a sign we were often refused access. Occasionally, when we'd look downcast or switch from foot to foot when encountering an "Out of Order" sign, a clerk would take pity on us. "Don't pay any attention to the sign." And we'd suddenly be one of the elite who was allowed potty privileges.

Some people (usually women) will say, "I could *never* use an outhouse." Poppycock. Let me tell you, when you are desperate, that outhouse gives privacy, and it looks pretty darn good. Certainly some are better than others.

A lock prevents being interrupted. Tight boards prevent peepers. High odor speeds up the business at hand. If the seat is set at an angle in a corner with a door that swings out and no lock, it makes for the acrobatic exercise of sitting, with your pants around your ankles, while stretching far out to hold onto the door while, at the same time, keeping your bottom over the hole. The best smelling is newly built of cedar and close to the road. The most beautiful are covered with flowers that climb up the sides and drift over and hang off the roof.

Yes, I prefer a clean, sweet-smelling, inside, flush toilet. However, when worse comes to worse, like this day in 1987, a cramping bladder and screaming intestine were gleefully and gratefully released by ducking into a roadside cornfield. The lesson to not be snooty was reinforced daily, 'cause *everyone* pees and poops.

Impressions

"Y' must come, Ghetel." A powerful spasm of shivering broke
Mary's voice as she said it.
    "No. I do not have to do vat you say."
    "Oh, but y' do." (FTR, p. 239)

Chip's father, Victor Stallard Sr., had appeared in Wayne Sourbeer's
docudrama *Mary Ingles: Indian Captive*. With a father and fire
department involved with Mary, it was no surprise that Chip showed
up to walk with us the last five miles into Winfield.

Chip's presence and implied protection made cars a curiosity
rather than a worry, especially when he pulled on an orange emergency
responder jumpsuit and walked, as gentlemen do, on the traffic side,
thus shielding Debbie and me. We had warned him about our close
calls with trucks. Yet, his face had an amazed, "That was a close one!"
look as he jerked his arm in when a truck zoomed from behind and
almost hit him—even though we were walking against traffic and the
vehicle should have been in the opposite lane. Was his bright clothing
protection or a target?

Local people all along our route had been kind. Yet I was constantly
on guard against inadvertently doing something to offend and thus cast
a bad light on The Walk. Having a "local boy" with us added a layer
of insurance. So when an old, rusted, and battered white car pulled
over and stopped behind us, and the door opened, my level of anxiety
was much lower than usual. Slowly, a balding man in a red-and-black
checked wool jacket emerged. As soon as I saw the arm canes, I realized

95

it was the same fellow who had shuffled passed Debbie and me the day before when we sat outside the truck stop.

Hobbling toward us, he repeated over and over, "I'm so sorry. I'm so sorry. I didn't know who you were. I'm so sorry. If I'd known, you could have stayed at my place." What he was talking about?

Alternately shuffling his canes and feet, he fumbled in his pants pocket, pulled out a fist full of bills and thrust them toward me. All the while repeating, "I'm so sorry. I didn't know who you were." And I kept repeating, "This is not a money-making project."

The man would not accept my "Thanks, but no thanks" until Chip, who recognized Harvey Cottrell, stepped in and assured him that the Winfield Fire Department was taking care of us.

Assured of our safety, Harvey relaxed and smiled. "I saw you yesterday, outside the restaurant. But, I didn't know who you were. I'm so sorry...I just thought you were truckers darlin's!" As Harvey drove away, Debbie chortled, "Instead of twenty miles on the road, he thought I put twenty miles on the sheets!"

Moving on toward Winfield, the river and road move close together, with a narrow strip of private property and cozy houses nestled between them. A two-story, old-brick house appeared abandoned. It was the kind I like to explore. However, a "No Trespassing!" sign kept my feet firmly on the road. Not so Phyllis' feet. When I saw her walk toward the house, I called to her. "There's a 'No Trespassing' sign!" Ignoring me, she walked right up to the door and looked in the windows.

Phyllis' pattern of walking with us was first you see her, then you don't. She would walk behind, catch up when we stopped for a break, then walk on ahead. When we would catch up with her, she would drop behind and disappear without a word. Whether it was the waterfront houses or the river, Phyllis seemed intrigued. To stand at the river's edge, she would walk between homes with "No Trespassing" signs posted on lawns and trees, stand, look around, then wander back to the road.

When Chip stopped to talk to a friend, I saw Phyllis again walking across private property. Maybe she would get back to the road before someone saw her. Or, if they did, perhaps a stranger's words of reprimand would sink in better than mine. As usual, I had not considered all the options. A man fishing nearby angrily approached *me*.

"What is *she* doing? This is posted!"

"Why don't you tell her?"

He snapped, "*You're* the leader!"

Furious that Phyllis put us in this position, I called to her again. I had worked hard to not offend people, while Phyllis went off in her own little world, with no apparent consideration of how her actions affected The Walk and therefore my ability to obtain safe lodging.

Bless Chip. Casually, he ambled up and chatted amicably with the fellow. Chip knew him, too. The homeowner's righteous anger evaporated. How could anyone be tense around Chip when he was constantly cracking jokes, blowing up balloons to make balloon animals for children, putting them in mailboxes, and squeaking them at horses? I silently thanked God for having him with us.

While Chip and I smoothed ruffled feathers and eased ourselves away and down the road, Phyllis once again had disappeared. Chip, with a straight face, looked around and asked, "Where's Gretel?" Debbie and I burst out laughing. Though not the first to compare Phyllis' obstinate behaviors to those of the Dutch woman who escaped with Mary, Chip was the first to name her.

Breaking Bread

*"With her hands free, she was able to pick up any shred or bit of
chewable material to put into her mouth—white filaments of root,
bits of inner bark from driftwood, winter buds, the pith of reeds,
a stinking half-frozen fragment of a dead fish left at the water's
edge by some feeding animal, and some little cold, squishy gray
globule that could have been anything from a turtle egg to a fish
eye, for all she knew or cared—for she would eat anything...."*
(FTR, p. 339)

For my group and me in 1987, food was not a life-and-death struggle.
While food sustained us physically, it also became an act of sharing,
communication, encouragement, recreation, and networking. And
occasionally, the food tasted so good and the conversation was so
stimulating that "breaking bread" became a sensual experience.

In some families, mealtime is filled with unspoken tension, and
food sits in the stomach as an undigested ball. As my companions and
I trekked along Mary's path, we left all that behind, because almost
every day, a kind stranger offered us food. Offering and accepting food
is a complicated process, because both giver and receiver are putting
themselves on the line. Unconsciously, food may be the physical
manifestation of a spiritual offering. It becomes more complex when
strangers negotiate.

For the giver the dilemma is this: If offered, will it be accepted? And
if accepted, is it good enough? For the recipient, the questions include
these: Who is this person? Why this offer? Do I need it? Is it safe? What

are my obligations if I accept? How do I repay them? Are the risks worth it?

If I had refused all offers of food, we would not have starved. We might not have eaten every day, but we would not have been famished, for the map showed enough small towns along the river (with gas station vending machines and grocery stores) to keep us from eating bugs. However, over and above retracing an historic route was my goal of making connections. Connections with the past and the present. And for me, that interaction meant meeting new people, people different from me.

Repeatedly, I found that the poor and average opened their homes to us much more often than did the rich and famous. The poor know how it feels to need help. For years I have wished that all those who helped me would travel through Bloomington, so I could return the favors. A few have. But, since it is impossible to repay all those kind souls, I have tried to be as gracious a host to others as those along the river were to me. And what did these strangers do?

Many wrote or called me before I left Bloomington, saying, "We live beside the river where Mary walked. Please stay/eat with us." Then I would call them the day before our arrival to confirm the invitation. Usually the only prior communication with these bearers-of-goodwill was a scribbled note or a brief phone conversation.

Such was the case early in the walk, when Debbie and I searched a narrow street for Pat Ackerson's address. In an area of modest homes, the address I had matched that of a small house clad in gray imitation stone. The lawn was newly cut. In front of a small patio stood a plywood cutout of a woman bending over showing her bloomers. The Ackersons had a sense of humor. A good sign. I held my breath and knocked.

The door opened. Mouth-watering smells flowed out before we saw the warm smiles or the farmer's breakfast filling a small kitchen table. As hungry as we were, Debbie and I hardly made a dent in the huge dishes of eggs, bacon, potatoes, biscuits, and gravy. This couple, dressed unpretentiously in T-shirts and slacks, offered the best they had to strangers, then stood and watched them eat. And the only thing I could give in return was a "Thank you."

Day after day, for at least 500 miles, anonymous angels held out cold drinks as we walked by. People in cars and trucks tooted horns and smiled encouragement. Ralph Madden dipped up a free ice cream cone. Dotty Devila gave us a treat from her snack wagon. Cheryl Styer and

Bertha Wallace refused payment for soup and bananas in their stores. Joyce Taylor, with a husband recovering from heart surgery, cooked up a buffet supper for us in her kitchen.

Others, like Erma Keeney, tracked our progress, then spread out "tea and crumpets" in advance and invited us in as we walked past their houses. And there were those, such as Amos and Nell Plumley, who not only opened their homes to me and my walkers, they spread out their best silver and china, and invited in family and friends to fill the house and served a Thanksgiving-style dinner.

Our sustenance included black beans and rice in an old log cabin, breakfast in a Kentucky mansion (occasionally the rich and powerful came through for us), a sandwich from someone worried about our diet, homemade bread from busy school teachers, steak eaten with river guides, spaghetti in a fire house and a Sandstone Falls dream cabin, a pitch-in dinner in a Virginia museum, and coffee and treats walked in (three times) by an Indiana friend. These and many other acts of kindness came unexpectedly and always seemingly at just the moment when we most needed help or encouragement.

This night, on Day 22, our host was Eleanor Henson, who planned to begin walking with us the next day. She invited Debbie, Phyllis, Lisa (my daughter who drove over to sag for the weekend), and me to spend the night. She not only invited all of us strangers into her home, she planned an open house, a kind of historic reenactment.

A group of muzzleloaders, wearing buckskins and moccasins, set up camp and fired off their long rifles. Beside a blazing bonfire, the women cooked up parched corn, venison stew, and hoecakes; food Mary and Ghetel might have eaten. As the sun dropped behind the mountain, night began wrapping its black cloak. Golden sparks from the fire floated up and mixed with the stars overhead. I wanted to stay outside with Lisa, Debbie, and Phyllis and soak up the smoke and listen to stories, but the house drew me inside like a magnet.

Eleanor bustled around in her kitchen. She brought out more food and drinks, all the while encouraging the lively banter of her friend Doug Cooper. and a stranger to her, Doug Wood, who worked for the West Virginia Department of Natural Resources. Doug Wood had dropped in after reading in the newspaper that I would be at the Hensons'.

It is always awkward for me to join an existing conversational group. However, soon the two Dougs and I were sitting on the couch like old friends. Doug Cooper, tall and thin with that rugged attractiveness that some outdoorsy men have, flipped pages of a photo album featuring his dream cabin. It was no rough-it place. It had comfortable beds and a complete kitchen. Huge windows looked out at the New River and Sandstone Falls. No wonder he was enthusiastic. The place was gorgeous.

As our comfort level grew, Doug Wood, whose boyish good looks and impish smile masked a keen mind, tentatively asked, "Is this walk just for women?" "Goodness no!" It never occurred to me that men might be interested in joining us. Could they? Would they? Now I was excited.

Doug Wood quickly made plans to join us in the New River Gorge near Thurmond. His knowledge of natural science and local history would make him an outstanding addition. Doug Cooper's father was ill, keeping Doug close to home. But he wanted me to let him know when we were close to Sandstone Falls, because he might try to join us. And Doug offered us the use of his cabin. Even if he weren't there! Then Doug Wood asked if we'd like to stay at an Appalachian Trail cabin in Virginia. Stunned at their generosity, I was near tears. Two men, whom I had just met, had offered me safe lodging for days when I had none. It seemed like a miracle—as though unseen angels had listened in on my unspoken thoughts and needs.

If you are *really* lucky, breaking bread with strangers can turn them into generous friends who answer silent prayers.

Day 23
Sunday, October 18, 1987
Coal River to South Charleston, West Virginia

Religion

"Thank 'ee O Lord in Heaven, for another little miracle." (FTR, p. 255)

To sag both ends of the day's walk and head back to Indiana at noon, Lisa dropped us off at a small strip mall, where we had stopped walking the day before. Our goal was the state capitol in Charleston. The plan was for Lisa to drive ahead, park the car and run back to meet us. We estimated 10-plus miles upriver, now an easy walk for Debbie and me. However, instead of our accustomed two walkers, this day, we became an unwieldy group of 10: Debbie, Phyllis, Eleanor Henson, John Smithson (who brought Doug Wood over to Eleanor's cook out the night before), Rick Ransom (who we met back in Huntington), Rick's four elementary-age children, and me.

Feeling a guilt pang, I decided we'd skip church. While there was no "believing in a God" litmus test for being accepted into the group who were helping retrace Mary's escape, personal beliefs were discussed. It would be nearly impossible to review the Ingles family experiences without delving into questions of unseen powers. While unexplained phenomena and angels frequently floated through our conversation, debating organized religion carried an unspoken taboo.

Before I began The Walk, I had planned to stop each Sunday for church. (Be nice to God and maybe he/she would help me.) However, as The Walk proceeded, my need for formal worship dwindled. Except for the Sunday service back in Huntington with the Jacksons, which felt right, as though I had given thanks and received a blessing, someone

102

else's idea of how I should honor my creator seemed an intrusion. (You may remember that 48 hours after that service we narrowly escaped being hit by a train.) However, compared to my instant and personal thanks to God, most organized worship seemed to put my creator at a distance.

"Thank you for the dry weather."

"Thank you, God. I didn't break a bone when I fell."

"Thank you for helping Debbie's feet heal."

"Thank you! We have safe lodging for tonight."

"We aren't lost. I see the river! Oh, thank you, God."

"Ohhh, that the truck was close, but it missed us. Thank you, God."

"They let us use the bathroom. We don't have to squat in a corn field. Thank you God!" And on and on. So, around 9:00 when Rick Ransom asked if he could lead a short, ecumenical worship service, I had mixed feelings about granting his request.

On one hand, a delay might help. Though the river ran close to the road, we couldn't see it because of a dense fog. A group of 10, walking beside a fog-shrouded road is dangerous. Car drivers couldn't see us until the last moment, even though the children, wrapped together in my red blanket, looked like a large stop sign with legs. If we waited a short time, the fog might lift. On the other hand, I did not want to risk offending the nine other walkers by agreeing to a worship service—even an ecumenical one.

While Debbie had discussed spiritual topics before, I did not think she espoused any one religion, though I concluded that her ideology was Christian. Eleanor was Roman Catholic. I didn't have a clue about Phyllis' or John's beliefs. I was an open-minded Methodist. Back in July, Rick had sent me a hand-printed note on a scrap of paper saying, "We wish to match up with you as you come through St. Albans-Charleston." It never occurred to me that "we" included four elementary-aged children, and until he asked to do the service, I had no idea that he was a clergyman or what kind.

Now, for me, ruffling the religious sensibilities of humans was minor to offending the creator and angels that had seen us safely more than halfway through this trek. Taking time for a short worship service couldn't hurt and might help.

So, we perched on the stone wall of a park shelter. The river ran unseen on one side and speeding cars on the other. A plaque indicated that the spot had been part of John Morgan's 600-acre estate. In the shelter of the former kitchen, we could imagine it feeding Union troops in 1861. Surprisingly, the stop and rest and learning calmed my compulsion to cover miles.

The world slowed down as Rick read from Ecclesiastes, chapter 3: "To every thing there is a season, and a time to every purpose under the heavens...." Luke, chapter 10, verse 29: "Who is my neighbor?" began the story of the Good Samaritan in which the rich and religious step around an injured man. It is a poor outcast who stops to help. Rick concluded with Matthew 25:35: "I was hungry and you fed me, thirsty and you gave me a drink; I was a stranger and you received me into your homes...." We sat silent and still. Experiences of Biblical record were reality 2,000 years later. With eyes brimming, I silently prayed. "Thank you, God, for helping us this far. We're a few days from the New River Gorge. Please be with us."

When we set off again, the fog had indeed begun to thin. Eleanor, who had trained well, stepped off a good pace, while the children brought up a slow tail-end. I stayed back, talked with the children, and tried to encourage a little speed.

Around 11:30 Lisa ran toward us—she had jogged to meet us from Charleston. Assuming that we were almost to the Capitol Building, I greeted her with smiles and relief. Lisa stopped in front of me, looked hard into my eyes, and said quietly and firmly, "You have eight more miles." Then she turned and began walking beside me, as my stunned brain tried to assess the situation.

Eight more miles. I had made a miscalculation of distance and the group's ability. In addition to the adults, I was now responsible for four minors, because Rick, their father, was now nowhere to be seen. It made no sense that the man who brought his family to meet us in Huntington and Eleanor's last night, and had arranged for our lodging and food near St. Albans would go off and abandon his children to us...but strange things do happen. Debbie, Eleanor and I could walk the eight miles in two hours. It was unlikely that the children and Phyllis could finish eight more miles, even at a slow pace.

It was now impossible for Lisa to leave at noon for the seven-hour drive back to Bloomington. She was a good runner, but her planned six-mile training run would now total 16. It would take her a little over an hour to run back to her car and return to us.

Yet, the best worst (maybe only) solution was for Lisa to run back to the Capitol Building, drive back to pick us up and drop us off at Eleanor's. I worried that Lisa would be exhausted before she began the drive back to Indiana. And what about the children? What if Rick did not catch up? Call the police? The fact that we would not make our goal became a minor concern. I felt trapped in a circle of bad choices. With a resigned, "Why did I ever commit to helping my mother?" sigh, Lisa jogged away from me.

Then several things happened in quick succession. I saw Lisa run about half a block when another jogger, running toward her, stopped her. It was unusual, because runners do not like to stop and break their stride. Why didn't Lisa get going? While I was ripe with agitation at this guy wasting her time, he delayed her just long enough for a car to pull into the driveway of the South Charleston Funeral Home that was right beside us.

The car door flew open as excited, petite, dark-haired Sara Cotto-Thorner stepped out. "I've looked all over for you! I want to walk with you! I'll go home and change!" Crushing disappointment clouded her face when I explained that we were quitting as soon as Lisa could get the car. I had no way of knowing that she had seen a photo of Debbie and me spread across the front page of that day's Charleston *Sunday Gazette-Mail* and had not told anyone of her strong desire to join us. She just climbed into her car after church, and with the few details from the paper, headed downstream to find the Mary Ingles walkers. And she *had* found us, only to have her desire denied. But we *had* to quit.

Then, as I was giving regrets to a sad Sara, and Lisa was finally saying good-by to the runner, my brain decided to work. "I know you wanted to walk with us, but it would *really* help if you would drive my daughter back to her car.... And can you take the children to their mother at the Capitol?" Though not at all what she had set out to do, Sara agreed to the scheme. However, when we discovered there were insufficient seatbelts, I decided to keep my new charges with me. At least one problem solved.

As Sara and Lisa drove off, another car pulled into the driveway, and a woman called out, "Where's Rick?" It was Rick's wife! After bundling the children into her car, we moved faster. However, I carried the mixed emotions of relief and regret. Though I was frustrated that Rick had left our group without a word, I had not properly thanked him for finding us food and lodging.

Then, although we would not reach the Capitol Building, it seemed no time before Lisa drove my red Firenza to a stop in front of us, right across from the historic Indian mound in South Charleston. Rick and his family followed and pulled in behind her. After saying, "Thank you," and learning that Rick had only dropped out for a pit stop, there were more smiles and hugs and photos as we bid another regretful farewell. Life is strange that way. We share wonderful experiences, then go our separate ways.

A narrow road beside the Coal River led us back to Eleanor's home in Booger Hole (what the locals call this area). If Mary had to detour, it would have been along this stream. Would she have noticed the breathtakingly beautiful yellow, orange and red, leafy patchwork cover on the mountains? Or would she just have said, "Thank you, God. We're alive"?

Back at Eleanor's, I began another separation. Instead of packing the topographic maps on my back every day, I decided to send them back with Lisa. They wouldn't be needed until the following weekend when we entered the most difficult terrain, the New River Gorge. Might as well lighten the load. Besides, in the daily shifting of gear, I didn't want to take any chance of losing them. They would be safe in the car that Lisa would drive back five days later. Carefully placing the round map case on the floor of the trunk, I kissed my daughter good-bye and said a silent prayer.

Thank you, God, for guiding the people and the decisions.

History Lessons

"One of his [George Washington's] most vivid memories among the harrowing experiences of the last three years was his own five-hundred mile winter ride to Fort LeBoeuf in the winter of 1753, whose accomplishments had made him famous throughout the Colonies. He had done it mostly on horseback, with a guide, interpreter and armed escort, yet it had nearly killed him. And now here before him sat this little woman of his own age with her haunted eyes who, without provisions or weapons, had made a far more awesome passage, through utterly uncharted territory."
(FTR, p. 388)

Ever wonder about the history of an area? Books are helpful. But, better yet, get out of your house and car. Take a walk. Stop, look, and listen.

On our journey, we figuratively and literally walked through history as we informally learned about local history from people who had lived their entire lives in one county. Unsung historians, like Patty Nugent of Pratt, West Virginia, whose very pores are filled with love of their family or town or mountain, pass on stories that don't make the history books. Ask the right question and local lore spills out like sugar from a sack.

My history lessons began the first day in Big Bone Lick, Kentucky, amid the dinosaur bones and the salt-making camp from which Mary and Ghetel escaped. Then, moving up-river, I learned that strong Confederate elements had been active just across the river from Cincinnati. When the Kelsches took us into the cramped underground railroad hiding place, I felt the desperation of people whose skin was a color different from mine. And I began to understand their need to struggle for freedom and equality, a struggle that later became personal when my son announced his interracial marriage.

Walking along, we read all the bronze plaques that dot the roadside. About 30 years after Mary and Ghetel walked through the area, Maysville, Kentucky, was settled on land whose property owners once included Simon Kenton and Daniel Boone. And 40 years later, the first macadamized road west of the Alleghenies would stretch from Washington to Maysville.

Near Point Pleasant, West Virginia, a plaque said that we stood on soil that had soaked up the blood of Virginia riflemen and the federated Indian tribes led by Chief Cornstalk in what some call the first battle of the Revolution.

One day, we ate lunch near a plaque that announced that we were sitting on land surveyed by a young man who would later become our first president. George Washington and Mary Draper Ingles lived in the same time and in the same part of the country. It is conceivable that they might have met, as Jim Thom described in his fictionalized account.

On this 24th day, when JoAnn Oakes, Chip Stallard, and John Taylor all urged me to visit the West Virginia state capitol and museum, I decided to make it a day of culture and learning. Besides, this day would not yield many miles since I was scheduled to visit with the gifted and talented class of Pat Gilbert and Ruth Ann Pershing. So, beside the river and right across from the State Capitol Building, the children and I sat on the lawn of the University of Charleston. I spread out maps, and we talked of dreams and struggles.

Afterward, Debbie, Eleanor, JoAnn, Phyllis and I stood high on a mountainside at Spring Hill Cemetery and looked at Charleston far below. At the grave of Dr. John Hale, JoAnn handed me a copy of *Trans-Allegheny Pioneers,* the book in which he wrote about his grandparents, Mary and Will Ingles. When I read from it and from *Escape from Indian Captivity,* written by Mary and Will's son John, the voices of Mary's son and great-grandson brought me as close as I could get to what really happened in 1755.

In a dark and quiet part of the state museum, we looked at a lovely grandfather clock, eight feet high, with a walnut case and silver face. Family tradition holds that William Ingles left it to his wife Mary, who left it to her son John, who left it to his daughter Lockey, who left it to her son Dr. John Hale, who gave it to the Capitol in Charleston. (*Trans-*

Allegheny Pioneers, pp. xviii, 153) I had expected to hear about Mary in Virginia, but was surprised at the way West Virginians revered her.

I was also continually amazed at the connection of people from the past to those in the present. For example, Sara McCorkle Cotto-Thorner (the young woman who found us after church and gave Lisa a ride to the Capitol the day before) was the great-great niece of former West Virginia governor W. A. MacCorkle. (The governor changed his name back to the old Scottish spelling to better relate to the Scotch-Irish settlers.) Sara grew up in Governor MacCorkle's brother's home, a mansion high on the mountain overlooking Charleston and the Kanawha River. While living in Charleston, Governor MacCorkle had attended the First Presbyterian Church where, in 1987, Sara's husband worked as Director of Youth and Recreation. An added irony is that Sara's father, Sam McCorkle, is descended from the Virginia McCorkles who, in 1754, settled near Ingles Ferry. (*Trans-Allegheny Pioneers,* pp. ix, 252-253) Sara's ancestors were important enough that, in the closing pages of *Follow the River,* James Alexander Thom has Adam Harmon take Mary to the McCorkle home.

After the museum tour, Eleanor Henson trucked our gear over to Pat Gilbert's. Pat, after a long day of teaching, prepared supper including hot, out-of-the-oven, homemade wheat bread, set up our beds, and fixed breakfast for us. Like thoughtless children, Debbie, JoAnn, Phyllis, and I went to a movie.

Matewan, billed as one of the best films of 1987, was a sober eye-opener about the history of the mountains we were trekking through. After the initial attraction of lush foliage, and powerful rivers and rapids, it seemed that the New River Gorge handed out hardship to anyone who dared walk through or tried to stay. Long after Mary and Ghetel fought their way upstream, we learned that, in the 1920s, miners with faces and lungs blackened from coal dust struggled with coughs, mine collapses, and the company store. In addition, there were deadly clashes when workers had unionized in an attempt to wrest just treatment from those corrupted by power. Amid all the struggles, the miners attempted to love and learn, make a living and raise a family. We walked and talked with the descendants of these pioneers.

Today, some still live in what would be called shacks. If you are trusted enough to be invited in, beyond the crooked floors and walls you will find a home. A home filled with the love of someone who, like Mary, grew strong in these mountains. She would grow her own vegetables, put in her own wood stove, and create beautiful quilts. So, when you drive past a "shack," don't look down your nose. Inside may be a very smart and classy lady, someone's mother or sister, and one of my best friends.

Repeating and Resisting

"Am I imagining all this? Mary wondered." (FTR, p. 221)

A problem depends on perspective. The fact that the stock market had dropped 500 points in one day floated over me with the impact of a gray cloud. Financial news and life back in Indiana seemed in another world. My present circumstances were more important, and my immediate concern was to move me and my companions farther upriver.

Before breakfast, Phyllis started the day by asking me if she could ask Pat to keep her car. My head screamed, "Didn't you hear me yesterday at Eleanor Henson's and last week at Joandel's?" My mouth and throat formed what I hoped was a firm and normal-sounding "no." Was she dense or self-centered, or had I mentally slipped a cog and just thought I'd repeated the "Don't ask..." message to her several times before? If retracing Mary's walk was the object, then why not put the car in long-term parking? For me, Phyllis' car was a problem. For Phyllis, it appeared to be a security blanket.

As Bill White, our Fire Department helper of the day, assisted, and we loaded gear into his van, I overheard Phyllis ask Pat if she would keep her car. Phyllis had refused to take my "no" for an answer. My blood pressure shot up. When Pat declined her request, I felt vindicated.

So Phyllis, in her car, followed Bill's van to The Mound, an historic Native American site in South Charleston, where we had stopped walking on Sunday. This teacher from Michigan deserved credit, for she was the most determined person I had ever met. In an effort to keep conflict out of the public eye, I did not tell anyone of the growing tension I felt between us.

Debbie, Phyllis, and I waited in a light drizzle to see who would show up to walk with us. I'd learned early on that many say they will walk, but few follow through. Susan and Eleanor arrived with hugs and smiles. Their goal was to walk with us for two weeks. Becky Straight, a shy nurse from Gandyville, arrived with a thick West Virginia accent, a big smile, and plans to walk one week. Day walkers Ene Purre and Sara Cotto-Thorner (our angel from Sunday) drove up just as we were ready to leave. They were friends of Susan's. Sara would finally make her dream of walking part of Mary's route come true. We were now a group of eight.

Given the difficulty I was having with Phyllis, I felt it was essential that the five new walkers receive the same "Don't ask…" message, and I hoped it would be a reminder to Phyllis of how important the rules were. Climbing onto the back of Bill's van, I thanked everyone for coming and began, "The rules are simple. You come along at your own expense. Stay off private property and respect 'No Trespassing' signs. Don't obstruct traffic. Only ask for a restroom and a safe place to pitch a tent. We've been lucky so far with sag wagons to carry our gear, but be prepared to carry everything on your back tomorrow. We've had close calls with cars and trains, so be careful. Any questions? Let's go." Promptly at 8:00 a.m., we set off to test our rain gear, and the legs and will of the newcomers.

Bill transported our gear to the Rand Fire Department, our safe lodging for the night. I was to call Bill about noon and tell him where I thought we'd be at the end of the day. Phyllis said she'd drive ahead and walk back to us.

Eleanor, Becky, and Susan had trained by walking laps around their mountain property and along access roads several times a week and were prepared for an all-day trek. On the other hand, Sara and Ene were walking on a whim, with little or no conditioning. While I remembered the pain and blisters of previous new walkers, Ene's and Sara's eager faces silenced my reservations. It was only one day, and they were close to home and help.

Rain hindered conversation, but Sara managed to pass word up to me that if we crossed the river, we could walk closer to the water and be away from the treacherous traffic through downtown Charleston…and, that her office, with a clean restroom, was near the blue bridge. A clean restroom? Say no more.

Mary had crossed the river in a canoe, near the Bluestone River. Since I couldn't recreate Mary's exact situation, I felt it was better to be safe and adapt to the world of 1987. So with only a slight pang of guilt, the slowest walker became the leader as we crossed the blue bridge. Sara's office *was* nearby, and the facilities were welcoming and spotless.

As Sara ushered us through the family's business as honored guests, we all became better acquainted. Also, by taking a longer than usual pit stop, we hoped the rain would stop. It didn't.

However, often less is more. Precipitation had eased a little, and Charleston's river walk was quiet and reflective, albeit foggy. Suddenly, shrouded in fog, there walked toward us what appeared to be an apparition with shoulder-length hair, wearing a long overcoat and army boots and carrying a paper bag. A street person? No. Phyllis. She had parked her car and for a while was part of the group. She flitted in and out of our life all day.

We took a mid-morning break on the steps of the gold-domed Capitol. Sara shared her homemade granola, and we added another recipe to our collection. Lunch found us between the road and the edge of a mansion's pristine lawn. We expected a gardener or maid to shoo away the eight bedraggled women who were having such a negative impact on the aesthetics, if not the safety, of the neighborhood. Instead, we were ignored.

In the afternoon, rain and traffic increased. With the initial excitement gone, Sara and Ene walked more and more slowly. At about 2:30, as we hunkered down in the shelter of an overpass, I decided to call it a day and wait for our sag. The Marmet Ambulance stopped and asked if we wanted a ride. I told them we'd wait for the Fire Department, which I had called after lunch. An hour and a half later, the Marmet Ambulance came by again, and this time we climbed in. There was a miscommunication with the Fire Department. That's life.

However, to reduce the chance of more misunderstandings, when John and Joyce came by that evening, I carefully went over the schedule and logistics for the next week. When they learned I had not identified a safe place to tent, they offered me two nights in an apartment next to their house…. Thank you, God.

We said good-bye to Sara and Ene, who at times had wondered if they would last the day. Ene said she'd try to join us the last day in Virginia…if we made it that far. Phyllis again asked for help with her car. What was there about "no" that she could not understand? My ability to obtain safe lodging depended on the goodwill of strangers, which I felt Phyllis was jeopardizing.

Debbie, Susan, Eleanor, Becky, and I gratefully laid our sleeping bags down on the cement floor at the Rand Fire Department. Phyllis slept by herself in her car. In the slumber party atmosphere, interrupted by an occasional fire alarm, I listened to my comrades and realized that I was not the only one confounded by Phyllis or who thought she, at times, appeared disoriented. Throughout the restless night, it became clear that it would be a challenge to keep this hostile element away from reporters, while maintaining the group's upbeat spirit. Yet, though aggravating, Phyllis' refusal to respect me as the leader had caused only minor problems...so far. What was important was that we ended this day with everyone intact and we had safe lodging. Troubles come and go. Don't sweat the small stuff.

America's Finest

"It was a place of health and happiness." (FTR, p. 2)

Maybe I'm exaggerating when I say that my 1987 retracing of Mary Draper Ingles' escape would not have happened without John Taylor and the Volunteer Fire Department, but he provided both immeasurable encouragement and assistance. John and I were both volunteer firefighters. Our friendship began at a Fire Department Instructors Conference in Memphis years before and was renewed each year at the annual conference. In January of 1987 I was one of several instructors John invited in for one of his state fire conferences at West Virginia's Pipestem State Park. It was there that John, I, and Mary Ingles came together.

If the Fire Department was John's first love, history came in a close second. So when I handed him a copy of *Follow the River*, it should not have surprised me when he said, "I've already read it," or that he had firsthand knowledge of the West Virginia areas where Mary had trekked. Full of *"Deliverance* Country" images, I asked, "Do you think someone could safely hike the river through West Virginia to retrace her route?" John quickly replied, "Sure. We'd just have fire departments along the way keep watch." With those words, a faint dream grew into a possibility.

As winter melted into spring, the possibility grew into a plan. I hung onto John's words and friendship the way a blind person clings to a guide dog leading them through unfamiliar territory. West Virginia was the longest segment of Mary's trek, and its New River Gorge was the roughest terrain. If West Virginia were doable, then a retracing of Mary's entire route was a realistic goal. However, I knew it was not reasonable to expect everyone to be as accepting and helpful as John.

Even today, there are individuals who chafe at the idea of a female firefighter. And as an idea made real, I was all too familiar with the mean hostility, unjust criticism, and cruel lies of some men and their spouses when a female enters a male conclave. In spite of that, some of my best friends (who just happened to be some of John's friends) are those I met and worked with in the fire service. As a result, I became an honored member of the informal 6:00 O'clock Breakfast Club that John and his friends convened at conferences. Each day began with laughter, war stories, plans, politics, and put-downs. Occasionally, we would meet for lunch or dinner, but it was those 6:00 o'clock breakfasts where I learned acceptance and respect. So I believed in John's connections and the dependability of his word. If he said the fire departments would help, I could bank on it. Of course, the fact that I was a 10-year veteran of the volunteer fire service didn't hurt.

In August, I was going full steam ahead with excitement and plans to launch the retracing of Mary and Ghetel's escape in September. Then when John called, I knew from his voice that something was wrong. He was having heart problems and was scheduled for bypass surgery. He wouldn't be able to help. I went numb.

Was it all over, the end of a dream? All the planning and work and training out the window? John felt not. He was confident that another firefighter, his friend Chip, whom John had introduced me to briefly in Memphis back in March, could fill his shoes. I was not so sure. John was my security blanket. Now, filled with apprehension, I was not sure I could transfer my trust in John to someone I had only shaken hands with a few months before. I had no choice.

A week later, John came through quadruple bypass surgery smiling and joking. And Chip (willingly or unwillingly) took over as organizer of West Virginia sag support. Chip asked for an itinerary. He wanted to know where we planned to be each night so he could line up safe lodging and gear transport. I did not have a clue.

I didn't have a clue, but I had to give him something. So, laying a West Virginia road map on the table and using the distance between the first two knuckles of my index finger to estimate 15 miles, I "walked" along the river and wrote down the name of the towns. It proved to be amazingly accurate.

From the minute I set foot in West Virginia, the volunteer fire services came to our aid. Gordon Merry from Ceems-Cabel Emergency Medical Service toted gear, gave us shower privileges (another bath!) and, with his recommendation, Clara Knight ultimately provided food and safe lodging.

The Winfield Fire Department let Debbie, Phyllis, and me sleep on the floor of the station. The Marmet Ambulance gathered eight soggy walkers out of the rain and transported us to the Rand Fire Department where we again, gratefully, slept on hard, but safe and dry, floor space. When Chief Charles Veasey okayed our staying over one night at the Pratt Volunteer Fire Department, Handy Handwork made us a huge spaghetti supper. Nathan (Buster) Byars of the Montgomery Fire Department transported gear and Dave Hartung walked along with us one day as an unannounced protector. Former Chief John Taylor, though still out of work, from heart surgery, opened the apartment behind his house to provide us with two nights of safe lodging. Steve Crukshanks and the Fayetteville Volunteer Fire Department acted as sag wagon, set up army cots, turned their day room and kitchen over to six women, and allowed us to use the showers....Oh, luxury!

Then, when I could find no safe lodging for our first night in Virginia, I made another call back to John Taylor. He referred me to Chief Tom Francis of the Peterstown, West Virginia, Fire Department. They allowed us to lay our sleeping bags within their safe walls and my parents (who were now providing our sag wagon) to park their trailer in the parking lot.

And, though not in the volunteer fire service, Jon Dragan and the crew of Wildwater Unlimited in Thurmond, who gave us food, lodging, sag support, guides with two-way radios and invaluable information about the terrain and history, also qualify as the finest of volunteers.

On this twenty-sixth day, we moved into the Pratt Volunteer Fire Department, where our tired bodies happily collapsed on the floor and we bathed in laughter all evening. I heard that some of the firefighters affectionately and bawdily referred to me as the lady who slept her way across West Virginia. I wish I could remember all the names of those who allowed me that privilege.

It may sound sappy, but my heart aches with appreciation when I think of how men and women who did not know me at all opened their facilities and lives to the strangers in their midst. *"Deliverance* Country" took on a new meaning.

On September 11, 2001, the whole world learned in a significant way what I experienced in a small way 14 years before. The fire service and unsung volunteers are truly America's Finest. They will be there when you need help. You can count on it.

Equipment and Training

"Look. We have blankets. This axe. Shoes. No Indians around.
We could go. Just go!" (FTR, p. 146)

Hiking in the New River Gorge tested both hikers and equipment.
Debbie and I, with almost four weeks under our belts, had worked
out the kinks. Debbie had learned her lesson about socks, her feet had
healed, and she had toughened into a hiking machine that, had she
desired, could have left me in the dust.

On the contrary, Phyllis did not appear to be gaining any physical
stamina. Her Jazzercise classes had not developed the aerobic strength
for her to walk all day, day after day. Even after a week, she did not
appear any stronger. Though she was struggling, her fierce independence
denied her the ability to ask for, or accept, help...at least from me.

On the other hand, Eleanor Henson, Susan, and Becky were strong
enough to keep up, despite openly nursing blisters. While hiking, they
compared notes: "I have a blister." "You want to see blisters? Look at
mine!" They made adjustments and seemed to enjoy the process. I found
it interesting to observe how each person came into the experience with
different training and equipment, and to see them adapt and grow.

Hiking, like swimming, is essentially a solitary sport, unlike
baseball, for example, which requires a team to play. However, every
sport requires training and equipment if it is to be enjoyed rather than
endured. When I read *Follow the River* in 1986, I thought I could just
walk out my front door as Mary had walked away from her captors.
Fortunately, I also read *The Complete Backpacker* by Colin Fletcher

and *A Walk Across America* by Peter Jenkins. Both authors were strong advocates of training.

Knowing that I did not have Mary's drive or desire, I decided to opt for training. The first three-mile walk in the hills of southern Indiana had me dragging. It was obvious that I needed to set up a serious workout schedule if, in four short months, I intended to carry a backpack and hike all day, every day, for 43 days. So, I began two or three short (three to five miles) hikes each a week, with one 10-to-20-mile hike on the weekends. Each week more weight was added to the backpack, and canned fruit and vegetables gave way to real equipment. Louise, who drove our sag wagon in Kentucky, said, "Think how strong you'll be!" She was the only one to suggest that The Walk might make me stronger... unlike Mary, who became physically wasted from her struggle.

Hiking boots were my first purchase. Because my skin abrades easily, I chose Vasque Sky Walkers, a flexible, leather and Gore-Tex ankle-high boot.

After boots came socks. Thin, cotton, off the shelf from the grocery wouldn't do. Serious hikers frequently recommend some type of two-layer system that allows the layers to rub against each other, rather than a single layer that rubs against skin, producing heat and blisters. Many prefer wool socks worn over a thin liner sock. Susan swore by a combination of thin cotton liners and wool socks handmade by her son-in-law's mother. I stumbled onto Blister Busters: one sock with two layers that rub against each other. They also wick away moisture. Originally I found them in a mail-order catalogue. One time I saw them in a department store. These days, I have Lisa or a friend who is running a marathon pick up a pair or two, because they always seem to be for sale at these events. Since I began using Blister Busters, the only blister I've ever had was on Day 2, when I put one foot into a stream and walked in the wet sock the rest of the day. SmartWool socks also work well. Be careful to get the correct weight. I ended up with black toenails the day I walked 20 miles in socks that were too thick for my boots.

While we're discussing feet, I need to mention that I also rubbed my feet with alcohol two or three times a day. It cools and dries the skin, helps to toughen wear areas and cleans any little skin irritations. Also, receiving a foot rub beside the trail, even one you give yourself, is priceless.

For my home on my back, I'd intended to use my son's well-used Boy Scout backpack. However, after several hikes carrying canned goods for weight, I realized that even at a mere 20 pounds, the metal cross-bars were causing me back pain and bruises. Don't just grab a pack off the shelf because it's big and has lots of pockets, or let someone talk you into the first one you pull on because it's on sale. Try out several stores and clerks. It took four outfitter stores before I found someone who, I felt, knew how to fit a woman. A smaller, exterior frame Kelty felt like part of me, and it had enough divisions for my kitchen, bathroom, bedroom, and clothes closet items. However, were I doing it today, I'd go for a pack with an internal frame made for females. (Women generally have larger hips, which gives them a different center of gravity than men.) In 1999, I used an internal framed Gregory pack on a week's Outward Bound trip in the Big Bend. At 110 pounds, I carried a pack weighing over 50 pounds and made it with no sores or bruises.

When buying clothes for all-weather backpacking, I go by the "cotton kills" rule. The only cotton I wear is white, cotton underpants. (Recommended by my urologist.) For shorts, slacks, shirts, and jackets, synthetics are lightweight, wickable, breathable, and warm or cool, depending on the item.

My other rule regarding equipment is this: Try it out before you leave, in as near trail conditions as possible. Given my experience with the Boy Scout backpack, I tried to train in all weather conditions. That meant a six-mile hike, with a full pack, in pouring rain, two days before I left. My son's old poncho whipped around in the wind, making it almost worthless because I became soaked inside and out. A North Face Gore-Tex rain jacket and waterproof pants, with a heavy-duty plastic bag slipped over the pack, worked much better.

On this twenty-seventh day I realized that Louise was right; I was much stronger than when I began. But just think of all the time, effort, and money it took for me to do what Mary had done with only a blanket, a hatchet, and the clothes on her back.

Day 28
Friday, October 23, 1987
Kanawha Falls to Cotton Hill, West Virginia

Reporters

"Every step back was twice as hard as any step in the right direction, and Mary would almost despair whenever she had to expend her waning strength backtracking...." (FTR, pp. 281-282)

Trees wearing golden crowns stood on an amber-speckled carpet of leaves, framing the river below and to our left as it rumbled over room-sized rocks. Trying to detach from the day's confrontations, I hardly noticed the beauty. Although we had advanced only six miles, I was exhausted as we neared the end of the day's walk where the trail crossed the road at Cotton Hill. The last thing I wanted to see was there to meet us. Struggling under the weight of several cameras, a young guy and gal brightly hailed us. "We're from Channel 4 in Oak Hill and want photos of you for the evening news. Back up and come toward us."

Each day—usually several times each day—I realized how lucky I was to have accidentally made it into the newspaper last August. Walking companions, safe camping, shelter, food, and sag support miraculously appeared from those who had read an article about me, heard secondhand from someone else who had read an article, or had an article handed to them.

It was a symbiotic relationship, so I gave interviews. Reporters gave me coverage that resulted in an enlarging circle of contacts and unimagined assistance, support that was impossible from my limited circle of family and friends. I knew I needed them. However, it was not always an easy relationship.

Generally, the reporters I met were hardworking and intelligent and tried to write factual stories. Many, such as Larry Incollingo of the Bloomington, Indiana *Herald-Times,* Paul Long of the *Kentucky Post,* an edition of the *Cincinnati Post,* Su Clauson of *The Roanoke-Times,* Joe Myers of the Montgomery, West Virginia, *Fayette Tribune,* and Regina Villers, writing for the *Cincinnati Post's Tri-State Magazine,* were sensitive and able to reach beyond the obvious. However, no matter how hard they tried, inevitably an error appeared. Given my experience, I now read all news wondering "Where are the errors?" Reporting accurately is a tough job.

I say what I mean. The reporters hear what they think I said, then condense down their interpretation for publication. The editor tweaks it. The public reads and makes another interpretation. It's no wonder there are so many misunderstandings and twisting of facts.

I missed a chance to rub elbows with George Clooney's father. In September of 1987, Nick Clooney was a Cincinnati TV personality. His advance man made all the arrangements for an interview at Big Bone Lick the night before I was to leave...before confirming it with me. (This was before George Clooney was a big star, so the Clooney that impressed me was George's Aunt Rosemary.) Nick's advance man just called and said, "We have it all set up." Now, Nick Clooney may be as nice as his son is handsome, but on September 24, I still felt the sting of rejection from when his representative had canceled an appointment with me six weeks earlier. I lost a day's pay and drove three hours to Cincinnati only to be told he was too busy to see me. In August I was unimportant to him. Unfortunately, in September when I became important, Mr. Clooney paid the price for a staff member's rudeness. The advance man sounded almost hysterical when I told him I would not be at Big Bone Lick for the interview. *"But it's all arranged!"* Too bad, you should have asked me first.

I wasn't just being difficult or vindictive. I was not packed and I *had* to work. The only person financing this project was me. I could not work my shift and drive to Big Bone Lick in time for the interview.

Occasionally a reporter appeared a little dense. Such was the case on Saturday, October 17, when we walked from Winfield to the mouth of the Coal River. The two-lane road ran close to the Kanawha. With me carrying the red Hudson Bay blanket, we were visible and easily recognizable. When a white car painted with the Channel 8 logo on the side slowed down, we did the same, assuming we'd been found again.

After 22 days Debbie and I were accustomed to interviews. A young, eager fellow leaned out of the car window. "Have you seen the Jenny Wiley walkers?" He did not ask who we were or what we were doing. He just asked if we had seen the Jenny Wiley walkers. Debbie and I smiled, shook our heads from side to side, and walked on. Several times during the day, the same white car and driver cruised past. Were there really Jenny Wiley walkers, or was the guy just confused? Giving interviews, an almost daily occurrence, had long since lost its excitement, so neither Debbie nor I were disposed to assisting the incompetent.

The next day, seven additional walkers accompanied me with the identifying red Hudson Bay blanket. We were walking through a thick fog when the same Channel 8 car and driver drove slowly by, turned around and stopped beside us. "Are you the Jenny Wiley walkers?" Trying to help him, I answered, "Sorry, we are the Mary Ingles walkers." His face sagged in disappointment as he drove away. If there were no Jenny Wylie walkers, he must have felt pretty stupid when he opened the *Charleston Sunday Gazette-Mail* and saw a colored picture of Debbie and me stretched clear across the top of the front page proclaiming, **"MODERN-DAY PIONEERS PASS THROUGH KANAWHA COUNTY."**

At times a reporter, for instance, Paul Long from the *Kentucky Post,* who drove in to walk with us three times, was unable to make a connection in his reporting between his experience and that of Mary and her companion.

Figuring that no one would die of starvation or thirst in one day, I never checked his equipment. The day's hike was short, but rugged. A mountain crossing and an always difficult railroad walk. Sun beat down all day. Under these conditions, the body loses a great deal of water. Mouths become dry. At noon we sat between the railroad and the river. With the sun at our backs, we looked down on white-capped Kanawha Falls and three, large wooden crosses on an island. The locals gave us a history lesson on the mine wars and the diversion tunnel near Gauley Bridge that killed hundreds of people from silicosis. Popping open water bottles and canteens, we drank deeply. All except Paul. He had neglected to bring water.

As he sat beside Debbie, Paul's eyes followed every movement of her water bottle as she opened her pack, removed the container, raised it to her lips, and let the refreshing liquid coat her parched throat. In silent, unblinking, animal desire, he stared. Noticing Paul's interest, Debbie, being a friendly gal, offered him a drink. Instead of the swallow or two she had expected him to take, he grasped the bottle and guzzled down the whole thing! In his article, Paul could have described, from personal experience, how a starving Mary and Ghetel might have felt as they struggled through the New River Gorge in search of food. But the story went unreported.

Thankfully, other stories, such as my inability to communicate with Phyllis and a frightening confrontation with two property owners when we missed a No Trespassing sign, did go unreported.

By this day's end, the accumulated pressures left me with little patience. The reporters sounded so matter of fact. "Now back up and come toward us." As if we should be willing to not only go back, but to do cartwheels to please them. Back? *Back Up*?!?! Were they kidding?

We had just finished a strenuous mountain crossing and railroad hike. Every muscle ached. And my mind and emotions were taut from confrontations that I was trying to keep out of the news. I could hardly put one foot in front of the other and they expected us to back up for some dumb TV show?

"You back up!" The words flew out of my mouth.

"But the camera is heavy."

"Well, we're walking to Virginia!" Sharp, grumpy, and testy, I was looking out for the project and the group. Most of the women were growing painful blisters. Their feet needed rest, not a command performance. Then, remembering our need for safe lodging in the days ahead, I relented. This TV crew was just doing its job. They didn't deserve abuse because I was nervous, frustrated, and frayed. We retraced and retraced again the "end of the day," smiled for the camera, and answered questions. I learned more than I wanted to about "spontaneous" news stories.

When The Walk was finished, after my 15 minutes of fame, I walked back into obscurity. I feel sorry for those who can't.

Day 29
Saturday, October 24, 1987
Cotton Hill to Wolf Creek Bridge, West Virginia

Tensions

"I think she be a needin' a lecture." (FTR, p. 259)

The previous day had started badly. I'd told everyone that they could sleep in, but before we headed off for Cotton Hill, I needed to get up early to talk to the children at the Valley Elementary School. The alarm in our room rattled us to consciousness. Susan and I, sharing a bed, fought with the alarm. Stifling laughter, we finally stuffed it under a pillow. Muffled beep-beeps continued as we frantically tried to find the "off" button. So much for my quiet departure.

Susan asked to use the toilet before I took a bath. Of course. Then, before I got into the only bathroom, Phyllis jumped in. A quick bladder emptying would not have been a problem, but she didn't leave. She stayed and stayed and stayed. Finally I knocked on the bathroom door.

"Phyllis, I need to get in."

"I'm busy."

"Do you want to go talk to the children?"

"No."

"I need to get ready."

"Well, I have some things to wash."

She was washing clothes? She decided to wash clothes when she knew I needed to leave early? Was she deliberately trying to delay me? What in God's name was the matter with this woman? I wanted to break the door down. Instead, I took a deep breath, went back to bed, and tried to practice yoga. Susan's reassurance that I had told *everyone*

126

that I needed to be out early and her commensurate outrage helped quiet my frustration.

After a few, fretting minutes we heard Becky's bare feet pad up to the bathroom door. She beat on the door with her fist and yelled, "Phyllis! I have to go...*bad!*" That got Phyllis out and me standing next to the door and rushing inside as soon as Becky left. Debbie and Eleanor, realizing that Becky had used a ruse to help me, held their sides with their own stifled laughter.

Conflicts are something I avoid at all costs, but I could no longer delay confronting Phyllis about her hostility toward me. As soon as I finished dressing, I called her into the tiny bathroom. We stood almost toe to toe. If my voice was not shaking, my insides were.

"Phyllis, we have a personality problem. If you cannot follow the rules you will have to leave."

"I don't think I've done anything for you to kick me out."

"It's not any big thing, but little things like a stone in a shoe. I don't like feeling uneasy, wondering what you'll do. You are taking advantage of hospitality extended to me. You *must* be kind and considerate."

Phyllis' face came close. Fear screamed for me to run as I felt her hot breath. She hit me with all her anger, resentment and determination. "*I will not bow down to you like everyone else!* I *will* stick this out. We will *have* to get along."

With a jaw locked and fighting for control, I shot back, "Then you will *have* to follow the rules." Then I turned and walked out.

With rubbery legs, I walked downstairs to the Taylors' kitchen. I couldn't tell if I was visibly shaking or if it just felt that way. When Joyce said there would be newspaper reporters and a TV crew at the school, I wanted to run away. Now the challenge for me was to give a presentation and interviews, and appear as though my only problem was the New River Gorge. Knowing I needed emotional support, Susan and Eleanor quickly agreed to accompany me. Disjointed and lacking flow, it was the worst talk I have ever given. But I got through it. I will remember the school and the students who filled that gymnasium long after they forget me.

Walking the river and the woods works off tension, and that day it did decrease the pressure, until we tried to climb from a road up the side of a railroad bed.

Dave Hartung, from the Montgomery Fire Department, was familiar with the area and walked along as a guide. A narrow dirt road ran alongside the railroad. A fence separated us from the railroad above and to our right, then turned near a house on our left and stopped us from going ahead. Dave had used the road before and said there was a hole in the fence. Eleanor found it and started through on her hands and knees. About halfway under, like Peter Rabbit in Mr. McGregor's garden, Eleanor's backpack caught on the fence. She couldn't go forward or backward. We were laughing at her predicament when an elderly couple rushed out of the house and began yelling, "This is posted! You're trespassing! Didn't you see the sign? We heard about you! Get off our property!" This wasn't a road. It was a private driveway. Trespassing sign? What trespassing sign? Oh. The one on a pole about 15 feet overhead? Not one of us saw it. And considering the hole in the fence, we weren't the first ones to miss it.

As screams and threats swirled, Dave, Debbie, Susan, Phyllis, and reporter Paul Long, along for another day, attempted to untangle Eleanor, squeeze themselves under the fence, and get off private property as fast as possible. At the same time, Becky and I tried to calm the couple before they had a stroke or shot us. Thank goodness for Becky. Her thick West Virginia accent and experience with agitated people when she was a Vietnam flight nurse with the Eleventh Aerovac, Aeromedical Squadron, saved the day. While slowly backing away, she talked calmly and slowly. We apologized profusely, and promised never to do it again. Dave apologized to us all afternoon. The rest of the day, Phyllis kept up, and we didn't have to send out a single search party for her. It seemed that we were all trying to be good.

That was the previous day.

On this day, Lisa and her friend Jennifer Oprise came in at about 2:00 a.m. to sag for the weekend. My eyes popped open, and the first thing I asked for when I saw Lisa was the topographic maps.

"I forgot them."

"You what?!"

"I don't have them. I took them out when I cleaned the car. I didn't think you'd need them."

She didn't think I would need them?! Going into the worst terrain of the trip, and she didn't think I needed them?! This on top of the confrontations of the day before? Disappointment, frustration, anger, and fear raised my blood pressure. Rage surged through my body as adrenaline pushed me to fight-or-flight. Tears welled up. My throat constricted. From the shocked look on Lisa's face, as I took it all out on her, I must have been a boiling thundercloud. Then, sounding close to tears, my daughter snapped, "I'm doing the best I can." Then she spun around and, like Phyllis, avoided me.

The Mary Ingles Trail Club and walkers bushwhacked through the New River Gorge.

Damn it. We were all doing our best. The confrontation with Phyllis the day before had left me strung tight as a bow. And now, going into the most difficult terrain, the comfort and reassurance of my maps would be denied me.

Like Mary, I would just follow the river and hope.

Breaks

"...they prepared a makeshift splint...(and)...braced the arm as well as they could in the splint..." (FTR, pp. 37-38)

Back in Kentucky, Kate had chastised me for taking The Walk too seriously. I didn't know how *not* to take it seriously. After 30 days of trekking, responsibility for the group's safety weighed on me, and repeated good-byes pushed my emotions to the surface. Laughter reduced pressure, but I didn't know how to initiate the release. Wolf Creek Bridge was another good-bye. A wall of boulders edged the small parking lot. Black, leafless trees stood in stunning silhouette against the trees across the river that dressed themselves in brilliant orange and yellow. But all beauty was lost on me.

People and gear were unloaded as Mary Ingles Trail Club members Brian Elkins, Alfred Falls, Bettie Mahan, Stanley Moore, Stella Stump, and Liz Watson waited to join us. Those who were leaving took photos. Time flew. Within minutes, Lisa would leave…again. Today I might slip and fall, break a bone, or die in this gorgeous but ominous New River Gorge. This might be the last time I held one of my children. Repetition did not make leaving easier. Time for the last hug.

Wrapping Lisa in my arms, I wanted to melt her into me. My weekend support, forgetter of maps, cheerleader, washer and shredder of clothes, my little girl. She'd be embarrassed if I cried. Besides, no one must see Eleanor cry. Searching Lisa's face I tried to memorize every line before releasing her with a breezy "See you next weekend!"

Feeling as if a knife had cut away my heart and lungs and soul, I watched her drive away. I wasn't sure my legs would hold up or my breakfast stay down. A voice in my head cried, "I love you, Lisa. Don't leave. I need someone to love me. Please believe your mother is okay. I'm afraid of this gorge. Don't forget me." Turning my back on the walkers, I tried to regroup. Words that sounded far away jolted me back, "Are you okay?" "Yes." It was no time to lick wounds of self-pity.

Like yesterday, trail club members who collectively knew the gorge like the back of their hand joined us. Born-and-bred mountain woman Stella Stump was most familiar with this section and volunteered to guide. She had snow-white hair that framed sparkling eyes and square jaw. Gentle words softened, but did not hide, her strong feelings. Wit, kindness, strength, and an elegant spirit earned her everyone's respect and affection. The day before, this spry 70-year-old had stumbled, fallen, recovered, laughed, supported Alfred Falls' leadership as an equal, and set the pace for those much younger.

Under the shadow of the imposing New River Gorge Bridge, Stella led us out of the parking lot, across the Wolf Creek foot-bridge, then eased around a room-sized rock outcropping to pick up a well-worn path. Unlike yesterday's narrow, bushwhacked trail, this was wide enough for a truck.

The Department of Natural Resources seemed to bulldoze wide trails to open access, then install chain-link fences to keep people out. At least that appeared to be the case at Kaymore, an active coal-mining town until the 1960s. About halfway up the mountain, trees, weeds, and flowers grew in, out, and over the once-active community. Steps climbed the mountain from top to bottom. A coal tipple hung overhead. Stella and Alfred identified crumbling buildings, chimneys, scales, and foundations with the knowledge of lifelong neighbors. I tried to remember their lessons and failed miserably. Mostly, I wondered about lost jobs and broken dreams.

Curiosity tempted me to explore the stairs and ruins. However, the Department of Natural Resources was reluctant to give us access to this route until someone assured them we *would* stay on the trail. So I had to stay out. Credibility was vital. With at least two more weeks to go, I had no idea what help I might need...or from whom. So, against all natural urges, we were good boys and girls, and left the enticing ruins to the ghosts.

After Kaymore the trail was less "improved." An old roadbed forgave trips and falls when dry leaves that hid sticks and stones rose to our ankles, and rustled with every step. Breathtaking vistas of the New River, far below, begged to be photographed. Here the river nestled at the bottom of a golden valley. Around a bend, dark branches outlined a silver ribbon peeking from behind a ruby-red lacy-leafed curtain. Each view seemed more beautiful than the one before; and beyond the river, always beckoning, a shadowed, blue-gray mountain to be crossed. Did Mary's physical or mental state allow her to appreciate the beauty, or could she only see the struggle?

One thing Mary did not deal with was kudzu. Imported from Japan, in some areas, this green, leafy alien covered every rock, shrub, and tree from the top of the mountain down to the river. Although it has a beauty of its own, it kills native plants, smothering them with its uncontrollable growth. The lesson I learned was, plant native plants.

The energy required for walking and maintaining smooth group dynamics soon overwhelmed my self-indulgent worry. At times the day felt surreal. Stella, who frequently rode her horse through here, guided our group of 12 through the rocky and rugged Gorge as though it were her backyard garden. Still well up on the mountain, we were working our way down. It took a conscious effort to remember that the dangers of the mountain were real. One step at a time. Be careful. You can't take care of others unless you take care of yourself.

At a shady spot in the trail, on a thick blanket of leaves, we stopped to eat lunch. Stella's wisdom and gentle acceptance of life's difficulties come out if you are lucky to be near her at a quiet time. Widowed nine years before and living alone, she housed chickens, dogs, cats and horses in her barns. Talking proudly of her only child, she mused, "Bud can't come in as often as I'd like…. He's got his life to live…. He can't live his and mine too…. If I need him, he comes."

Some of the walkers became chilled and moved on to a sunny bend in the trail with a river view. White rapids appeared to run into the V of ebony tree limbs. Orange and bronze leaves cuddled the river. A strip of white clouds floated through a blue sky. Ahead rose the ever-present dark mountain. Everyone with a camera clicked away. Then, like children soaking up sun in their front yard, we oohed and aahed, relaxed, solved the world's troubles and forgot our own. Too soon, Alfred, Brian, Debbie, and I broke the spell and rose to leave. The rest slowly gathered themselves to follow.

Around the corner from our oasis, the wide trail disappeared. Ahead yawned a foot-wide path across a creek and landslide. Tripping here would mean a fall to rocks hundreds of feet below. Single file. No mistakes. Alfred led the way. My eyes hugged the trail, except for one quick look. Yep, it went straight down. Slowly, carefully, thankfully, I made it across. Then down a short but steep embankment.

At the bottom, I heard a distant voice and stopped to listen. Was it Liz? Looking back, no one was following us. Another shout. We froze. Did she say, "Someone's down"? With anxiety-driven hearts and legs, we scrambled back. Near the tree, where moments before we were laughing and carefree, I realized Liz had not said, "Someone's down." She said, "Stella's down!"

Stella lay on the ground, conscious but dazed. Becky wiped a trickle of blood from Stella's cheek with one hand while feeling for a pulse with the other. Phyllis held her head. Liz knelt beside Stella, deep concern clouding her face. Dropping beside Becky, I saw in Stella's wrist a textbook example of a silverfork fracture. Both the radius and ulna were broken. While we hovered like mother robins around a fallen chick, Stella began apologizing for causing trouble and tried to sit up. Nausea stopped her.

My EMT training kicked in. Pale, conscious, and alert. Vital signs normal. No apparent internal injuries. The bleeding, from biting her tongue and lip when she fell, was minor. Wrist pain and waves of nausea were Stella's only complaints. Not life threatening, but a problem, since we were five miles from the nearest road. The bones had to be splinted before she could move.

The air splints and wide flat boards of first-aid class are unavailable in a wilderness. Sticks were abundant but crooked and heavy and did not give the needed support. Without hesitation, but with concern, I dug into my backpack and pulled out a Ziploc bag holding maps and my yellow legal pad. All the names and addresses of people we met and those who might have safe shelter in the days ahead were in that bag. Telescoped, the maps and legal pad made a splint from Stella's hand to her elbow, thereby stabilizing the joints above and below the break. Tightly knotted bandannas secured the splint around her arm, and several tied together formed a sling.

With the bone ends immobile, nausea subsided, and Stella was on her feet. Liz stood in front of her. Looking and talking quietly and directly, Liz explained the situation in factual, unemotional terms. No helicopter could land. A stretcher could be walked in over the top of the mountain, but that would take as long, or longer, than us taking her out. While I was unsure of what was best, Stella was firm. She would walk out. She would continue her job as guide and lead us out by going forward to Cunard rather than backtracking to Wolf Creek. Questioning this, I conferred with Liz. She was equally firm. "Stella knows *exactly* where she is."

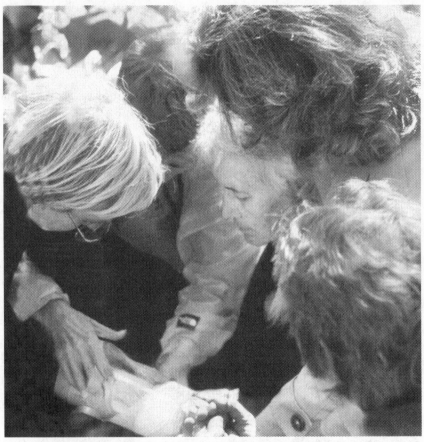

Becky Straight, Phyllis Hyde, Liz Watson, and I used my precious maps to make a splint for Stella Stump's broken arm.

Now the challenge was to make our way down a rugged mountain while not moving the broken bones. Stella had fallen when an egg-sized rock, hidden by leaves, turned under her foot. It could happen again—to any of us. Stella held a walking stick in her right hand as a stabilizing leg; Becky, following closely behind, held onto the back of Stella's shirt.

I supported her left side. We moved off like an awkward three-headed, six-legged insect. Stella's tolerance for pain and nausea would determine the outcome. It would be an interesting five miles.

Perceptions change when we are concerned for others. As we concentrated on Stella, tried to walk as a three-part unit and stay upright, we crossed the landslide, for the third time, almost without fear. While Stella paid a high price for our passage through the Gorge, she eased the tension with her main concern, "I bet my doctor will tell me I can't go skiing this winter!"

Day 31
Monday, October 26, 1987
Cunard to Thurmond, West Virginia

Attitudes

"...they were blessed with mild, dry, southerly winds, sun-gilded, fleecy clouds cruising across a pearly blue sky. The wind soughed high in the trees above them, sent shivers across the surface of the river and stripped off the first loose leaves of autumn. A gust would boom in the crowns of the towering hardwoods; leaves would spill off and whirl away like yellow snowstorms. Deep drifts of ochre and orange and crimson leaves deepened on the forest floor, fragrant and crisp and easy underfoot. Docile wasps and weary flies stitched leisurely through slanted sunbeams." (FTR, pp. 190, 191)

And our day deep in the New River Gorge looked just as Jim Thom described it. Warm sunshine filtered down through dry, rippling yellow leaves, and the last drop of rain we had felt was back in Kentucky. Hiking doesn't get much better. As we chatted and walked, local history poured out of the Mary Ingles Trail Club members who directed the way to easy hiking on an abandoned railroad bed that wound through the mountains.

We learned that as late as 1950, the creeks and hallows that are now wilderness had bustled with activity. In one half-mile stretch, hundreds of beehive coke ovens had once spewed smoke. We saw the remnants of four. Because of the coke and coal business, more trains had come through Thurmond than Richmond and Cincinnati combined. But these days Thurmond was struggling for survival.

As she had the day before, Liz Watson packed a Wildwater Unlimited two-way radio. Her employer, Jon Dragan, generous with company resources, also provided food, sag wagon support, lodging, and hot showers. It should have been a trouble-free day, but, as usual, Phyllis repeatedly wandered off or lagged behind.

In spite of all the Phyllis searches, we enjoyed a glorious walk near the rushing river and through a forest turned to gold by the autumnal sun and leaves. At times, the extraordinary beauty of walking through a tunnel of shimmering golden leaves and into the glowing rays of sunshine felt like what entering heaven might be like, and it took my breath away.

Our 15-mile-day ended, near Thurmond, at the trailhead of the newly dedicated Mary Ingles Trail. The waiting reporter and cameras took a back seat to a smiling, J. C. (Eleanor's husband), who held a hand-lettered, cardboard sign on a stick.

COME HOME
ELEANOR
WHEREVER YOU ARE.
STOP HERE.

J. C. thought his wife's idea to walk the river was a little goofy. Here, he good-naturedly tried to change her mind. When Eleanor saw J. C. and the sign, she ran into waiting arms that locked her in a "gosh, I love you" embrace. However, J. C.'s sign, humor, love and sacks of food would not deter his wife. Though thrilled to see her husband, Eleanor said, "I'm not ready to quit, yet. I'll let you know when."

J. C. not only brought love for Eleanor, he brought a huge snack to share: bananas, bread, ham, turkey, apple juice, etc. Nutritious food and grateful bodies spread out over a large, flat-topped boulder. After sharing food, grins, belly laughs, and hugs, J. C. reluctantly drove away.

Later I inquired about Eleanor's marriage. Though she and her husband practice different faiths, they appear to support and respect those differences. Eleanor's modern/independent assessment was, "I'm my own person." It seemed the same for Susan and Dave. Susan described Dave as a frustrated architect and traditional artist while she worked bronze into modern art creations. It never seemed to occur to these men to be other than supportive of wives searching for a dream.

These and the couples I was yet to meet knew how to make marriage work. On the other hand, I was struggling.

In the first interview on June 23, a reporter had asked, "Will your husband take his vacation and go with you?" It felt as though I'd been stabbed. How could I say, "He has said nary a word to me about this project"? After a few seconds I spoke words that I would repeat over and over, "I'd appreciate it if you did not mention the children's father in the article."

When the relationship between two seemingly good people is in trouble, it is painful for both participants and observers. The first words I heard my husband say about The Walk were not directed to me. Rather, he was speaking to a friend, but loud enough for me to hear. "I think we should go along and heckle her." Stunned and hurt, I pretended not to hear. Would Will Ingles do that to Mary? After a pause came the soft reply, "I don't think that would be a good idea." I will forever be grateful to our friend for his sensitivity. In his way, my husband was probably trying for humor. Any humor in his statement escaped me. However, there was plenty of bad behavior for us to share.

One day at the end of July, after I had worked eight hours, hiked eight training miles, and walked into the house at 7:30 in the evening, I expected supper to be ready, particularly since the man of the house was home all day. It wasn't. Seething in anger, I banged pots and dishes around in the kitchen as I fried hamburger and onions for a quick chili supper. My spouse came downstairs and said, "Oh, I was going to do that." Instead of a lighthearted, "Great! It's all yours!" and heading upstairs for a soak in the tub and feet up with a book, I wrapped the mantel of martyrdom around myself and snapped, "It's almost done." I prepared the meal alone, sucked on my hurt, and ate chili that went down to my stomach like a lead sinker. I seemed incapable of accepting either my spouse's humor or his assistance. Communication was strained and unappealing.

Though my husband's support was not what I wished for, he was not openly hostile. We did not publicly fight. While I longed for someone with whom to share my highs and lows, and my hopes and fears, he may have felt threatened with fears of his own. Fears he was afraid to put into words. Fears that would ultimately come true. With his silence indicating tacit willingness to stay behind and keep the home fires burning, I plunged ahead with my plans.

On the trail, relationships and men were frequent topics of conversation. Referring to Mary's struggle, Debbie said, "I've never met a man I thought was worth it." However, cynicism had not totally hardened my heart. I could think of a few men who might be worth it: Will Ingles and my Uncle Cal instantly came to mind. Of course, one was dead, the other a relative, and Eleanor's and Susan's husbands were taken. Always to be remembered was the woman in 1755 who thought one man was worth it.

> *"She clawed at the cliff with her fingernails as the current tried to lift her feet from under her and pull her down into its cold, gentle, final embrace. She tried to grip the bottom with her toes, but they were rigid and numb as wood. She stood there for an immeasurable time, afraid to move, the cold again penetrating inward toward the feeble lamp of her heart.*
> *Then she thought of Will." (FTR, p. 343)*

The tears that had brimmed in my eyes as I watched Eleanor and J. C. were not just sorrow for desperately wanting what I would never have—they also sprang from joy. We were through the worst of the New River Gorge. So far, only one casualty, and Stella was on the mend. Thirty-one days ago, I had had grave doubts that we would make it this far. Now it seemed a real possibility that we just might make it all the way.

Day 32
Tuesday, October 27, 1987
R & R, Thurmond, West Virginia

Disappointments and Hope

"Mary, her heart high with hope..." (FTR, p. 185)

The disappointments began early. Back in the spring, when this trek was just an idea, I fed on the notion that with Mary as an excellent role model for women, the Girl Scouts would be interested in following my progress. I imagined Girl Scouts all along the river researching their local history while watching for and participating in a retracing of the escape of the woman who some say was the first white female in Kentucky. Some girls would walk a little way or help me find safe tent space. It seemed like a natural fit. Barbara Light, who worked in the Girl Scout office and had given this volunteer much help in the past, was interested enough to take the proposal out of the local office up the chain of command. Unimpressed, the executives refused any association with my project with a "She can't do it without offending the Indians." The sting of disappointment was eased by Barbara's private support. She even talked of being a sag wagon driver for a few days. Then, as the day for me to leave grew nearer, I tried to avoid the actual words, but we both knew she wouldn't be coming.

Then there was the enthusiastic support of Larry Incollingo, freelance writer for the Bloomington *Herald-Telephone,* and Marion, former teacher of my children. They had a small trailer that they could use for a sag wagon. However, as the days ticked off and September 26 drew near, it became apparent that though the spirit was willing, the flesh wanted to stay in Bloomington.

Shelly Gregg, my Department of Natural Resources cohort at Lake Monroe, planned to walk the whole way. We trained together by hiking the state park trails, carrying her son on our backs for weight, and asking her mother to baby-sit. Shelly was smart and pleasant to be around, and I felt that my chance of completing the trek would be greatly improved with her on board. I was particularly pleased when I learned that Shelly's given name was Bettie, the same as Mary's sister-in-law who was captured with her. It seemed that a guiding hand of fate meant for someone who I knew and trusted, and who had a link to Mary (albeit a distant one), would go with me. Shelly even crocheted soap holders for us to use as washcloths. They had loops so they could be hung in a branch to dry. Sadly, the week before we were to leave, Shelly's mother suffered a heart attack. Fortunately for me, by that time Patti, Brenda, Eleanor Henson, Phyllis, Debbie, Becky, and Susan had contacted me and each asked to walk from a weekend to a week or more. But, without Shelly I was suddenly left with only strangers who might, or might not, show up.

Then there was John Taylor's heart attack in August that knocked him out as my West Virginia coordinator and the Kentucky State Policemen who assured me that they would drive by *each day* to check on us—when we saw them maybe once or twice. With each disappointment, the message became clearer.... I was the only person I could count on. If I wanted this adventure, I better be willing to do it alone.

This thirty-second day was planned for R & R, and as luck would have it, a steady rain fell most of the day. Because Jon Dragan let us camp beside the river in the Wildwater Unlimited bunkhouse used by his river guides (site of the famous Dunglen Hotel), there were no wet, muddy boots and tents to dry out. So, there I was: high and dry, resting, shopping, exploring the history of Thurmond, giving interviews, and making phone calls and arrangements for the days ahead. One of those calls went to Steve Trail, upstream in Hinton.

Steve was one of the historians featured in WSWP's docudrama *Mary Ingles: Indian Captive*. Ever since I telephoned him before leaving, Steve's knowledge of the New River/Greenbrier/Bluestone area and his assurance that he would help me make it to Virginia, were linchpins in my confidence. After we left the security blanket of John Taylor's fire-fighting friends in western West Virginia, I counted on Steve being with us from Hinton on to the Virginia state line.

Now that we were through the worst of the New River Gorge, a stomach-knotting anxiety concerning the stretch after Hinton began to tighten. And the call to Steve, telling him we were about three days away, did nothing to relieve my tension. While still *saying* he would help, he sounded vague and unorganized. If he did not come through, there was no backup. While the air was thick with bad vibes, I kept the worries to myself and enjoyed delightful dinners with Jon Dragan, his wife Melanie and son Joshua. Jon was a pleasant surprise. For as Becky said, when she observed Jon at the Mary Ingles Trail Club meeting a couple nights before, she had *never* thought he would give us *any* assistance. But there he was, the unlikely angel. So, surrounded by the Dragans' good company and laughter, for a while my anxiety disappeared. Then, three days later, a few miles from Hinton, my fears were realized. Steve could not help.

It took years before I understood that even those who disappointed me were also angels who helped me down the trail. For, by the time they backed out, I was committed. They gave me hope and that hope kept me planning and walking.

Searches

"Mary grew impatient, and was constantly coaxing her on." (FTR, p. 261)

Sending out search parties for a lost or lagging hiker took its toll on time and patience, both mine and that of those providing support. Phyllis, who disappeared on an almost daily basis, was the only hiker to exhibit this behavior. "Where's Phyllis?" was heard so often it almost became a mantra. "Where's Gretel?" was the quieter, surreptitious call.

The first time I heard that phrase, it startled me. Although I never repeated it to anyone, given her attitude toward me, I did wonder if Phyllis were consciously or unconsciously playing the role of Mary's troublesome companion.

I concluded that disappearing, without a word to anyone, was Phyllis' way to gain attention and/or control. Bad enough when it inconvenienced me, but when it infringed on the patience and goodwill of those "angels" providing food, lodging, and transportation, I became downright angry. After the first week of it, I was willing to walk away and let her find her own way out, for she seemed to prefer walking alone. However, no one else wanted that responsibility. Some kind soul would say, "What if this time she is *really* lost or hurt?" And I would think, "What if she slipped and has broken a bone like Stella?" We couldn't just leave her. Then, forward travel would stop, and another round of calling searchers would spread out.

The possibility of serious injury was real. It seemed that Phyllis was oblivious to the dangers of the Gorge and the trouble she caused. Perhaps

143

she didn't care. If she wanted to walk alone, why had she hooked up with me? Why not just walk the river by herself? I was mystified. Eventually, about 20 minutes or so later (after a search for her was undertaken) an unconcerned and unapologetic Phyllis would surface around a curve in the trail or from behind a small hillock.

Each time she reappeared, my sympathy shrank and resentment grew. Neither coaxing, explaining, cajoling, reasoning, or pleading changed her behavior. At this point in The Walk, I did not care if she were hurt. I wanted this human millstone gone.

The Protector

"[She]...suddenly was drawn out of herself by a great wave of pity." (FTR, p. 195)

As my frustration and exasperation with Phyllis increased, so did the friendship and bond between Phyllis and Debbie. During a pool game at the Fayetteville Fire Department, they became friendly rivals. Debbie's skill at banter and billiards engaged Phyllis in an activity in which she showed surprising skill at knocking balls in a pocket. Phyllis "let her hair down," and a sad family history spilled out. A wounded child emerged. One could see the vulnerable sister and daughter who developed an armor of defensiveness to survive, while becoming her mother's caretaker.

That knowledge made it easier for me to understand Phyllis, but it did not make her one iota easier to deal with. On the other hand, Debbie, free of any trip responsibilities and not trying to make Phyllis conform to a rule or schedule, was open to Phyllis' need for sympathy and friendship. So, day by day, link by link, they forged a bond. Debbie became the shield who excused, explained, and joked away the actions of the thorn in my side. And, day by day, little by little, the bond between Debbie and me loosened. Though Phyllis talked of driving east to see Monticello (with my full encouragement!), it never happened. Two and a half weeks, and she was still counting.

After sharing another big breakfast with the rafting guides before 7:00 a.m., Jon Dragan showed up to load our gear. Tensions floated away on the wings of laughter as Jon teased everyone. Even Phyllis laughed when he referred to her as "Coffee-mate." We headed for Prince in high spirits—and without Phyllis' car.

When we arrived at Prince, my heart sank. There was no Doug Cooper, nor the truck he had said would take our gear to his camp at Sandstone Falls. Jon drove to the other side of the bridge, toured us around Quintamont, and regaled us with local history of the Berrie family. When we arrived back at the bridge, a car waited, but it wasn't Doug's. Stanley Moore and Betty Mahan had decided to join us, for the fifth day in a row. The day before, Betty was concerned about her husband's reaction if she walked again. This day he drove their shuttle car and became part of the party. (I must have been doing *something* right.) With the addition of Stan and Betty, the group increased to nine.

As delighted as we were to see our trail club friends, something had to be done with the gear. Jon couldn't wait any longer; he had a business to run. So, beside the road, he unloaded our packs, Debbie's Diet Cokes, and miscellaneous food and gift bags that the gals couldn't get in their packs and headed back to Wildwater Unlimited. Now I had nine people to move 15 miles upriver, a mountain of gear that belonged to people I doubted could carry it, and a stomach full of nervous knots.

It was a distinct possibility that Doug had decided not to walk or make sag wagon arrangements for us. His father, who was ill when we met at Eleanor Henson's party 12 days earlier, had died. A saddened son suddenly had free time on his hands. But if Doug decided he wasn't ready for a day of physical exertion and contemplation, several women would carry more than they ever thought they could, or leave it behind. Though I was the one in the best shape to carry her belongings, I seemed to be the only one concerned about the lack of gear transport.

At a wide place in the road where it approached a bridge, I looked up and down the road, straining to hear the sound of a truck motor. Our little group fought against the chill in the early morning air. Mouths and minds worked at reliving and relating experiences and wondering what the day would bring. Arms wrapped coats tightly to bodies. Feet stomped. Hands clapped.

Then my gaze caught Debbie wrapping her arms around Phyllis to keep her warm. Phyllis' head lay on Debbie's shoulder, while at the same time Phyllis stuffed food in her mouth. It struck me as the portrait of a guardian angel caring for the weak, abused, and hungry.

Then, a few minutes before 8:00 o'clock, a truck pulled to a stop, and Doug Cooper stepped out. Like a cork out of a bottle, my tension released, and I ran up to a man I had met only once and give him a huge hug. Today, our angel wore blue jeans, a plaid wool shirt, and freshly oiled hiking boots. Thank you, God! The gear, cartons of Diet Coke, and most of my anxiety disappeared down the road in the back of that pickup.

But all day, I remembered the tender vignette of Phyllis and Debbie huddled against the world. And I knew, without a shadow of a doubt, that Phyllis would stay around as long as she wanted, because Debbie was now her protector.

Day 35
Friday, October 30, 1987
Sandstone Falls to Hinton, West Virginia

Rainbows and Promises

"And finally the sun's entire orb was freed from behind its bars of cloud; and the storm receding across the river made a vast, bruise-colored backdrop for a perfect rainbow that seemed to straddle the river. Even through her misery, Mary felt she was seeing the work of a God whom she had not thought much of for many weeks." (FTR, p. 197)

Sitting just upriver from Sandstone Falls, Doug Cooper's "camp" was everything the pictures had promised. Mary and Ghetel could never have imagined such comfort and luxury. A wall of windows, a deck overlooking the river, electricity, clean beds, microwave, television, and a telephone.

While I could have done without everything else, almost daily telephone calls to contacts, well-wishers, and helpers were what kept this band moving safely upriver. A call the day before confirmed my premonition that Steve, a historian familiar with the area, would not walk with us and that he had no lead for someone else to assist. While I was deeply disappointed, Steve surprised me with two free rooms for two nights at the Coast to Coast Motel, right beside the river...and he asked if I would be his guest for lunch at the Rotary meeting at the Episcopal church. "Okay...if I can bring the five women walking with me," I said. (If I got a free meal, the women would have one too.)

So, instead of taking the day off, we walked eight miles into Hinton. It was dry and sunny. The walk, now out of the gorge where the New River flows wide and much slower, should have been pleasurable, but

148

hordes of flying gnats made it nearly impossible to appreciate the hills and houses that sported orange, gold, red, and brown leaves, and jack-o'-lantern and scarecrow decorations ready for a holiday I'd forgotten. Stopping for a drink of water was agony. The gnats were in our eyes and noses and mouths.

Entering the civilization of Hinton, a little town nestled at the foot of a mountain just below where the Bluestone River empties into the New River, we left the bugs behind. Mary would have recognized this junction. At this point, did she fight the gnats, or just concentrate on how close she was to home?

I was concentrating on finding the Rotary Club. We crossed the bridge, and soon found the old, red-brick church. Immediately we were deluged with a swarm of questioning people.

I had walked in carrying a load of worry. Making nice to a crowd of eager strangers was not high on my list of afternoon entertainment, because I knew that every step out of Hinton would be strictly on our own. No sag wagon for gear. No local guides to clear the way. Again I told the women we'd have to carry our packs, but they kept buying cartons of soft drinks and bags of souvenirs, in a naive certainty that a vehicle would come along. As the pile of gear grew, I continued to be the only one concerned about the unknown terrain and the walkers' ability.

My worry was not imagined. Eleanor Henson's knees were badly swollen; Phyllis continued to drag behind; and JoAnn Oakes, with little training, planned to begin walking with us when we left Hinton. The Corps of Engineers said if we entered the area upriver from Hinton, we had to be out the same day. No overnight camping. I tried to hide my concern and be upbeat with all questioners. The challenge was to be polite, swallow a little food, and get us out before the Rotary program and business meeting began. Then, just as I finished eating, Steve rose, thanked everyone for coming and said, "Now, Eleanor will say a few words."

Now, Eleanor would have liked to have been informed! I should not have been surprised that this was a "sing for your supper" meal, but I was. Breathing deeply, I rose slowly and tried to figure out what I could say to this roomful of expectant faces.

The main message was my heartfelt gratitude for all who came each day, out of nowhere, to provide a safe place for us to stay. They were my "angels in everyday clothing." One of them being Steve. (I might be disappointed that he would not assist us as a guide, but he provided two nights of lodging and a meal for six walkers. A generous contribution.) Then, unplanned, my concern about the next two days came out.

Hinton to the Virginia state line was a wild, undeveloped stretch. The Corps of Engineers, in control of most of the land, though not hostile, resolutely refused any physical assistance to anyone walking through the area. Many said it couldn't be done. (Well, I knew two women who *had* done it 232 years before.) Then my mind went blank. There didn't seem to be anything else to say, so I thanked the Rotary for their interest and was about to close, when Connie Newton and her Hinton High School Appalachian Studies class arrived. They presented me with a school sweater and said they wanted to walk a little with us. Local students interested in local history—perfect. When I sat down, Susan said I had sounded good. But it felt awkward, as though I had messed up on a pop quiz.

Wilber Farley, a helpful angel, wore a rainbow and offered us a promise.

As I left the meeting room, out of the crowd, a man about 80 years old, with a little round belly, strode up to me and held out his hand. Unpretentious, in a plaid-flannel shirt rolled up to the elbows and blue jeans held up with rainbow striped suspenders, he gave a firm handshake, looked me straight in the eye, and said, "I'm Wilber Farley. I'll see that you get to the Virginia state line."

Sometimes I go through life doubting that there is a God who cares, let alone angels that help or hinder my existence. At other times, it seems obvious that there is an unseen force at work, saying "Yes" or "No" or "Not now, I'll get someone else."

Just as I believe that in 1755 there were forces who assisted Mary and Ghetel to accomplish the impossible, along the river in 1987, there were times when I felt there were spirits giving me aid and comfort. On this day, there wasn't a doubt in my mind that an angel stood before me wearing rainbow suspenders and bearing a promise.

Waterfalls and River Rides

*"It was a canoe....It might require more strength than she had.
But, strengthened by hope, she set to work." (FTR, p. 314)*

Eleanor Henson's knees continued to be painful and swollen. She didn't complain, but she rested every chance she could. Taking the weekend off might help them recover. (It had worked for Debbie's feet back in Kentucky.) A couple days to rest and think of where we were, had been, and were headed would be good for all of us. And the two days of rest would have us walking out of Hinton on Monday, when the Appalachian Studies class could join us. Two nights at the Coast to Coast Motel were perfect for an R & R weekend. We could sleep in, play around the camp, and move into the motel after lunch.

As early risers, Doug and I cooked breakfast. It was pleasant working with a male who was comfortable enough with himself and women that he did not have to "prove" himself by boasting or talking down to me. I liked listening to him talk about his wife, Joyce. We missed meeting her because she was back in Dunbar recovering from mononucleosis.

After kitchen cleanup, I walked down to Sandstone Falls and found it essentially unchanged from when Mary walked through hundreds of years before. There were no "improvements" such as walkways and benches for tourists. I just stepped from one table-top-sized rock to another, picked one, sat down, and watched the endless river flow past.

Here, the river spreads out and meanders through a wide valley. The water is relatively shallow and appears deceptively calm. Low foamy rapids suck hard as inexperienced canoeists, caught in its grasp, use all their strength to pull free. Huge, flat stones let you walk out above, yet into the current. Except for fishing camps upstream, it is isolated and peaceful, until fishermen and canoeists wander through.

It was probably upriver from here that Ghetel, driven mad with hunger, tried to eat Mary. After Mary broke free and hid out, she stumbled upon a canoe. Using a piece of flat wood as an oar, she managed to steer it across the river and away from the one who so hated her.

As owners of Cooper's Canoes, Doug and Joyce rented and gave canoe lessons. They talked of one day opening a bed and breakfast. When Doug casually asked if I'd like to take a canoe ride, I looked at him in disbelief. Like Mary, access to a canoe to cross the river came to me serendipitously. Fortunately, unlike Mary, I would not have to fight off my nemesis to get it.

Blue skies gave way to a gray haze of clouds mixed with smoke. The air was dry. Good for walking and playing and forest fires. This day the fires were far west of us, and we had no worries. We had safe lodging and food, the promise of assistance when next we took to hiking, and two days to play.

While Phyllis and Eleanor, like little girls, took turns swinging on a fat rope swing hanging from a tall sycamore tree, Doug picked up a pretty red canoe from under the deck and carried it to the river bank. He held it steady while I stepped in. Then, with a practiced motion, he pushed off and stepped in himself. Sandstone Falls sounded its muffled roar just below us, but Doug's strength and skill took us out to quiet water. I thought of Mary, her struggle, her crossing, and how another similarity in our journeys was again coming to pass. Mine was a symbolic ride. I knew that. But it seemed important.

I wondered about the history of this valley. Doug said that according to Dewey Adkins, who used to live in the area, it was called Longbottom. In the '20s, about 12 to 15 houses dotted the area, with a small sawmill providing work. Dewey's job was to push the finished lumber across the suspension bridge that had sat upriver from where Doug's camp now sits. Today, the lumberyard and bridge and jobs were all gone. I wondered how much of what we were seeing would be gone in the next 50 or 60 years.

As we drew close to the opposite shore, Doug's eyes swept up the mountainside, along the shore, down the river and settled on me. "I wanted you to ride in the canoe, like she did."

Thanks, Doug. Thanks for everything.

Day 37
Sunday, November 1, 1987
R & R, Hinton, West Virginia

Surprising Abilities

"You are happy or not happy insofar as you belong...." (FTR, p. 152)

If all went well, this would be our last week. But first we needed to get through two long days of hiking, including the last wild section of the trip. So this Sunday was a day of both rest and preparation.

Debbie, Susan, Eleanor, and Becky washed clothes and checked out the town. Phyllis and JoAnn Oakes, who had arrived the evening before, dealt with car problems, shuttles, and repairs. Phyllis had said earlier that she would stop walking in Hinton. Now, with JoAnn's help, Phyllis planned to walk into Pipestem, if JoAnn could retrieve her car from Pratt. (I didn't even want to know what was going on.)

For me, the day was tense with numerous phone calls, adjustments, arrangements, and seemingly endless meetings. It was all necessary to learn about the land, people, and politics of the area. In addition to my unease concerning the isolated and unknown route from Hinton to Glen Lyn, my desire to walk as close to the river as possible, and the political pressure on me to stay away from it, I mulled over the continuing Phyllis factor.

The night before, Phyllis had been openly hostile to Becky. (Becky felt it was because she had defended me against Phyllis' complaints.) The result was that Becky refused to be anywhere near Phyllis, let alone sleep in the same room with her. To ease another Phyllis problem, I juggled sleeping arrangements. Instead of tensions easing because we were nearing the end, the quivering nerves in my stomach felt like dancing electrical wires.

From Hinton to Glen Lyn, the New River flows right through Army Corps of Engineers property. Because of the size of the group and our notoriety, I needed the Corps to believe in me enough that they would grant access. After numerous phone calls, I finally convinced a representative to meet with me. Past experience showed that I had better luck face to face than on the phone.

Wayne Riegor, from the Corps of Engineers, and his wife stopped by my motel room. They were nice people. He brought topographic maps, went over mine, and assisted with map orientation, but he steadfastly declined any physical help and continued to argue that we stay away from the river. Though I was not surprised by Wayne's position, my dark hole of depression grew.

Safety was the primary issue for me and the Corps. Eleanor's knee, though better, was iffy, and Phyllis and JoAnn had not walked even one complete day. If one of them gave out in an isolated area, the problem could be serious for everyone. Without telling him about our deficiencies, I struggled to reassure Wayne, while making a fair and reasonable decision. The Corps was obviously concerned about bad publicity if something happened to us, and that we might accidentally start a fire in the extremely dry conditions. With forest fires popping up between Hinton and Charleston, the danger was real. While I was dealing with Wayne, Wilber Farley called. It sounded as though he knew the area well enough to fulfill his Friday "I'll see that you get to the Virginia state line" promise.

In the middle of my conversations with Wayne and Wilber, Debbie, Phyllis, and JoAnn kept popping their heads in with questions or jokes. Then Melvin Plumley, the Rotary president, came by with "There is someone I want you to meet." While trying to negotiate the maze of mental messages, as if by magic, a compromise plan fell together, and Wayne granted reluctant approval.

With Wilber providing sag wagon support for two days, by walking 18 miles to Pipestem, I could honor the Corps' wishes to stay away from the river once we left Hinton. Then, if Wilber drove us to Bull Falls, we could walk the isolated 22 river miles to Glen Lyn, Virginia. We would have sag backup out of Hinton. If the weak walkers didn't make it from Hinton to Pipestem, I'd tell them they could not join the walk into Glen Lyn, and they should understand. With that decision, my depression cloud floated away, and, in a flash, Susan and I climbed into Melvin's green Chevy truck and were bouncing along narrow, two-lane roads to parts unknown.

A quiet, unassuming man, Melvin had a sensitivity and appreciation for beauty in both people and art that you would not expect in a yardmaster for the railroad. He braked to a stop at a wide place in the road. Our destination, the Wakerobin Gallery, was in the middle of nowhere.

Inside, clay bowls, glasses, pitchers, and plates were displayed on open shelves. You could stand at the counter and look across the open room to watch the artist throwing clay at her wheel, taking phone orders, answering customers' questions and making in-person sales. It was a one-woman shop. Marsha Springston did it all. She would be pleased to know that it was difficult to believe she was totally blind. Not only talented, she was warm and gracious. "You must meet my parents," she told us.

Across the road, in a beautiful old farmhouse that they purchased six years before, Dave and Connie Springston lived in retirement. It was obvious where Marsha got her artistic bent. After retiring, Dave and Connie discovered latent talents, skills they had never before tried. And they became famous in West Virginia: Connie for her weavings and Dave for his watercolors.

Connie toured us through the house, where looms of various sizes produced hand-woven placemats, runners, scarves, curtains, and bedspreads. Dave's paintings decorated every room. Then Dave led us out to the barn, and we climbed stairs to where a door opened onto an artist's loft. Up high, overlooking fields and sunsets, Dave could watch people and dogs and birds and life go by. No wonder his paintings held so much feeling.

This couple had spent their lives raising two blind daughters to adulthood and to independent lives, as a potter and teacher. Then in retirement, Dave and Connie found new, challenging, and rewarding abilities in crafts they had never tried before. Though they had different skills, each showed the other support and respect. Life had not been easy, but this family looked happy. I felt as though I were being shown beauty wrapped in love.

Riding back to Hinton, I carried my copy of an order for six handmade bowls to be delivered, if I survived the next six days.

This day of rest showed me that there really is more to life than merely existing, and perfecting plans, and rushing down the road. Sometimes you need to stop and relax and realize that you don't need eyes to see beauty and love, or to find happiness.

Day 38
Monday, November 2, 1987
Hinton to Pipestem, West Virginia

The Children

"Now, Mary thought. Just turn your back on it and go. Don't go look at the baby: y'll get all upset and they'll suspect something. Don't look at the baby!" (FTR, p. 155)

I ended this day as I began it, looking at a sea of shining, eager faces, and I remembered those who came before.

When the retracing of the historic event became public, many teachers seemed to instinctively understand that having even a modest adventure like mine would interest and excite their students. This little project was hardly more than an idea when Marion Fleener invited me to her fifth-grade Binford Elementary class in Bloomington. A few teachers who had read a newspaper article wrote to me and asked if I'd stop at their school when/if I made it to their area. Frequently, it was a last-minute request.

Day 4 of my adventure, Alma Wiley covered the gymnasium floor with children in California, Kentucky. I sat cross-legged and talked from a bare, raised stage, the kind you see in a '50s movie. As Debbie and I left, a selected group of about 40 children walked along with us through the field that safely lay away from the road and not too close to the river. Debbie's lonely arms reached out whenever a child was near. Soon her daypack, hat, and walking stick were passed around and proudly carried. It surprised me how quickly the children tried to emulate us. Picking up and using walking sticks was the most obvious display of their fascination. It made me realize how careful adults should be when the impressionable are near.

Day 21, as we walked into Winfield, West Virginia, 75 or so middle schoolers stood on a hill and greeted us, waving "Welcome Eleanor" signs that they probably had made in art class. Would they like to join us? (Was there a doubt?) Debbie and I looked like the Pied Piper as the mayor, teachers, and children followed behind us in a two-by-two parade to the elementary school, where another group waited for me to speak.

Enjoying more time away from lessons, the boys and girls stood, sat, and waited outside in the warm sun for other classes to join them. A young girl who appeared more poised than the mayor, or me, gave an introduction. Nerves and anxiety always fought for control, particularly when I stood in front of children. They'd never remember anything I said. So it was important that they remember something of the feeling. Understanding that neither I nor my words were memorable, I tried to avoid boring them.

Day 24, when we reached Charleston, West Virginia, another teacher was waiting. Pat Gilbert had written to me with an invitation for a night's safe lodging, if I'd talk to her gifted-and-talented class. Then she enlarged the hospitality to include supper and breakfast, and like others before her, Pat's generosity extended to those walking with me.

At Marmet Junior High, on Day 26, while searching for a recommended restaurant, the first teacher I ran into happened to be the one who had called Pat Gilbert days earlier. My little band of six (sans Phyllis, who was out with her car) could eat a free breakfast with the schoolchildren, if I'd "sing for our breakfast" by talking at an impromptu convocation.

In Pratt, West Virginia, though chomping at the bit to leave, on Day 27, I couldn't refuse Virginia Ivey's request that we open the school day for her third-grade class. Upriver, and on Day 28, the students at Smithers Valley Elementary filled one side of the gym. People had been exceptionally kind to us. Taking time for their children was the least I could do.

On this day, as we left Hinton, students from Connie Newton's Appalachian Studies class swelled our little band from seven to 25, for about the first mile. Polite, interested, and appreciative, they were a far cry from what most people think of as "typical" high school students.

At the end of the day, a detour put us near the Pipestem Grade School, where I signed 20 to 30 autographs. It gave me a minuscule taste of what the truly famous go through. Children are fun. Clamoring adults would be a nightmare. At every school I felt I was experiencing a lesson or a test.

I never knew where the question would come from. It might be the curly-headed girl in glasses or the boy with mud-spattered overalls or the shy child hugging his knees in the last row. It always hit like a sucker punch out of nowhere.

The teacher's smiling, enthusiastic request was for me to talk about Mary and The Walk. Tell about your training and what's happened. That was easy. They did not warn me about the question-and-answer session. After the first and second time, I knew it would come, sooner or later.

A hand would slowly rise. Voice tentative and soft. Body tense. Eyes riveted to mine. "What about the children?"

The children. Elementary-age students were supposed to be too young to grasp that part of the story. That part when Mary left her daughter and two sons behind when she escaped. They were supposed to be interested in blistered feet, eating bugs, catching poison ivy, slithering snakes, and death-defying escapes.

"What happened to the children?" Why did Mary leave without her children? There had to be an answer. And the words had to be right. Okay, Eleanor. Explain in 25 words or less why a mother would leave her children. And while you're at it, reassure this child looking deep into your eyes why his mother or father left him—and why it isn't his fault. This is no time for test anxiety and your brain's computer to crash. Come on, Eleanor....Think....*THINK!*

Culling

"We're but five days from home!" (FTR, p. 295)

As had happened almost every day, safe (and free) lodging was provided for us. John Taylor used his network of friends to finagle us two nights at Pipestem, one of West Virginia's country club-like state parks. One night in the campground and one in the lodge. Unlike Mary and Ghetel, we camped in style. And, unbeknownst to me, my parents had pulled their camper all the way from Florida and set themselves up three campsites away. I never understood how they had found us, but their presence meant we would have sag support all the way to the end. My hiking companions' blind faith of the past 38 days was justified. We would never have to carry a full backpack, and they would not have to jettison Diet Cokes and souvenirs. I should have been high as a kite and loose as a goose. I wasn't.

Responsibility and concerns again had me tense and anxious. The hike from Pipestem to Glen Lyn, Virginia, would be mentally and physically challenging because of the length of the day's walk and its wild nature. However, physical and mental challenges were minor considerations compared to my big worry. Unlike the past 38 days, the next day I would *not* be taking everyone who wanted to go. And, anticipating the disappointment, arguments, and hard feelings weighed heavily on me.

A combination of experienced hazards and unknown peril meant the welfare of the group was at stake. Because of a lack of rain, fire was burning some of the mountains we had crossed only days before.

The group had to be able to move rapidly. Topographic maps showed relatively flat terrain along the river. However, despite the flat terrain of the second day, it had turned out to be one of the most arduous days of the whole trip. Adding to the pressure were the Army Corps of Engineers, who continued to have grave reservations about my chance of success. There was also the ever-present possibility of an accident or injury. However, strong hikers are less likely to have problems than are the tired and out-of-shape.

Local property owners were incensed that I was reduced to begging permission from the Corps. (Had I been familiar with the adage "It's easier to get forgiveness than permission," I may have handled things differently.) However, in 1987 I worked at an Army Corps of Engineers facility in Indiana and as an interpreter at Monroe Lake, an Indiana State Recreation area, and my paycheck resulted from a Corps project, so I tried to follow the rules. Unlike the embittered locals, I'd never had my property condemned and local historical buildings gutted and burned by this government agency.

But I now had consent to walk through Corps property...*if, and only if,* we completed the distance in one day. The Corps refused to authorize an overnight camp. While verbally agreeing, I silently thought, I'll make the attempt, and if we don't finish in one day, we don't finish. We'll have to spend the night.... We'll just not have a campfire. What was I going to do, grow wings and fly out? Now it was time to decide who to take and who to leave behind.

Becky, Debbie, and Susan could make it. Eleanor Henson's swollen knees had not responded to R & R. The day before she had called J. C. and said the words he longed to hear, "Old man, come get this old woman." Day-hiker Stanley, if he decided to join us, was a strong walker; however, I was concerned about his hiking friend Bettie. She had always worked hard, kept up, and never complained. But her frequent labored breathing and flushed face worried me. The last thing I needed was a diabetic reaction or heart attack in the middle of nowhere. However, after a long-distance discussion with Stan, I decided to take a chance on Bettie. They would drive over and meet us the next morning.

JoAnn was unique. Her zany humor made a delightful addition to group dynamics, but she physically couldn't keep up, even on yesterday's short and easy road walk. I hated leaving her behind. Phyllis, on the other hand, had previously walked an entire day, but she was constantly lagging behind, and countless search parties had to be sent out to find her.

There would be no search parties or car rides from Bull Falls to Glen Lyn. In good conscience, I could not allow two weak hikers to jeopardize the rest of the group. We had over 20 miles of backcountry to traverse. If the terrain turned out to be like the second day, a rocky shore, thick brush, and blow-down would slow us and stress even the strongest among us.

JoAnn was obviously disappointed when I told her I thought she should not accompany us, but, explaining the situation to this pleasant, reasonable, and understanding lady was no problem. In fact, I encouraged her to join us in Virginia, where the hikes would be shorter and the terrain less rugged.

Phyllis was another matter. After our heated confrontation at John Taylor's, I feared she would react to my rejection with the same resentment and hostility. I dreaded talking to Phyllis and decided to take her aside, but well within sight of the others. My experience of the past 23 days told me she would not create a scene if other people were present.

It was early morning when I saw Phyllis standing alone, across the road from my campsite. Gathering a deep breath and all my courage, I walked up to her. Quietly, yet I believe firmly and gently, I said, "Tomorrow I will take only those people who have shown they can keep up day in and day out. Therefore, I am not taking you and JoAnn." Of course she protested with a strong "Why?" "It is unknown terrain," I explained. "You have not kept up for one complete day in the three weeks you have been with us. I am only taking strong, consistent walkers." Phyllis was surprisingly quiet. She said she disagreed, but she accepted it. Amazing.

Relieved that the confrontation was over, I felt my tension begin to melt away. A huge weight lifted. She hadn't yelled. There was no hostile protest or argument. Phyllis could be reasonable, after all. I could enjoy the day.

With a bounce in my step, I happily kicked through dry leaves as I ambled over to Mom and Dad's trailer. On the picnic table, they had spread a farmer's breakfast of bacon, eggs, fried potatoes, toast, and coffee for me and my five companions.

After eating, Debbie and JoAnn went horseback riding. I worked on arranging lodging for the next two nights. With luck, in 40 hours we would cross into Virginia. Our last state. My Virginia contacts, Mary Lewis Jeffries and Dr. Grace Edwards, didn't know of any safe place to camp there.

After more long-distance calls, leads and dead ends, and feeling at my wit's end, I called John Taylor...again. True to the word "friend," his network of firefighters would come to my rescue.

The goal for the next night was Glen Lyn, Virginia. Across the river from Glen Lyn sits Peterstown, West Virginia. Because John knew Peterstown Bank President and Fire Chief Tom Francis, John called Tom, who agreed to allow us to sleep on the firehouse floor. Chief Francis also offered Mom and Dad parking space for their camper. Again, a plan was coming together. We had a place to stay, and Phyllis said she would leave. However, over the last two weeks, Phyllis had said several times she would leave the next day or weekend, and she was still with us.

In the evening, we splurged at dinner in the Pipestem Lodge. Everyone, including Phyllis, bubbled with talk and laughter. Phyllis talked of going to see Monticello. Tension between Phyllis and me evaporated. Conversation sparkled as we relived our adventures: the blisters, the best socks, the train, guys who had fawned after Debbie, JoAnn's Santa Claus-like white fur boots and red-and-white nightshirt, the day's horseback riding, and car repairs with the help of Chuck Loonie. Spirits were high. The end was in sight.

Euphoric that I had once again found safe lodging for the next day, I was about to share the good news with my table companions, when a tiny voice inside my head insisted, "Don't tell *anyone!*"

Day 40
Wednesday, November 4, 1987
Bull Falls, West Virginia, to Glen Lyn, Virginia

The Antagonist

"She had made it. She had crossed the river! Ghetel could not get to her now." (FTR, p. 317)

Sometimes, we are not nice people. Sometimes, it seems that our animal instincts take over. Sometimes, it is what we don't say that screams loudest. Sometimes, we realize the fight has been not without, but within. And, sometimes, it takes years to realize what really happened.

As I walked into the lobby of the Pipestem State Park Lodge, a group of walkers, new friends and newly acquainted with one another, gathered for our early morning departure. Amid laughter and hugs, I stopped dead in my tracks. Phyllis stood in the middle of the group.

She was not supposed to be there. She had said she was heading to Monticello. Ever the manipulator, she smiled and softened her voice. "I couldn't bear to not walk this." Her words turned my blood to ice and my jaw to iron.

Was her pleasantness last night contrived to throw me off? Did I imagine that she had said she was leaving? No. No. She had said she would leave. Was I angry at myself for falling for her sociability of the day before or at Phyllis for accurately assessing that I (like her) would not make a scene in front of everyone?

My anger and frustration were not just a reaction to Phyllis. There was an old familiar feeling about the situation. She was treating me the way others had. The so-called friends and loved ones who ignored what I said and did what they wanted, as if I and my words were of no value. I was incensed at the lack of respect and at what appeared, to me, to be

165

her deception. Was part of my anger that Phyllis could assess me so well and that I continued to misjudge her?

Looking at Phyllis, my brain snapped a silent reply, Well lady, if you want to walk...so be it. But there will be no slowing down for you to catch up, and no search parties. Today it's keep up or find your own way out. Without acknowledging her presence, I continued preparations to leave.

Mom and Dad stuffed the gear of four walkers into their trailer. Debbie, Susan, Becky, and Phyllis climbed into the back of Wilber Farley's old blue pickup. Again ignoring the often-repeated rule, Phyllis asked Wilber to bring her back to Pipestem, so she could pick up her car. Although Stanley's wife would drive to Glen Lyn that evening to pick him up, and they could easily have taken her, Stan did not offer Phyllis a ride.

As I climbed in beside Wilber for the ride down to Bull Falls, concern for our safety overcame my anger and sharpened my concentration for the task ahead. Forest fires were burning the trail behind us. Though I had reluctant approval from the Corps, the locals seemed to agree that we could not hike Bull Falls to Glen Lyn in one day. "No one's ever done it," they told us. Their concerns were the reason I wanted only strong, proven hikers. If we got into trouble, I wanted people who would be a help rather than a millstone.

As we bumped along, Wilber's fascinating history lecture softened my exasperation and transported me to earlier, more difficult times. Wilber spoke as though he knew the area's early settlers personally. Here the first settlers lived in a cave. There the Corps of Engineers burned historic homes. And, without a doubt, Mary walked close to the New River just as we would, and somewhere along this stretch she may have fought for her life to escape the crazed, old woman who was trying to cannibalize her. One of my goals was to reach back into the past and here I was, sitting next to living history. Someone needed to record his words before it was too late. I cursed my sieve of a brain. Why didn't God give me a photographic memory so I could hold onto Wilber and his stories?

The road narrowed. Ruts jerked and directed the tires as we careened down a steep hill before landing in the small, isolated Bull Falls parking area. Concerned for our safety, Wilber said he would try to make it down the lone access road that came in upriver. Then, pointing out what appeared to be an old logging road that ran beside the river, he waved good-bye.

As I turned to leave, my mother walked up to me. Nodding toward Stanley, in confidential tones, she whispered, "I'm so glad you have a *man* with you." For the second time in an hour, I was speechless. She loved me, and I loved her, but my mother did not have a clue of what The Walk was for me, nor did she understand that for the last 40 days and even today, her little girl had been the one in charge.

I had not encouraged Stanley to join The Walk because I needed a leader and savior. I was the one who planned the hike and looked out for the safety of the group, including the men. The solitary man on this day's walk was not welcomed as a protector. He was there as an equal—a strong, intelligent walker, with a good sense of humor, who, like us, wanted to test himself in new territory. As in previous days, Stanley would give his thoughtful opinion when asked, but would not intrude with know-it-all advice. He was there to follow my plan for the day, to help if needed, but primarily to enjoy himself and the scenery. Mom did not understand that I was honored that Stanley was not only interested enough to walk with me once, but, like so many others, he came back again and again.

I gave Mom a warm, but sad, hug. Her words indicated that she would never be able to give me the respect I desperately desired from her. That day I realized that part of the growing-up process is to accept the fact that the words we want to hear may never come from outside. We may just have to feel them inside and know it's okay if they are never spoken.

As we headed out, on our left, the New River was wider and slower as it flowed north. Red, gold, and green leaves still clung to branches high overhead. Soon the road petered out, and we struggled over fallen logs, clawed through brush and bushes, and stumbled on stones covered by a thick blanket of dry leaves. We had to cover over 20 cross-country miles. I remembered day one, and the bone-weary tiredness as we finished in the dark...and that was mostly on the flat. Today, if we were to finish as promised, we needed to walk a steady, firm pace, with five-minute rests each hour and only 30 minutes for lunch.

As expected, Phyllis brought up the rear. From her silent, pained expression it was evident she was hurting, but she kept us in sight. After a few hours, Stanley mused, "Phyllis is doing better today." "I told her that there would be no searches or stops." Stanley quipped, "Maybe someone should have told her that before."

About noon, as we came around a curve, we saw a small dirt road descend a hill on the right. Sitting there was our paunchy angel wearing a plaid flannel shirt, camouflage hat, rainbow-colored suspenders, and a beaming smile. Wilber had negotiated the old dirt road to check on us…this time with a red truck because his blue truck had conked out. Surprisingly, no one accepted his tempting offer to quit early and ride back, although, as the day wore on, Susan and Phyllis may have wished they had.

Unbeknownst to me, that morning Susan had "tripped over a leaf" and sprained her ankle. She confided only in Becky, who had firmly instructed, "Don't tell Eleanor. If you do, she won't let you continue. And you're going to finish if I have to carry you!" Later I learned that the Susan and Becky were also annoyed at Phyllis' insisting on walking this day. "Because we knew if something happened to her, you would go on and one of *us* would have to stay behind," they explained.

At lunch, Phyllis sat on a log, away from the group. Her trench coat sagged low on hunched shoulders as she pulled items from the ever-present paper bag. A mid-afternoon stop found her collapsed on the ground, coiled in a fetal position. Hand and hair covered her face. I could only imagine the lead weight of her army-type boots and the pain of her blisters. As I stood looking down at her, satisfaction, not sympathy, curled my lips into a slight smile. My only thoughts were: You deserve this. You didn't believe me.

After sunset, but before dark, we neared Glen Lyn. With the end within our grasp, everyone gained strength. For one more day, neither fires nor darkness had overtaken us. Bodies and spirits soared as we tried to sprint into the gas station and to the open arms of Wilber, Stanley's wife, and my parents.

After the joy of completing those 22 miles came the pain of separation. This was the last Stanley and Betty would walk. We'd never again see Wilber: that stranger who had greeted me with an outstretched hand, beaming smile, and a promise. We stood beside the vehicles, hung our heads, and pushed dirt around with the toes of our shoes. Small talk led to promises and reluctant good-bye hugs.

Phyllis stood apart, beside Wilber's truck. (I assumed he agreed to take her back to her car.) Then she walked over and extended her hand to me in a farewell handshake. I stared at it and her.

I did not see the joy of accomplishment in this woman who supported and cared for her mother. I was oblivious to the teacher who played a mean game of billiards and the attractive, young woman (who primped and chose hairbands to match her dress) inside her aging body. I had no understanding of the pride of an unprepared hiker who had walked faster and farther than ever before. The fact that Phyllis, like me, struggled to find her place in life and made a dream come true was lost on me. No, I saw none of her positives.

All I could see then were 24 tension-filled days. At that moment, the woman before me was just a strong-willed, selfish individual who would do what she wanted no matter how much it inconvenienced or hurt someone else. I remembered the icy stare in her eyes when we first met in Huntington. Heard her continually tell me one thing, and do another.

I listened to myself repeat again and again the rule of The Walk: ask only for a place to go to the bathroom and space to pitch a tent. Those are the *only* things we *ask* for. We will not impose on people who are already going out of their way for us. No trespassing, particularly when an area is posted with signs. Yet, over and over, I watched her walk into property marked with "No Trespassing" signs. I felt the knot in my stomach as people complained *to me* about her trespassing and her requests for someone to store her car or to give her a ride. "Do something about her. *You're* the leader!"

The train almost hit me when I stayed on the railroad tracks to keep her company and tried to make her feel welcomed. I don't think she ever understood that my decision to stay on the tracks had saved her life.

I had seen lodging denied us after people met her. And I remembered the almost daily frustration and delays from sending out "Where's Phyllis?" search parties.

I would always feel her hot breath in my face and the fear in my stomach as she towered over me and yelled, "I've done nothing wrong! I will not bow down to you!!!"

Her attitude seemed to be a haughty, "Who do you think you are, trying to tell me what I can and cannot do? Your thoughts, feelings, and plans are of no consequence. I'll do what I want. You can't make me do anything."

Though she accepted the food, lodging, and transportation I provided, Phyllis did not appear to care about me or the group. She would jeopardize everyone else for her personal agenda.

I saw none of her courage and strength. I only saw a manipulative wench whom I needed to run from. To protect myself and the group, I had to get away from her. This day we were lucky. The next we might not be.

Looking at the outstretched hand, all my soft emotion congealed into steel armor, and I was not a nice person. This woman must not know where we were going to spend the night or our route in Virginia. My eyes narrowed into icy slits. Jaw muscles tightened my teeth into an iron vise. Her outstretched hand hung in mid-air as I abruptly turned away from my antagonist and crossed the river to finish on the other side. And I never laid eyes on her again.

It took years before I understood that two people can be both right and wrong, and neither right nor wrong. Sometimes it doesn't matter. Sometimes we just have to take care of ourselves at the time and understand later.

Cold

"Mary lay shuddering with cold in a deep drift of leaves and waited for dawn...." (FTR, p. 326)

Wind gusts pulled and yanked at hair, hat, coat, and tent. Like little needles, bits of snow stung my exposed skin. Fingers numbed by the resulting wind chill and muscles tired from a day of walking tried repeatedly to work the tent from a rumpled lump into some form of shelter. Over the howling wind, a silent, internal voice shouted instructions.

Sit on the collapsed tent. Find an end. Push in a tent peg. Move around to each corner. Secure the tarp. Now, raise the center pole from inside. Success! Then the tent walls snapped loudly, and several more pegs pulled loose. I crawled out from under the tent and repeated the process again and again. With each fight with the elements, cold and frustration slowed my body movements. Anxiety and self-doubt mounted. What kind of fool sleeps outside when she could be in a warm motel with her hiking companions or in Mom's and Dad's trailer? My mind filled with the remembered words hurtled at me since childhood: Dumb. Silly. Dreamer. The descriptions: Stupid girl. No skills. No common sense. And the questions: What do *you* know? *Why* are you doing this? *Who* do you think *you* are? Kawap! Again the tent fell on my head.

Was some invisible hand trying to fling me off the mountain? Was some force saying I should not be there? Now I fought tears along with the wind and snow and tent. If it came down again, I'd just let it lie on top of me. A collapsed tent was more shelter than Mary had in 1755.

Back inside, as the tent jerked and snapped, I dug into my backpack for dry clothes. Whether or not they felt damp, the clothes I had worn all day were full of sweat. Sleeping in them could chill me into hypothermia—even death. Giant goosebumps popped up as I changed clothes and pulled on everything I had: Two pairs of polypropylene long johns, wool-blend undershirt, long-sleeved T-shirt, Patagonia fleece jacket, wool hat, and down booties. Then, on the hard ground, I curled up in my blanket and hoped for sleep to rescue me.

Perspective returned as I remembered that, at this point in her struggle, Mary's dress was in shreds, and she had lost the blanket she carried away from the Shawnee camp. On this night 232 years ago, necessity had forced Mary to lie naked on the ground. I fought with the wind and the cold by choice. So, *why* was I crying?

I had walked a long way, over 500 miles. The fun parts were learning to treat all strangers as extended family, that my body would do more than I thought, that my personal influence was less than I would like, and that when life doesn't go as planned, there just may be a stranger waiting to make it better than ever. I could read maps, communicate with people of all social levels, feel the pride of local historians, garner the interest of the news media and find food, lodging, friends, and support in unlikely places. (For instance, just hours earlier, Ray Neeley had arranged for a pitch-in supper at the historic Johnston House and permission for me to set up a tent on the grounds.) The best part of the experience was discovering that there were people who liked me and my ideas, and that I could deal with and surmount the daily problems of twisted ankles, blisters, thirst, and broken bones. It took someone else to point out that I had also exercised leadership and managed the psychological ups and downs of an extended-mileage trip with companions of assorted temperament, all who started as strangers. The tough parts were fighting trucks for space on the road, barely escaping being hit by a train, searching for charisma to deal with reporters, and all the while trying to hide the personality conflict I had with someone I never understood.

By a long shot, mine was not the accomplishment of Mary Draper Ingles. However, it was no small feat. If all went well, in a day and a half it would be over. So, why was I curled into a ball sobbing instead of celebrating?

Icy air seeped through the layers of cloth. Shivers of cold and tears held off sleep.

All I could think of was Mary's lonely struggle for survival. What had kept her alive on such a night? What drove and pulled her along the river? Was it a mother's yearning for the children pulled from her breast and left behind? Or was it the remembered warmth of her husband's love?

Will Ingles had believed in his wife and had never given up searching. Unbeknownst to Mary, he had been out hunting for her that very night so long ago. Although Mary didn't know it at the time, if she could stay alive for another 36 hours, she would accomplish what rational minds at the time said was impossible. She would have walked all the way home, and be welcomed with open arms and undying love.

As sleep overcame the cold and wind and tears, I wondered, "If I stay alive for thirty-six hours, will open arms and love be there for me? Will open arms and love *ever* be there for me?"

Day 42
November 6, 1987
Pearisburg to Pembroke, Virginia

Friends and Neighbors

"Her soul, benumbed for so long that she had nearly forgotten what it was to experience an emotion, became a turmoil of memories, joys, regrets, fears, a bittersweet flood of gratitude and despair." (FTR, p. 346)

Morning dawned. Breathtaking and frightening clouds reflected brilliant orange colors across the sky. Smoke particles from fires burning the forest we had walked through just days before floated above in artistic patterns, hung heavy in the air, and irritated eyes and throats. Like an animal checking for danger, I scanned the mountains north and west. No thin red fireline was visible. Would the wind pick up? Would the fires catch us? Could we make it through the last full day?

Tension churned feelings of fight or flight. Concern for our safety and anxiety that the end of the trail was near hung like a coat of heavy armor. What I dreamed of and trained, planned, and worked for was within reach—and now I was dreading it.

With luck, in 24 hours it would all be over, and I would go back home. The daily dose of challenge, excitement, acceptance, laughter, and support would stop. I didn't want this experience, that had been wonderful for me and almost everyone who touched it, to end. Susan Wood said she now understood the camaraderie soldiers in battle feel for their buddies. We each had grown strong and changed in unexpected ways. As I struggled with my emotions, silent voices in my head were pleading, "Let me hold on to these good people and feelings. Please.

Please, don't take them away!" Breaking camp and preparing for the day took my mind away from sentimentality.

The last full day we would have two unseasoned walkers. Ene Purre, who had walked one day through Charleston, had arrived the night before. To celebrate their twenty-fifth wedding anniversary, she had asked her husband to take off work so she could walk two days with the Mary Ingles Walkers. In addition, Jo Ann Oakes would attempt her first all-day hike. If JoAnn started, she'd have to keep up, for there were few crossroads for an easy rescue. However, this day's hike would be a relatively short and easy. JoAnn and Ene should be able to make it; certainly they were stronger than Mary had been at this point.

Added pressure came in the form of phone calls with Mary Lewis Jeffries (a Draper/Ingles descendant) and Grace Edwards (professor of English at Radford University), who were making plans to welcome us in Eggleston and Radford. It's hard to be melancholy when thinking of others.

On this forty-second day of her trek, Mary was weak, starving, and nearly naked. Will was searching for her, not realizing she was so near. In 1987, to ward off icy winds, Debbie, Susan, Becky, JoAnn, and Ene pulled hats, coats, and gloves out of pockets and backpacks and onto their bodies. As we walked, a smoky haze hung thick in the air. But it didn't obscure the soothing effect of watching sheep grazing lazily on hillsides, sniffing the last flower to escape the frost, or marveling at the ever-running river eating away at the fingers of rock jutting into its path. We even poked around in a small cave, hoping to find hidden treasure.

We laughed at worn-out JoAnn sitting spraddle-legged on the ground, resting her blistered feet and recouping energy. She may have been slow, but she was a good sport. She laughed at herself. Then, we'd gape in open-mouthed admiration at Becky's ability to find money. This day, she spied a quarter lodged among the gray stones beside the railroad tracks.

On a grassy bank sandwiched between the New River below on our right, and the railroad tracks above our heads on our left, we stopped for lunch. In the river, like a brown and green carpet, a low island seemed to float out from us. To lessen the bittersweet taste of our last lunch together, we had a pitch-in.

Laying out my yellow rain jacket as a tablecloth, we piled red and yellow apples, a Three Musketeers bar, an orange, nuts, crackers, sardines, cheese, cookies, and water. A "Stone Soup" feast without the stone. We were the picture of relaxed, laid-back hobos as we reminisced about the past 42 days: How we joined the adventure, our training or lack thereof, pain, blisters, historic areas, colorful personalities, breathtaking scenery, hikers who of necessity left but were with us in spirit, and the times of anxiety and danger. We had developed a river of friends that sparkled like a priceless, jeweled necklace. Amid the conversation and laughter, I looked up.

A severe-looking man, carrying something in his hand, was walking down the railroad track toward us. Was it a railroad authority coming to fine or arrest us for being on their property? (We had walked past railroad "No Trespassing" signs for 42 days.) Had they finally caught us? Or was it an angry local bent on destroying intruders who dared walk across his land? (The memory of the irate, screaming couple back in West Virginia was not one to forget.) My blood ran cold.

No longer warm and idyllic, our picnic spot suddenly felt vulnerable. We were unarmed females in an isolated area. No one would hear our screams. The only defenses I had were a container of Mace, my hatchet, and 95 pounds of courage. It seemed the best first defense would be to look and act strong and unafraid. (At times like this, I wished someone else were "leader of the pack.") With a firm stride to look strong, I climbed the steep embankment up to the tracks and strode toward the stranger.

As we drew closer, the confrontation I feared came in the form of a gentle scolding: "Eleanor, I'm going to stop having coffee with you. You're getting harder and harder to find!" Dumbfounded, I blinked in delayed recognition. Tom Arnold? My Indiana neighbor and soul mate.

When I first began training and couldn't finish 10 miles, Tom picked me up beside the road and drove me home. With his wife, Beverly, he had found us beside the road in Kentucky, West Virginia, and now Virginia. Before I started The Walk, Tom seemed to understand my need to make the trek even more than I did. This kind and gentle electrician had found us once more in the middle of nowhere!

The ultimate delivery man, Tom had carried in coffee, cookies and 7-Up, and a tiny teddy bear for Debbie. What had been a lunch of memories tinged with the sadness of closure was now joyous with jokes and laughter.

After eating until we were stuffed came the climb up to the railroad tracks. Sliding down was *much* easier than climbing up. Pushing from behind and pulling in front, we took turns slipping on stones that rolled under our feet. The whole effort looked like a cartoon of a bunch of people trying to move donkeys off dead center. Butt heavy, we found that our full bellies and laughter only made matters worse.

Once everyone was up, with batteries recharged and Tom's enthusiasm to inspire, too soon we were in Pembroke. Mom and Dad, Tom's wife, Ene's husband, and Paul Long, a reporter from the *Kentucky Post*, waited with smiles and hugs.

Tonight, our last night, we would sleep in the Holy Family Hospice. On Doug Wood's recommendation of weeks ago, we had permission to spend the night. Maintained by the Catholic Church, with a wood stove, table, books and *shower*, it was one of the Cadillac shelters for Appalachian Trail hikers. We spent the night with old and new friends and rubbed elbows with *real* long-distance hikers.

There *were* new people to meet, places to see, and dreams to dream. It *wasn't* over. There was no end to the adventure.

Day 43
Saturday, November 7, 1987
Pembroke to Eggleston, Virginia

Endings

"She was too weak and shaky to walk." (FTR, p. 357)

After a restless night near the Appalachian Trail, a brilliant orange sun rose on a cloud-rippled sky, then quickly disappeared into the smoky haze. We didn't see the red fireline of flames crawling across the mountains. They were obscured by smoke. If Mary had had such a drought year, there would have been fewer tributaries for her to detour around, which would have increased her chances. Almost everyone has a theory of why she survived. That's one of mine.

In the Holy Family Hospice shelter, Debbie, Susan, Becky, and I huddled near the wood stove and tried to get warm. We discussed Mary and Will Ingles: How much food did she find? Were the tributaries as big a problem as described in *Follow the River*? Did Mary and Will stay together because of love, or necessity? We discussed everything except what was happening to *us*.

A unique experience was drawing to a close. What we struggled and sweated and searched for was within our grasp, yet there seemed to be a collective reluctance to reach out for it. What should have been a day of joy was opening with long faces and melancholy voices. Oh, we all tried to be perky, but the spark was missing.

For the last 43 days, we had struggled through extraordinary terrain, trials, and emotions. The sands of time were pouring unique experiences and relationships through my fingers, and I was a puny ant trying to stop the Sahara from shifting. This day—this last day—seemed anticlimactic. Where Mary eagerly fought for the final step, I wanted to skip the whole thing.

I needed to say something to these women had who stuck with me through thick and thin, but words were inadequate. I looked at this support team with pride, appreciation, and love. Becky, a Vietnam veteran, and Susan, a bronze sculptor, had each walked 20 days with me. Debbie and I had struggled together for all 43. Collectively, we survived blisters, broken bones, rain, snow, trains, hassles at work and home, and personality conflicts. This forty-third day was our last together. How could I possibly say good-bye and thank the exceptional people who had given me so much for my little project? "That's all, folks!" would not do.

Finally, with a deep breath and leaking eyes, halting words stumbled from a throat filled with lumps. We were changed women. We had discovered strength we did not know we possessed and had come further than anyone thought possible. Accomplishment was found in the struggle, not the conclusion. Success is sometimes painful because a conclusion is inevitable.

I wanted to hold each woman. I wanted to let their collective warmth and humor and strength melt into my body and soul, because after this day, I would have to go it alone. After this day, I would have only memories.

The real world came into focus with JoAnn and Ene's arrival. They had stayed at a motel. Soon Mom and Dad arrived to pick up gear, and the inevitable reporter appeared moments later. A quick, but heartfelt, "Thanks, I'll always remember you" was all I could manage. Then we headed out to pick up the river beside railroad tracks that ran out of Pembroke.

From the start that day, it seemed that everyone was holding back and walking slow. I felt as if I were trying to pull all of us through sucking mud. Everyone thought up reasons to stop—to delay the inevitable. Changing clothes, carving names in walking sticks, adjusting shoes, even flossing teeth! No excuse was too small. Finally, I decided that holding off the conclusion was worse than facing it. In words I'm not sure anyone heard, I said, "Let's get this over with." Then, clutching my walking stick and clenching my teeth, I strode out in a firm and steady pace.

With the building of the railroad, the 300-foot, vertical, stone cliffs that Mary climbed on her last day were blasted away long ago. However,

I kept looking for the wrinkled cliffs to jut out into the river. When I had talked to Jim Thom on the phone, he said, "Just pick one and climb." While John, my rock-climbing son, had said, "You've come this far. Don't do a vertical climb and do something to hurt yourself now." But I kept looking. Rain, Ene's husband, appeared on top of a hill at our left and shouted, "Here it is!" and tried to wave us up. Just walk up a little incline? That seemed ludicrous. Surely there were rocks that could be scaled.

Around a bend, we began seeing people. People smiling. People with cameras. My daughters, parents, friends, and strangers—lots of strangers. And everyone was smiling. A child I had never seen before walked up and put her hand in mine. Later, I learned she was 11-year-old Carrie Ingles, a descendant of Mary and Will. Purely by accident, I began and ended the walk with a Draper-Ingles family member at my side.

We passed security fencing that kept rocks from falling onto the railroad tracks. More familiar people and strangers, huddled in groups, appeared. A reporter wearing an NBC cap stood in front of me. Love and support flowed wide as the river, but one face was missing: Sue Kennedy, Mary and Will's descendant who had walked out of Big Bone Lick with me. The last thing she had said was, "If you make it all the way, I'll be there with the champagne!" As I stalled amid the joy and confusion, I heard several voices ask, "Aren't you going to climb the rocks?"

Without knowing it, I had passed *the* rocks. The ones beside me looked anemic. The toughest rocks were behind the railroad fencing. What a dilemma! I had planned to climb, had said out loud that I would. Now this looked silly—after the fact. We had walked right past them!

An inner voice was saying, "This entire walk was about *feeling* Mary and Will's experience, not *recreating* it. Don't worry about *the* rocks. Climb *something*." I kept looking around. Still no Sue. And no decent, handy rocks.

I felt pressure to try some type of climb. Without it, The Walk would not be complete. It was fish or cut bait time. Maybe Sue had lost interest or just couldn't make it. Perhaps I might try a symbolic climb up the rocky incline at the end of the fence?   On hands and knees, I clutched at dry flaking rocks and pulled up and over onto a steeply wooded incline that rose above my head. For only the second time in the last 43 days, I was alone. About halfway up, from far below, I heard a faraway voice calling. "Eleanor! Eleanor! It's me! Sue! I'm here!"

Stopping in place, I turned and looked down. On the edge of the river's giant horseshoe curve stood a small figure: Sue Kennedy, Mary and Will Ingles' great-great-great-great-granddaughter. I stood up, waved and yelled at the top of my voice, *"I made it, Sue! I made it all the way!"* Then turning back to the hill, I began hands-and-knees crawling up the steep slope. The people on the railroad tracks and reporters struggling up below me dropped away physically and mentally. It was just me and the hill.

Climb! Climb up! Work for the top! Fingers clawed at loose soil that slipped from under me, sliding us both backwards. Had to work. Had to hurry. Had to make it up. Pulling, clawing, breathing hard. Breathing faster—in and out. Lungs hurting. Arms aching. Fingers stinging. Look up. A steeper incline. A ledge. Got to get over. Pull. Slip. Claw. Breathe. Sand slips. Rocks roll. Pull. Heave. Up. Up and over—and finally collapse on the ground.

Over the ledge, out in front of me, the green hill gently fell away. Away into a cornfield? Adam Harmon's cornfield? The field Mary would have seen? Suddenly I was aware of sounds. Of sobs. My own uncontrollable, quaking sobs—it was over. All over, for Mary and for me.

What so many thought or said I could not do, I did. I did it! I really did it! Suddenly, all I wanted was to touch and hold my children. Then, slowly rising on weak, rubbery legs, tingling all over and holding onto trees for support, I gingerly made my way down the hill.

Back beside the railroad tracks, I reached for Janette and Lisa as they handed me a delicate bouquet of pink wildflowers and soft, plumy grasses—the most beautiful bouquet I've ever received. As grateful as I was for their thoughtfulness, all I wanted was to wrap them in my arms and feel their warm bodies. Holding tightly to my babies, all I could say was, "I did it. I did it."

Mirroring Mary's experience, my walk ended with two women completing the entire route from Big Bone Lick to Adam Harmon's farm. An old woman (me) and a young woman who had left her children behind (Debbie). Looking around, I saw smiling, proud faces. Hugs and friends came from far and near: Tom and Beverly Arnold from Indiana; my parents from Florida; George and Joandel Jackson, and Doug and Joyce Cooper from West Virginia; Marilyn Hopper from Kentucky; Sue, Chris, Lynn, and Ann Kennedy from Georgia; Pat Ingles and granddaughter Carrie from Ohio. When I saw Stanley, who had walked several days in West Virginia and whom I thought I'd never see again,

I was so surprised and overwhelmed that I ran into his welcoming, supportive, and congratulatory arms.

Of course there were locals, like Virginia Whittaker, taking pictures. I wanted to shake everyone's hand. To thank them all for coming, sharing and supporting us. For smiling on Mary's memory and our dream-come-true. For welcoming me with open arms and love.

Enthusiastically shaking hands around the crowd, I came to a man standing off to one side. Wearing rumpled work clothes, he appeared to be local. With cool eyes, firm jaw, and the feel of his almost reluctant handshake, I felt—more than heard—his contempt. "You're not Mary Ingles. You didn't struggle. You didn't climb the *real* rocks. *You didn't do anything!*"

I wanted to scream at him. Nothing? You think I did *nothing*? You may be a good ol' boy, but you are also a self-righteous prick! I am sick and tired of people who think they are superior and look down on me because I am a small woman, without a prestigious job and some framed piece of paper on the wall. You can think whatever you want buddy, but I *know* Eleanor Mary Lahr just did something special, because no one's ever done it before. She may be an average, ordinary woman, but she is also strong and honest and hardworking, and she deserves respect. And she doesn't need your or anyone else's approval. She also knows that there are good and supportive and understanding and caring men out there. You are just not one of them. But I didn't scream at him.

Without a word I moved on to the next person. He was right, yet oh, so wrong. I had not walked Mary's exact route, suffered as she did, nor climbed the rocks she climbed. (No one could. They no longer existed.) Blinded by expectations and limited knowledge, he would never understand. Too bad. For once upon a time, he touched a hand that had reached back in history and spent 42½ days with a multitude of angels.

Homecomings
(The Afterward)

Saturday, November 7, 1987
Eggleston and Radford, Virginia

Fortunately for me, there were many who thought I did do something special. After coming off the climb, most of the crowd moved to Payne's Store in Eggleston, where Erma McPeak had a cookie, sandwich, and lemonade reception. With shaking hands I sat atop one of the display cases and put the last knot in my belt. The Walk was over, but I had a special "thank you" to deliver.

With Dr. Grace Edwards driving, we led a long caravan to the site of *The Long Way Home,* an outdoor drama near Radford, where Mary and Will last lived and ran Ingles Ferry, property that is still in the family. Beside the foundation of Mary's cabin, one of her closest living descendants, Mary Lewis Jeffries, a smartly dressed, handsome, gray-haired woman with a strong jaw, greeted me with open arms, a huge smile, and a hug.

Mary Lewis led the group as we strolled down to a small family cemetery near the river. Using the bouquets Joandel had brought for us, Debbie and I laid flowers at an unmarked grave. Somewhere among the dirt and stones lay Mary and Will. The Walk was to honor Mary and Will; I wanted it to end with a "thank you" to them. However, with the crowd and cameras, our gesture seemed anticlimactic, even phony. It was not what I had envisioned. But then, none of this was what I had envisioned.

Immediately, we began our good-byes as Susan, Becky, and Ene headed west. They would miss the afternoon reception at Radford University, Mary Lewis' evening dinner at the Valley Pike Inn (where Mary Lewis theorized that Will spent the night when he returned from trying to find Mary), and the Ingleside reception the following day.

It all had a bittersweet feel. While I had my girls and parents and close friends around to be happy for me, not one of Debbie's family came to congratulate her. Janette and Lisa took Debbie back to the Best Western, and Mary Lewis took me up to the house that John Ingles, Mary's youngest son, had built for her. In the original section of the house, she literally tucked me into bed and kissed me goodnight. Mary, who preferred her small cabin, never slept in Ingleside. But she certainly had walked in its rooms.

Sunday, November 8, 1987
Radford and Blacksburg, Virginia

Before Mary Lewis' reception, Janette, Lisa, and I drove around Radford and stood before a stone monument at Ingles cemetery on Pendleton Street, made with stones from the chimney of Mary and Will's cabin. Then we stumbled onto a small sign that marked the Draper's Meadow massacre, now the site of Virginia Tech in Blacksburg. Most people walk by and pay no attention.

Back at Ingleside, we found it filled with family and friends spilling out onto the wraparound porch. A grand open house with smooth, southern hospitality. After several hours, people drifted away one by one. I said good-bye to Mom and Dad, Janette and Lisa, and Tom and Bev (who drove Debbie back to Indiana). Mary Lewis and I cleaned up party debris; then, beside a glowing fireplace we kicked off our shoes and soaked up in the warmth. It felt like home.

I called my son Jerry, who had a Navy assignment at the University of Idaho. Mary Lewis called her son, Bird Colonel Lewis I. Jeffries, who said his former executive officer was now at the University of Idaho. He would call him and tell him about Jerry. When I called Jerry back, he was amused at his mother's connections.

Monday, November 9, 1987
Radford, Virginia

The Walk was over, but not the interviews. Dr. Edwards organized a video interview at Radford University. Afterwards, Jeff Franklin, who hadn't come to Mary Lewis' open house "because there were so many people," gave me a historical tour of the Ingles property, the remains of the old ferry, and the original road to Tennessee. He also showed me another New River dam. It seemed as though the river was struggling at all these chains.

Back at Ingleside, I had several phone calls to return. John Taylor, continuing to make connections for me, said that our Connecticut firefighting friend Dick Sylvia was trying to reach me. Then another telephone interview with a Huntington, West Virginia, paper before I changed clothes for dinner with Mary Lewis' next-door neighbors, Bob and Monti Chapman. Back "home," tired from tension rather than effort, I fell into a deep sleep.

Tuesday, November 10, 1987
Radford, Virginia, and Charleston and Huntington, West Virginia

Finally rain. A steady soaking rain. Finally. I would not have to drive back through fire and smoke. I'm not foolish enough to think that the creator held back rain so I could have a good walk and homecoming. But it did work out that way. The rain mirrored my tears as I waved good-bye to Mary Lewis and Ingleside and drove away.

In Charleston, I stopped to have lunch with John Taylor. Rain had turned to snow. We drove up the mountain to Susan's Mountain Wool Trading Company, but the shop was closed. A call found Susan at home in Leon. With an inch and a half of snow on the ground, and many accidents, she had decided not to come in and open the shop.

Late in the day, with snow falling harder, I checked in at the Huntington, West Virginia, Days Inn instead of driving on to Bloomington. I called Joandel. No answer. Maybe someone was saying it was time for me to leave the river behind and head home.

Wednesday, November 11, 1987
Bloomington, Indiana

"Mister Harmon startled Mary out of her torpor with a sudden loud whoop." (FTR, p. 371)

Snow continued, making the driving slow. Slow was okay, since going home was something I did not look forward to. I was forcing myself toward home, and that was not a good feeling. Tears began to ooze out of my eyes as I drove slowly into Bloomington and my driveway. Nothing seemed to have changed. It looked the same. No one was home. It was cold and gray, outside and in. Then, as I stood in the kitchen, alone, trying to orient myself to my real world, the phone rang.

An unfamiliar, male voice asked, "Is this Eleanor?"

"Yes."

"Two hundred and thirty-two years ago, I picked you up and put you up."

It was Jim Connell, a descendant of Adam Harmon, the man who found Mary in his cornfield, when her adventure ended and a new life began.

Welcome home, Eleanor.

Postscript

The walkers and the angels, with the challenges of the New River
Gorge behind us, moved on to new dreams and accomplishments.

There never was supposed to be a book; however, from Day One
people began asking if I would write a book. My response was always

the same. "No. That is not the purpose of this walk; besides, I am not a writer."

I didn't believe I could write well and laughed at the thought of myself as an author. But no one else could write the story for me, so I began writing by telling myself I was only putting memories down on paper. I wasn't writing a book; I was attempting to sort out my feelings and actions and, thereby, find a purpose for the experience. Most authors sweat over their work—I cried through each and every day I relived and through each and every page I wrote. Understanding never came. Relief did.

After The Walk, many of my new friends and I were called upon to go places we never dreamed of going to. Some colored their lives with the blue and greens of lake and forest adventures; some used red for exciting cities and projects; while others picked the golden hues of serene sunsets. Too many of us were forced to pick the black of death and divorce.

Then we fought against feelings of despair and failure. We struggled with life's tragedies and pleaded for God to give us strength and to take away the hurting. Eventually, we moved through our private pain to different lives—peaceful lives, but perhaps ones still colored by imperfect answers. I had tried my entire life "to do it right": to do what my friends and family and community seemed to expect of me. I struggled to interpret silences in my family and prayed to God for help, but God was also silent. It seemed as if I was climbing the mountain of life by myself. That is why The Walk was ultimately so important to me. Each day I realized I was not walking alone after all.

The primary impetus for this book came from the deaths of so many of those who made The Walk so special. Each loss brought me crushing sorrow; however, before our last good-bye, many told me how much their participation in retracing Mary's escape had helped them through life's difficulties. With each friend's death, I felt the pressure to write weighing heavier upon me—I needed to write my story so that the extraordinary people who participated would be remembered.

When I returned home in 1987, I felt no different, physically or mentally, than when I started. It would be years before I realized the full impact of the experience. It would take five years for the self-confidence and courage that I gained to allow this over-50 female to leave her marriage, with a temporary job as her only income. Within a few months, Indiana University hired me in a professional position.

Building on the success of the walk, losing some of the fear (and going on in spite of it), in the succeeding years I signed up for an Outward Bound Wilderness Adventure for those over 50, trekked the Himalayas to Gokyo, Nepal (so I could see Everest with my own eyes), canoed in the Boundary Waters, backpacked and had close encounters with moose on Isle Royale, camped out alone in an old fire tower high above the trees and mountains in northwest Montana, and went horseback riding across the steppes of Mongolia. On the home front, I added central air conditioning, remodeled the kitchen and added a screened-in porch— all are dreams I had before 1987, but had thought were unattainable. I retired in early 2008 and promptly prepared for a backpacking trip in the High Uintas of Utah.

Others who touched my adventure also made significant changes in their lives. To mention a few: Debbie reached her dream of being an emergency medical technician. George and Joandel Jackson traded their home by the river for rest and relaxation in Florida. Susan Wood moved her Mountain Wool Trading business to downtown Charleston, West Virginia. On November 23, 1987 Phyllis sent me a kind note thanking me for the fine trip; I heard that she retired and moved to Alaska. Eleanor Henson now spends winters in Florida golfing with her husband. Becky Straight retired from nursing and, when not tending her garden, scares mountain lions and bears away from her mountain home. Sara Cotto-Thorner, after an untimely widowhood, remarried and purchased the Safety Caution Equipment Company, which makes safety signs and sells safety equipment. Doug and Joyce Cooper opened a bed and breakfast near Valley Head, West Virginia. Sue Kennedy began her own real estate appraisal business. Patty Hons moved from classroom teaching into elementary school counseling and then wrote a children's book, *Mary Draper Ingles, a True Story about Courage and Family*. Mary Lewis Jeffries' son, Lewis Ingles (Buddy) Jeffries, now manages the Draper/Ingles property as a productive cattle farm and, with his son John participates in Radford Heritage Days and occasionally opens the original Ingles home site for living history interpretation.

Sometimes it takes years and years to notice that life experiences have affected us. If I learned anything from 43 days along the river, it is that I am stronger, both physically and emotionally, than I thought and that fear doesn't have to immobilize me; it can just as easily be my protective caution. Working through fear can bring incredible, though sometimes painful, growth; however, with a new friend or helpful stranger, confronting one's fears can also turn into a glorious adventure.

As I end this book adventure, I feel both accomplishment and relief. Mark Twain said it best in *Adventures of Huckleberry Finn*, "If I'd a knowed what a trouble it was to make a book I wouldn't a tackled it and ain't agoing to no more."

The Begats

In the beginning, I tried repeatedly and unsuccessfully to find Draper/Ingles descendants. Ultimately, Mary and Will's offspring found me. Each was intelligent, handsome, kind, and generous. To this day, the ones I met remain strong and proud. Each, carrying genes of their long-gone grandparents, are truly outstanding individuals. With the charisma that they all display, it is understandable why Thomas returned to the white world only when he had seen and talked with his father. In meeting their descendants, who all contributed to the success and uniqueness of the 1987 retracing, I came as close to Mary and Will as anyone could.

Mary Draper and William Ingles begat Thomas, George, Mary, Susan, Rhoda, and John, who begat the following descendants.

Esther I. Saunders, descended from Thomas, was the first family member that I was fortunate to meet. She graciously welcomed me into her Ohio home and reverently handed me an original copy of *Trans-Allegheny Pioneers*, written by Mary and Will's grandson, John P. Hale. Esther begat Sue Saunders Kennedy, Patty Saunders Hons, and James Saunders.

Sue Saunders Kennedy, who lives in Georgia, was the family member who happened to see a Kentucky road sign and reacted with, "Big Bone Lick. I've never been to Big Bone Lick. Let's stop at Big Bone Lick." A quick detour led her to see the WSWP television station's *Mary Ingles: Indian Captive* video at the visitors center, where she learned of my idea to retrace Mary's route. And she couldn't resist signing the guest book as "Sue Kennedy, sixth great-granddaughter of Mary Draper Ingles." Then, spreading the word among her kith and kin, Sue dragged her sister Patty and young daughter Lynn away from family plans to see me start walking at Big Bone Lick. Sue and Patty had a Mary Ingles sweatshirt made to identify me on The Walk. Sue's initial phone call and her and her sister's approval became the family blessing I desperately desired. Walking beside me as we headed out of Big Bone Lick, Sue and her family made real my wish to have Mary's family participate in the project.

Patty Saunders Hons, an elementary school teacher in Ohio, allowed herself to be caught up in her sister's enthusiasm. As gracious and lovely as her mother and sister, Patty came to Big Bone Lick when I began, and, after I completed The Walk, she invited me to talk at an Enrichment Day program where I spent all day talking to several hundred children. She was one of the models for the statue of Mary at the Boone County, Kentucky, library.

James Saunders attended a dinner after a Walk reunion near Big Bone Lick, Kentucky, in 1988.

Sharon Ferguson, descendant from John, provided lodging at the Radisson Hotel in Huntington, West Virginia. Kind and caring, she also spent a delightful breakfast with us.

Patricia Carle, a descendant from Virginia, waited for me at the Radisson when I arrived in Huntington. Imagine, one of Mary's family going to such an effort to meet me. I was touched. Unfortunately, I mislaid her address and lost contact.

Al Castanoli, a descendant from West Virginia, dug up a copy of his family tree and invited Debbie and me to the Reverse Raffle in Huntington. Before I had climbed into Al's car, I had Debbie take our picture—just in case something happened to me. I was trusting of strangers, up to a point.

Carrie Ingles, granddaughter of Pat Ingles, whose husband was a descendant of Thomas, was 11 years old when, below the Eggleston, Virginia, cliffs, she put her hand in mine and walked beside me to the end of Mary's walk and mine.

Mary Lewis Jeffries, descendant of John Ingles, called after her husband died to offer me "...a bed and hot water for your feet, when you finish." Beside the ruins of Mary's cabin, she greeted me with the smile and open arms of southern hospitality. Mary Lewis was all the more appealing because of her evident internal strength, intelligence, and pride of her pioneer heritage. For 18 years, she played Mary's mother, Elenor Draper, in *The Long Way Home,* an outdoor drama about Mary's experience. It was produced on Mary and Will's land in Radford, Virginia. Mary Lewis begat Louis Ingles Jeffries.

Louis Ingles (Buddy) Jeffries continues the long line of descendants who defend country and family. After retiring from the army, he moved to and farms Ingleside, the Virginia land on which Mary and Will lived, died, and are buried. He holds the copyright to Earl Hobson Smith's *The Long Way Home* from which the outdoor drama was based. He is the male descendant with whom I have had the most contact. To me, he displays a strength, sensitivity and devotion that I imagine in Will Ingles.

Roberta Ingles Steele, descendant of John, who, before The Walk was defensively offended by my letter and proposal, was genuinely kind and helpful after I finished. She continues the legacy of keeping the land in the family by residing at LaRiviere, and she owns the Ingles Ferry Tavern and farm with her niece and nephew. She holds the copyrights to *Escape from Indian Captivity,* as told by John Ingles Sr., and *Trans-Allegheny Pioneers,* by John P. Hale.

Andrew Lewis Ingles, Roberta's brother, came to Ingleside the day after I finished the walk. His wife Frances poured coffee at the reception. I wish I had had more time to get to know them.

Sylvia Franklin, a descendant of John, lives in Florida. A couple years after I finished The Walk, she visited me in Indiana. Then, in 1990, to touch back to her famous ancestors, Sylvia and her husband walked along the New River from Charleston, West Virginia, to Eggleston, Virginia.

Ingles Maddox, a descendant of Rhoda, read an article about my project in *Walking* magazine and called me from her Louisiana home. We met at a family/Walk reunion at Ingleside and, true to the Draper/Ingles hospitality, a couple of years later, Ingles treated me to a three-day tour of New Orleans and the bayou. There is nothing better than experiencing a city and people and history through the eyes and heart of one who loves them.

The descendants of Adam Harmon, the man who found Mary in his cornfield, are less visible. I met only two: Mrs. Bentley Hite, the only Harmon descendant at Mary Lewis' reception, and Jim Connell, who telephoned me minutes after I returned home. Several years after I completed The Walk, to recapture part of his personal history, Jim purchased property that was part of Adam Harmon's farm. He planted a cornfield, and in the fall has had reenactments of Mary's return. I had

E. M. Lahr

the pleasure of being there one year to see Jenny Jeffries, Mary and Will Ingles' great-great-great-great-great granddaughter, crawl barefooted and scratched into the field one cold November day. For those who are familiar with the story, it is a goosebumpy experience.

A Partial List of Angels

It's risky to try to list those who are significant, because inevitably someone vital is left out. But I have to try. If your name isn't on the list, remember that you were important too; it's just that I have a bad memory.

Ackerson, Pat: Food and warm fuzzies, Kentucky.

Adkins, Leigh: Draper descendant.

Alexander, Miss Evelyn: Encouragement in Virginia.

Arnold, Beverly and Tom: Walked, food, my Indiana friends.

Arrasmith, John: Native American, from Kentucky.

Ash, Beth: Encouragement, Jenny Wiley descendant.

Babbitt, Rosie: Toilet privileges in Mount Carbon, West Virginia.

Barlow, Linda and Randy: My Kentucky friends, formerly from Bloomington.

Bates, Robert (Bobby) Allen: Walked, Mary Ingles Trail Club.

Bell, Ann: Encouragement, National Park Service.

Blevins, Ruth: Lodging, Johnston House, Pearisburg, Virginia.

Blythe, Jim: Amateur radio communications in Kentucky.

Bogucki, Ray: Lodging in Augusta, Kentucky.

Breeze, Joseph: Kentucky State Police.

Brown, Mary and Enos: Food and sag wagon, my parents, Florida.

Bruce, Chester: Ego-builder near South Shore, Kentucky.

Brunner, Bob: Reporter, WSAZ-TV, Charleston, West Virginia.

Buck, Mary Neil and Richard: Encouragement in Virginia.

Byars, Nathan: Sag wagon, Montgomery, West Virginia, Fire Department.

Carle, Patricia: Descendant of Mary and Will Ingles, encouragement in Huntington, West Virginia.

Cartmell, Harriet: Mayor of Maysville, Kentucky.

Castanoli, Al: Descendant of Mary and Will Ingles, encouragement in Huntington, West Virginia.

Chapman, Monti and Bob: Encouragement in Virginia.

Childs, Mrs. H.: Encouragement at the Johnston House, Pearisburg, Virginia.

Clauson, Su: Reporter for *The Roanoke-Times.*

Clooney, Nick: Television personality from WKRC-TV Cincinnati, Ohio.

Connell, Jim: Descendant of Adam Harmon in Virginia.

Connell, Sister: Lodging, Vanceburg, Kentucky.

Cooper, Doug and Joyce: Food, lodging, walked in West Virginia.

Cotto-Thorner, Sara McCorkle: Sag wagon, walked in West Virginia.

Crossman, Kate: Eleanor's cousin from South Carolina, sag wagon in Kentucky.

Crukshanks, Steve: Sag wagon and lodging, Fayetteville, West Virginia.

Davila, Dottie: Food in Montgomery, West Virginia.

Davis, Zoni: Parking and outhouse privileges, Quincy, Kentucky.

Dillard, Patti: Walked in Kentucky.

Dragan, Jon, and Wildwater Unlimited: Food, lodging, sag wagon, Thurmond, West Virginia.

Duncan, Nina: Owner of the everlasting spring, near South Portsmouth, Kentucky.

Eads, Rick: Washed our clothes in Hinton, West Virginia.

Edwards, Dr. Grace: Radford, University, TV show *Mary Ingles: Indian Captive*.

Elkins, Brian: Walked, Mary Ingles Trail Club.

Epplen, Marsha and Gary: Walked, food and lodging, lives beside Licking River.

Falls, Deloris and Alfred: Walked, Mary Ingles Trail Club.

Farkus, Tom: Reporter for *Ledger-Independent*, Maysville, Kentucky.

Farley, Wilber: Sag wagon, directions, West Virginia.

Farmer, Miss Frances: Encouragement in Virginia.

Ferguson, Sharon: Draper/Ingles descendant from John, lodging in West Virginia.

Fleener, Marion: Fifth-grade teacher from Bloomington, Indiana.

Francis, Tom: Lodging, Fire Chief and Bank President, Peterstown, West Virginia.

Gardner, Mrs. Lewyn H: Encouragement in Virginia.

Gibson, Earl: Encouragement in West Virginia.

Gilbert, Pat: Food and lodging in West Virginia.

Gilreath, Jim: Reporter for *The Virginia-Leader*.

Graham, Scott: Appalachian hiker at Holy Family Hospice, Pearisburg, Virginia.

Gregg, Shelly: Encouragement from my Department of Natural Resources co-worker.

Haddox, Diana: Encouragement in West Virginia.

Handwork, Handy: Food at Pratt, West Virginia, Fire Department.

Hanson, Robert: Winfield, West Virginia, videotape.

Hardyman, Anne: Friend of Harriet Cartmell, Maysville, Kentucky.

Harshberger, Kathleen and Richard: Encouragement in Virginia.

Hartman, Brenda: Elementary school teacher, walked in Kentucky.

Hartung, Dave: Walked in West Virginia.

Hastings, Lori: Encouragement in West Virginia.

Henson, Eleanor: Food and lodging, walked from Charleston to Hinton, West Virginia.

Hensley, Marie: Drinks in Kentucky.

Henson, Jim: Food in Kentucky.

Hite, Mrs. Bentley: Adam Harmon's descendant, encouragement in Virginia.

Holland, Russell: Encouragement, Mayor of Point Pleasant, West Virginia.

Holroyd-Dolin, Elizabeth: Reporter, *The Herald-Dispatch*, Huntington, West Virginia.

Hons, Patty: Draper/Ingles descendant of Thomas, Ohio.

Hooper, Marilyn: Contact for lodging, Kentucky.

Horten, Harry: Encouragement at Point Pleasant Mansion House.

Hyde, Phyllis: From Michigan, participated from Huntington, West Virginia, to Glen Lyn, Virginia.

Incollingo, Larry: Reporter for *Bloomington Herald-Times*.

Ingles, Carrie: From Ohio, Draper/Ingles family, walked.

Ingles, Andrew (descendant of John) and wife Frances: Encouragement in Virginia.

Ivey, Virginia: Teacher, Pratt, West Virginia, Elementary School.

Jackson, Joandel and George: Food and lodging beside the Ohio River.

Jarvis, Litz: Encouragement in West Virginia.

Jeffries, Mary Lewis: Descendant of John, from Virginia.

Jones, Hilarie: Walked, Mary Ingles Trail Club.

Justice, Judy: Encouragement, Greenup, Kentucky.

Keeney, Erma: Food, East Bank, West Virginia.

Kelsch, Pauline and Bill: Food and lodging, Kentucky.

Kemp, Louise: Sag wagon and food in Kentucky, from Ohio.

Kennedy, Annie: Sue and Christopher's youngest daughter, Draper/ Ingles descendant.

Kennedy, Christopher: Sue Kennedy's husband, from Georgia.

Kennedy, Lynn: Walked, Sue and Christopher's oldest daughter, Draper/ Ingles descendant.

Kennedy, Sue: Walked, Draper/Ingles descendant of Thomas, from Georgia.

Klene, Debbie: From Indiana, walked Big Bone Lick, Kentucky to Eggleston, Virginia.

Knight, Clara: Food and lodging in West Virginia.

Kwaczala, Evelyn: Augusta, Kentucky, *The Times* reporter.

Lahr, Janette: Sag wagon, my #3 child.

Lahr, Jerry: Encouragement, my #2 child.

Lahr, John: Made map for this book, my #1 child.

Lahr, Lisa: Sag wagon, my #4 child.

Light, Barbara: Contacts, encouragement, Bloomington, Indiana.

Lindy, Bob: Manager, Big Bone Lick State Park.

Long, Paul: Reporter, *Kentucky Post.*

Looney, Chuck: Assistance with tents and cars at Pipestem.

Loyd, Karen: Food at Marmet Junior High School.

MacGee, Father Jim: Lodging at Holy Family Hospice, Pearisburg, Virginia.

Madden, Ralph: Ice cream cone, Lloyd, Kentucky.

Mahan, Bettie: Walked, Mary Ingles Trail Club.

McPeak, Erma: Pyne's Store reception, Eggleston, Virginia.

Merry, Gordon: Creems/Cabel Emergency Medical Service Director, West Virginia.

Mileski, Florence: Encouragement in West Virginia and Virginia.

Miller, Rusty: Chef, Pipestem State Park, West Virginia, food.

Mock, Donna: Contact in West Virginia.

Montgomery, Tom: Muzzleloader Association, encouragement.

Moore, Stanley: Walked, Mary Ingles Trail Club.

Morrison, Glenda: Bloomington friend with mayoral advice.

Myers, Joe: Reporter for *The Fayette Tribune.*

Neeley, Ray: Food and drinks in Virginia, friend of Wilber Farley.

Newton, Connie: Appalachian Studies, Hinton High School, West Virginia.

Nibert, Judy: Encouragement in West Virginia.

Norton, George: Encouragement in Kentucky.

Oakes, JoAnn: Walked in West Virginia and Virginia.

Pladies, Ann and Bill: Food and lodging, Kentucky.

Plumley, Amos and Nell: Thanksgiving dinner, Hinton, West Virginia.

Plumley, Jan: Fruitcake recipe.

Plumley, Melvin: Food, contacts, Rotary President, Hinton, West Virginia.

Price, Jim: Lodging at Coast to Coast Motel, Hinton, West Virginia.

Purre, Ene and Rain: Walked in Virginia.

Purshing, Ruth Ann: Contact in West Virginia.

Ransom, Rick: Food and lodging, walked in West Virginia.

Riegor, Wayne: Directions and permission, Army Corps of Engineers.

Rollins, Walter (Lefty): West Virginia House of Delegates, encouragement.

Sauer, Alice: Telephone privileges in Point Pleasant, West Virginia.

Saunders, Esther: Encouragement, descendant of Thomas Ingles.

Schweiser, Gertrude: Food and lodging, Augusta, Kentucky.

Shaw, Abrey: Encouragement in Virginia.

Shoue, Harry: Encouragement at Point Pleasant Mansion House.

Sourbeer, Wayne: WSWP-TV interview at Big Bone Lick, Kentucky, and Beckley, West Virginia.

Spelock, Maron: Encouragement in West Virginia.

Sprigg, Daisy: Food and lodging, former mayor of Concord, Kentucky.

Springston, Dave and Connie: Encouragement, Forest Hill, West Virginia.

Springston, Marsha: Encouragement, Wakerobin Gallery, Forest Hill, West Virginia.

Stallard, Chip: Coordinated sag wagons and safe lodging, and walked in West Virginia.

Stallard, Victor: Walker in West Virginia.

Steele, Roberta: Descendant of John Ingles.

Stivers, Carol: Walked lunch to Maysville, Kentucky, from Ohio.

Straight, Becky: Walked from Charleston, West Virginia, to Eggleston, Virginia.

Stuart, Muriel: Walked in West Virginia.

Stump, Stella: Inspiration, Mary Ingles Trail Club.

Styer, Cheryl: Food in Mentor, Kentucky.

Taylor, Fred: Sag wagon in West Virginia.

Taylor, John and Joyce: Food, lodging, encouragement, and firefighter colleague, West Virginia.

Thom, Dark Rain. Wife of James A. Thom, consulted on recipes.

Thom, James A.: Indiana author of *Follow the River*.

Tongret, Doris and Charles: Encouragement.

Trail, Steve: Contacts and encouragement, and historian in *Mary Ingles: Indian Captive*.

Varney, Clayton: Muriel Stuart's brother from Florida.

Veasey, Charles: Lodging, Chief of Pratt Volunteer Fire Department.

Veasey, Steve: Encouragement, West Virginia.

Villiers, Regina: Contributing reporter for *Cincinnati Inquirer*, neighbor of Louise Kemp.

Wallace, Bertha: Banana, Mt. Carbon, West Virginia.

Watson, Liz: Maps, encouragement, Mary Ingles Trail Club contacts and walked in West Virginia.

Weaver, Mary Jo: My neighbor who recommended lambswool for blistered feet.

Weekley, Maxine and Roy: Refreshment in West Virginia.

White, Bill: Sag wagon in Charleston, West Virginia.

Whittaker, Virginia: Took photos in Eggleston, Virginia.

Wiley, Alma: Teacher, California, Kentucky.

Williams, Patti: Directions in Hinton, West Virginia.

Williams, Susan: Reporter for *Charleston Gazette*.

Williamson, Claudette: Encouragement in West Virginia.

Wilson, Steve: Encouragement.

Wirthlin, Fran: Walked near Concord, Kentucky, friend of Louise Kemp's.

Wood, Doug: Walker and contacts, West Virginia.

Wood, Susan: Food and lodging, walked Charleston, West Virginia to Eggleston, Virginia.

Wood, Vera: Walked, Mary Ingles Trail Club.

Worthington, Dr. Jan and Gary: Encouragement and clothes washing privileges, West Virginia.

Wylie, Mark: Lodging, Pipestem State Park, West Virginia.

Eating Along the River

A sample of what the angels provided to Debbie, guests, and me. Some Mary would have eaten, most only in her dreams. *(My notes in italics.)*

Debbie's Jerky
Day 1

6 pounds of beef brisket, sliced like bacon, with the grain. *(For one batch, a 3-pound brisket filled four cookie sheets and three shelves in my oven.)* Trim off all fat.

Mix together:
    ½ cup soy sauce
    ½ cup water
    dash to ¼ teaspoon garlic powder

Marinate slices of beef brisket in mixture for at least 20 minutes. *(One cup of mixture worked for a 3-pound brisket.)*

(Note from Dark Rain Thom: In an 8 ½ x 13-inch pan, lay one layer of beef strips; then pour on a small amount of mixture. Add alternate layers of beef strips and mixture until used up. Marinating for 8 hours is not too long.)

Then, place slices on a cookie sheet. Do not layer. Bake at 150 to 200 degrees for 8 hours. You may want to put a wooden spoon in the door to keep the oven from becoming too hot.

On the afternoon of our longest day (28 miles), Debbie shared this jerky. I could feel energy surge through my muscles.

Ann's Red Beans and Rice
Day 3

1 pound dried kidney beans
2 or 3 chopped onions
2 cups chopped celery
3 cloves garlic
1 pound Hillshire Farms or Andouille-type sausage
4 to 6 cups water
rice
cheese, grated
hot sauce

Soak beans according to package directions. Add onion, celery, garlic and sausage *(cut into bite-sized pieces)*. Add water as necessary. Cook until beans are mushy *(2 to 3 hours)*. Serve over rice with hot sauce and grated cheese. Good with taco chips or cornbread.

Like vegetable soup, this can be adjusted to taste and what is in the kitchen cupboard. For a Louisiana flavor add a little green pepper, bay leaves, cayenne pepper, dried thyme, sage, parsley, and Cajun seasoning.

Joandel's Chocolate Delight Dessert
Day 16

1st layer, the crust:
  2 cups flour
  1 cup margarine
  ½ cup chopped nuts

Mix *(rub with hands or use pastry blender)* and press into 9 x 13-inch pan. Bake 15 to 20 minutes at 350-375 degree oven until light brown. Cool.

2nd layer:
  1 (8 oz.) package softened cream cheese

1 cup confectioner's *(powdered)* sugar
½ of a large *(9 oz.)*, thawed Cool Whip

Mix cream cheese and sugar together, then fold in Cool Whip, and spread on crust.

3rd layer:
3 small *(3.9 oz.)* boxes instant chocolate pudding
4 ½ cups cold milk

Mix and spread on cake. *(Let pudding set about 5 minutes before adding next layer.)*

4th layer:
Spread on remaining Cool Whip.
Sprinkle top with chopped nuts.

Tom's Parched Corn
Day 22

Pull husks back on fresh sweet corn and hang to dry. When corn is dry on the cob, shuck. In a greased frying pan, heat kernels until they *barely* puff. It's like popping corn, only using less grease. Add salt to taste.

Pat Gilbert's Whole Wheat Bread
Day 24

6 cups warm water
3 packages dry yeast
1 cup honey *(molasses, Karo syrup, or whatever)*

Combine and let stand until foamy.

Add 10 cups whole wheat flour. Stir 100 strokes. Add ½ cup oil, 2 tablespoons salt, 4 to 6 cups white flour. Stir 100 strokes. *(I worked most of it in with my hands.) Place dough in a warm, greased bowl; turn to grease top. Cover loosely with cloth.*

Let rise until it doubles. *(About 1 ½ hours.)* Turn out on floured counter. Knead about 10 minutes. Divide into 4 (occasionally 5) oblong shapes, pressing out all air. Shape into loaves. Place in greased bread pans. Let rise about 1 hour. Bake 45 minutes at 375 degrees.

Sara's Granola
Day 25

Mix together:
    3 cups regular oats *(Quaker Oats)*
    1 cup coconut
    ½ cup wheat germ
    1 cup sunflower seeds
    1 box (1/4 cup) sesame seeds

Mix and heat until peanut butter melts into mixture:
    ½ cup honey
    ¼ cup salad oil
    ½ cup peanut butter
    ¼ teaspoon vanilla

Mix dry and wet ingredients. Spread on jellyroll pan *or cookie sheet,* and heat in 250 degree oven for one hour; stirring every 10 minutes.

Add raisins as desired after mixture cools.

Doug's Garlic Bread
Day 36

Heat cast-iron skillet
Melt butter or margarine
Spread slices of bread with butter

Place bread, buttered side down in hot skillet and fry until golden brown. Remove from skillet and sprinkle browned side with garlic power to taste.

Doug's ease as cook and host while his wife was ill made him and his garlic bread winners.

Mary Lewis' Oyster Cracker Appetizer
Day 43

12-16 oz. plain oyster crackers
1 package, buttermilk ranch dry dressing mix
¾-1 cup salad oil
½-1 teaspoon dill weed
¼ teaspoon garlic powder
¼ teaspoon lemon pepper

Combine dressing mix and oil; add dill weed, garlic powder, and lemon pepper. Pour over crackers, stir to coat. Place in warm oven for 15-20 minutes.

At Mary Lewis' Ingleside home, after everyone was gone, we sat by a blazing fireplace, musing about the day's events and munching oyster crackers. Mary Lewis said, "I always keep some in the freezer, to bring out for company."

Acknowledgements

The inspiration I received from Mary Draper and William Ingles would not have been possible without James Alexander Thom's *Follow the River*. My book would not be in your hands without Jim's kind and gentle encouragement.

The Walk would not have been the spiritual journey it was without the hundreds of people along the Ohio, Kanawha, and New Rivers who helped and inspired me. Lack of your name in this book indicates my feeble memory and organizational skills, not the level of your importance or the degree of my appreciation. This book is in honor of all the spirits who otherwise might go unrecognized. Not only those who walked along, and provided food, shelter, and sag support, but those who waved from a vehicle or house, smiled out from a crowd, left phone messages with good intentions, and also clerks in stores who permitted toilet privileges, just to name a few.

First, I must thank my children. Lisa and Janette gave up many weekends and drove many hours to help their foolish mother fulfill her dream, Jerry gave encouraging words when my spirits sagged in the middle of the writing, and John came through with graphic skills when I needed a map.

My daughter-in-law, Darcelle Lahr, helped me realize that racial and personal interaction and interpretations are more complex than I thought. And, the racial and gender prejudice I experienced as an adult was more subtle than when I was a child, but it was there and needed to be addressed—even when I was reluctant to admit it.

Susan Wunder, a freelance writer and neighbor, listened to my sobbing, frustrated anguish over the phone, read a few of my very rough drafts, and said, "There is good stuff here. You need to get this off your back."

When I asked Carol Beal Stone, a grade school friend and science writer for editorial advice, she replied, "I tried editing for a friend one time and it nearly ruined our friendship. I can't do it for you, but I'll try to put you in contact with someone." Everyone should be lucky enough to have a friend of 55 years whom they can call on and know they will offer assistance.

And Carol's friend of a friend came through! Without Karen Garinger's professional and kind editorial handling of me and the manuscript, these pages would still be in a box.

The St. Mark's Book Club's enthusiasm after hearing me read a few pages kept me at the computer for months.

Nancy Baxter's rejection words, "We aren't the ones to publish this book, unfortunately...[but]...this book is definitely publishable," were propped on my desk as a constant reminder that at least one publisher thought this work was worth reading.

Tonya Matthew, poet, and Susie Takach, artist, allowed me to sit in on their monthly writing table. Their honest and helpful encouragement and criticism made this a better product.

When I couldn't afford to pay an editor, Dr. Timothy Tilton read the manuscript, gave valuable suggestions, and kept nudging me toward publication.

Without Susan Roth, garden photographer, writer and soul mate, I would never have kept my nose to the grindstone to finish the last page. Susan not only read and spell- and grammar-checked each and every page, she gave rewrite feedback so the work would sound more professional when I sent it off to an editor. Equally important, Susan was at the other end of the telephone when emotion seemed too much to bear.

The computer I reluctantly purchased for the sole purpose of putting memories to paper was a source of many hand-wringing minutes and hours. Everyone needs at least one available expert when the thing sends weird messages or just refuses to respond. I was blessed with three. Over the years, John Clear calmed me from his home in Texas. TYG gave up many hours including lunches to bail me out of minor and major glitches, and an anonymous friend helped me find a new computer when mine bit the dust and I thought all was lost.

This is more accurate because of all the hikers who were there in 1987, who listened to these words, corrected my foggy memory, gave insight and affirmed my interpretation. We remembered many things the same and some things differently. This happens to be my interpretation—for better or worse.

And last, but not least, my everlasting appreciation for Richard P. Sylvia, who opened his house and heart to a friend. He gave me space to put the first words to paper and made publication possible. One never knows where a handshake will lead.

As the years pass, and the body declines, I am frequently reassured by a quote from an unknown person named Schnitzer. I read it while visiting Susan Wood and Eleanor Henson in West Virginia, one cold November day in 1989: "It will be painful when frailty prevents me from climbing mountains. Yet, when that time comes, I hope I find serenity in wandering through valleys, looking at the realm of distant summits not with ambition, but with loving memories."

Thank you all for helping me on the incredible journey of completing the book I said would never be written.

About the Author

Eleanor Mary Lahr has enjoyed the outdoors since she was a child. Her first serious hike was when she retraced the route of Mary Ingles' escape. Now retired, she divides her time between tending gardens around her home in southern Indiana, staying in touch with friends, and exploring new places.